In *Digital China's Informal Circuits*, Elaine Zhao offers an exciting and informative analysis on the often-neglected informal economy, secondary market and alternative forms of production and practices of digital culture in China. From open source cultures and piracy to amateur labor and media, Zhao argues that such informalities – and the dialectics between the informalities and the formalities – have hammered out a more complex and dynamic cultural condition in contemporary China.

Anthony Fung, *Chinese University of Hong Kong and Beijing Normal University*

Digital China's Informal Circuits: Platforms, Labour and Governance provides readers with a critical perspective on how China's information and communication technologies are at the leading edge of disruptive innovation. In this readable and comprehensive book Elaine Zhao describes how multiple players and publics strategize to position themselves between formal and the informal economies against the backdrop of a society undergoing massive digital transformation.

Michael Keane, *Curtin University Australia*

Digital China's Informal Circuits

From open source cultures, piracy, to amateur media and on-demand labour, informal media activities are vibrant in circuits of cultural production, distribution, consumption and labour utilisation in China. They come in different sizes and shapes, involve multiple actors, often with transnational ties and tensions, and challenge polemic views. Why do these informal activities occur, and how do they evolve? What cultural and social consequences do they have? In what ways do they pose challenges to governance and provoke us to rethink the notion? This book engages with diverse forms of the informal and their equally diverse interactions with the formal in the broader context of the rise of digital platforms, the contingent and complicated state–market interactions, and evolving roles of users. The book provides a vivid and original account of how digital platforms navigate formal and informal boundaries at both operational and discursive levels; how enthusiastic fans, aspiring amateurs, 'ordinary' users and necessity-driven labourers become integral to the formal/informal interface; and how state and non-state actors intervene in governing the formal/informal dynamics. In doing so, the book opens up new insights into the ongoing digital transformation in China.

Elaine Jing Zhao is Senior Lecturer in the School of the Arts and Media, Faculty of Arts and Social Sciences at the University of New South Wales, Australia.

Media, Culture and Social Change in Asia

The aim of this series is to publish original, high-quality work by both new and established scholars in the West and the East, on all aspects of media, culture and social change in Asia.

58 Cultural Policy in South Korea
Making a New Patron State
Hye-Kyung Lee

59 Television in Post-Reform Vietnam
Nation, Media, Market
Giang Nguyen-Thu

60 South Korean Popular Culture and North Korea
Edited by Youna Kim

61 Russian Nationalism
Imaginaries, Doctrines, and Political Battlefields
Marlene Laruelle

62 Digital China's Informal Circuits
Platforms, Labour and Governance
Elaine Jing Zhao

For a full list of available titles please visit: www.routledge.com/Media-Culture-and-Social-Change-in-Asia-Series/book-series/SE0797

Digital China's Informal Circuits

Platforms, Labour and Governance

Elaine Jing Zhao

Routledge
Taylor & Francis Group
LONDON AND NEW YORK

First published 2019
by Routledge
2 Park Square, Milton Park, Abingdon, Oxon OX14 4RN

and by Routledge
52 Vanderbilt Avenue, New York, NY 10017

Routledge is an imprint of the Taylor & Francis Group, an informa business

British Library Cataloguing-in-Publication Data
A catalogue record for this book is available from the British Library

Library of Congress Cataloging-in-Publication Data
A catalog record has been requested for this book

ISBN: 978-1-138-73710-5 (hbk)
ISBN: 978-1-315-17379-5 (ebk)

Typeset in Times New Roman
by Wearset Ltd, Boldon, Tyne and Wear

MIX
Paper from responsible sources
FSC® C013056

Printed and bound in Great Britain by
TJ International Ltd, Padstow, Cornwall

Contents

Acknowledgements

Many people have accompanied me along the journey leading to this book. First and foremost, I would like to thank all the individuals who kindly shared with me their experience in formal and informal circuits of cultural production, circulation, consumption and labour utilisation. These include amateur developers, parallel dealers, rooting and jailbreaking service providers, enthusiastic fans, aspiring internet literature writers, professionalising online video producers, taxi drivers, on-demand drivers working with ride-hailing apps, and industry practitioners, all witnessing the trajectories of various digital platforms in China. I am indebted to Xiaoxiang Shi and Marina Guo for their assistance in arranging part of the fieldwork.

The idea for this book germinated during my time at the ARC Centre of Excellence for Creative Industries and Innovation, and the Creative Industries Faculty at Queensland University of Technology. I owe an eternal debt to Stuart Cunningham and Michael Keane, who have provided invaluable mentorship in my academic life. Many other researchers in this cross-institutional research environment have been a continuing source of inspiration, particularly Terry Flew, Jean Burgess, Patrik Wikström, John Banks, Ramon Lobato, Julian Thomas, John Hartley and Lucy Montgomery.

Much of this book was written and researched at the School of the Arts and Media, Faculty of Arts and Social Sciences, University of New South Wales. I wish to acknowledge the financial support of the Special Research Grants, which allowed me to conduct fieldwork in China. Many thanks also to my colleagues for their support and encouragement.

I am extremely grateful to Michael Keane, Ang Peng Hwa, Anthony Fung, Stuart Cunningham, David Craig, Ned Rossiter, Jack Qiu, Tom O'Regan, Tarleton Gillespie, Yu Hong, Jung Sun and Kelly Hu for providing insightful comments, asking stimulating questions and pointing me to useful resources. I am also indebted to the anonymous reviewers for the generous and helpful feedback. Of course, the responsibility for any omissions or errors remains entirely my own.

Beyond the academic circle, my former colleagues in the mobile internet industry, particularly Marko Vänskä, Mike Ding, Joseph Zheng, Kristal Li, Yifeng Chu and Scott Li, have continued to provide advice, inspiration and emotional support, although we have parted ways.

My special thanks go to Stephanie Hemelryk Donald, the series editor, for her enthusiasm and support from the first moment. I must also thank Peter Sowden, Commissioning Editor at Routledge, for his gracious welcome of the book, and together with his team, including Rebecca McPhee, for their professionalism and patience in bringing this project to completion.

Some ideas in this book have appeared, in different forms, in previous publications: 'Writing on the assembly line: Informal labour in the formalised online literature market in China', *New Media and Society 19*(8) (2017): 1236–1252; 'Between formal and informal: The shakeout in China's online video industry' (co-authored with Keane, M.), *Media, Culture & Society 35*(6) (2013): 724–741; 'Professionalization of amateur production in online screen entertainment in China: Hopes, frustrations and uncertainties', *International Journal of Communication* 10(2016): 5444–5462.

Finally, I wish to dedicate the last line to my parents, Zhigang Zhao and Meizhen Zhang, for their unsparing support and enduring love.

Abbreviations

AFA	Anti-Fragmentation Agreement
AOSP	Android Open Source Project
API	Application Programming Interface
APK	Android application package
ARPU	average revenue per user
CAC	Cyberspace Administration of China
CCAC	Central Cyberspace Affairs Commission
CNNIC	China Internet Network Information Centre
CWA	China Writer's Association
EFF	Electronic Frontier Foundation
FOSS	Free and Open Source Software
GDP	gross domestic product
GPL	GNU Public Licence
ICT	information and communication technologies
ILO	International Labour Organisation
IPO	initial public offering
IPR	Intellectual Property Rights
MADA	Mobile Application Distribution Agreement
MII	Ministry of Information Industry
MIIT	Ministry of Industry and Information Technology
MMORPGs	massively multi-player online role-playing games
MOT	Ministry of Transport
OECD	Organisation for Economic Co-operation and Development
OHA	Open Handset Alliance
OS	Operating System
ROM	Read-only memory
SAPPRFT	State Administration of Press, Publication, Radio, Film and Television
SARFT	State Administration of Radio, Film and Television
SDK	Software Development Kit
SIIO	State Internet Information Office
SMTC	Shanghai Municipal Transportation Commission
SOE	state-owned enterprise

SPC	State Planning Commission
TRIPS	Trade-Related Measures on Intellectual Property Rights
UGC	user-generated content
UNESCO	United Nations Organization for Education, Science and Culture
UV	unique visitor
VV	video view
WAPI	WLAN Authentication and Privacy Infrastructure
WLAN	wireless local area network
WTO	World Trade Organization

1 Introduction

After more than 30 years of surging growth, China's economy is slowing down. While the country became an economic superpower through its capacity to manufacture and export cheap goods to many parts of the world, it is now in desperate need to find a new engine. The role of information and communication technologies (ICT) in facilitating innovation and stimulate economic development has figured prominently in state policies since the 2000s (Zhao, 2008; Hong, 2017). Most recently, the state has charted the path towards digital future through the 'Internet Plus' (*hulianwang jia*) blueprint, proposed by Chinese premier Li Keqiang in his Government Work Report in 2015. As a prescription for the ailing economy and China's aspiration for leadership in the world's digital economy, the plan manifests the state's intention of capturing the full potential of the internet, or of ICT more broadly including the mobile internet, cloud computing, big data and the internet of things, as a force to promote productivity and innovation.

Since the mid-1990s, the internet in China has undergone rapid diffusion and commercialisation. Almost a decade ago, China became home to the world's largest internet population. In recent years, digital conglomerates such as Baidu, Alibaba and Tencent and Xiaomi (popularly known as BATX) have joined the ranks of the world's leading technology companies. Largely funded by transnational and domestic private capital, they are fundamentally shaping the Chinese internet (Jia and Winseck, 2018). Digital platforms have taken a central role in media and cultural transformations in China, as the boundaries fade between professionals and amateurs, commercial and non-commercial, corporate R&D and grassroots creativity. China's digital economy reached 22.58 trillion yuan ($3.4 trillion) in 2016, ranking second globally and accounting for 30.3 per cent of national GDP (*Xinhua News*, 2017). While leading platforms take the spotlight, informal circuits in cultural production, distribution, consumption and labour utilisation are often overlooked. Yet the informal media economy is vibrant and increasingly visible. Parallel trade, unauthorised file sharing, free and open source software development, amateur cultural production and on-demand labour are but a few examples. In order to understand media and cultural transformations in digital China, it is timely and important to include the informal in the analysis.

This book is about these informal circuits and their interactions with the formal in China's digital media economy. Approaching informality as inherently diverse and mutually constituted with the formal, this book reveals various forms of vibrant informal activities, and traces flows of people, ideas, content, technologies and capital between the formal and informal in the broader context of the rise of digital platforms in China. Digital platforms provide a rich site for analysing such interactions and their impacts on cultural and social transformations in China. This book draws on case studies of digital platforms for open source smartphone production, mobile app distribution, online literature production, video streaming and sharing, and on-demand ride hailing to map the coevolution of the formal and informal in digital China. While the proliferation of digital platforms has made informal activities more visible, it must be recognised that informality is not unique to digital economy. Focusing on digital platforms, this book seeks to map the connections between digital informality and their precedents, and to consider their impacts on society.

For digital platforms, it is crucial to carve out their positions as they attend to multiple publics for strategic purposes (Gillespie, 2010). As digital platforms move across formal/informal boundaries, they interact with multiple actors in China and across the border. At both operational and discursive levels, digital platforms strategically take different approaches to informal elements in the circuits of cultural production, distribution, consumption and labour utilisation. Multiple users including developers, hackers, parallel dealers, fans, pirates, entrepreneurial content creators and on-demand labourers participate in the informal circuits with different motivations and experiences. Various forms of labour exhibit varying degrees of informality and coevolve with platforms. The evolution of digital platforms also involves negotiation with regulatory interventions, both formal and informal. The diversity of the informal and its interaction with the formal presents governance challenges. In China's context, the state's multi-pronged approach to the internet and its dual role as market regulator and participant, the central–local dynamics, competing authorities and China's increasing integration into the global economy complicate state–market dynamics. Further, non-state actors such as digital platforms and user communities add further complexity to the question of governance.

This book cuts across three levels of analysis – the state, the market and user communities – to explain how various actors play their roles and interact with each other in shaping the coevolution of the informal and formal in China's platform economy. Going beyond the dichotomies of the formal versus informal, professional versus amateur, state versus market, local versus global, it provides a broad and dynamic perspective on digital transformation in contemporary China. It reveals multiple actors in the informal circuits, their complex interactions with the formal, and the varied consequences for media production, consumption, distribution and labour utilisation. Through these analyses, I hope to open up new ways of considering the ongoing digital transformation and its cultural, social and policy implications in China.

The informal economy

If informality was once associated with the margins, it is no longer. The informal economy is penetrating into many parts of today's world (OECD, 2009). In the words of British economic anthropologist Keith Hart (2002), the informal economy is going mainstream. What, then, is the informal economy? Over the past four decades, the concept has been defined in myriad ways. While definitions and classifications vary in different studies, a general consensus on the concept lies in that it refers to economic activities taking place outside of state statistics and regulatory scope (Hart, 1973, 2010; Portes *et al.*, 1989; Portes and Haller, 2005). This includes activities such as domestic do-it-yourself work, unregistered employment, tax evasion, bartering and street trade. Illegal activities such as smuggling are approached by some researchers as part of the informal economy and are treated as a separate category by others. Some researchers categorise the informal economy with a further dimension of legitimacy: 'a generalized perception or assumption that the actions of an entity are desirable, proper, or appropriate within some socially constructed system of norms, values, beliefs, and definitions' (Suchman, 1995: 574). In other words, informal economic activities can couple illegality with legitimacy. The inherent heterogeneity and indeterminate boundaries may pose analytical challenges. However, as Manuel Castells and Alejandro Portes (1989) compellingly argue, the informal media economy is best understood as 'a common-sense notion whose moving social boundaries cannot be captured by a strict definition without closing the debate prematurely' (p. 11).

Keith Hart's seminal work on informal economic activities in West African cities first brought it to public attention. As an anthropologist, Hart documented off-the-books activities in his 1973 study based on his fieldwork in Ghana in an attempt to reveal the capacity of informal economic activities to generate growth for the poor. In Hart's words (1990), the concept 'bridged the gap between my experience there and anything my English education had taught me before' (p. 14). In this sense, the concept not only highlights a long-neglected, complementary part of the formal economy, but also critiques Western notions of economic development and growth. The concept became institutionalised when International Labour Organization (ILO) adopted it and commissioned studies to investigate the size, characteristics and composition of informal economic activities and recommended incorporation of the informal within the formal. Often characterised as an excluded sector in less developed economies, informal economic activities became recognised as a key pathway to promote growth and reduce poverty. Since then, research on the informal economy has grown prominently.

Once dismissed as an obsolete form confined to premodern societies, the informal economy has proven to be 'a fundamental politico-economic process at the core of many societies' (Castells and Portes, 1989, p. 15). Since the late 1980s researchers have analysed informal economic activities in developed economies (Portes *et al.*, 1989; Sassen-Koob, 1989; Stepick, 1989). This body of literature offers rich insights into the diversity of informal economic activities, which can be understood as survival strategies, dependent exploitation and growth opportunities (Portes and Haller, 2005). Notably, the earlier term 'informal sector' has given way to the notion of an informal economy, a broadened concept with a view to include informality manifested in both Global North and Global South, and to reflect the intersection and dynamics of the formal and informal (Hart, 2009).

Research in economic anthropology, sociology and urban studies has offered important lessons in understanding the informal economy. The earlier notion of the informal economy as a residue that is only to be replaced by the formal economy as the economy develops, has proven to be flawed. Equally problematic is the idea that the informal exists separately from the formal. In fact, the informal intersects and interacts with the formal in various ways, constituting what Castells and Portes (1989) call the 'variable geometry' of formal–informal relations. The diversity and complexities of these interactions require further empirical analysis. As Hart (2010) reminds us, researchers should beware the risk of incorporating informal economies into abstract models without knowing what is actually going on.

Policy doctrines have swung back and forth in the past four decades (Hart, 2009). Informalisation in the context of the economic liberalisation of the Reagan and Thatcher years in the West was a decisive departure from the Keynesian state of the previous three decades. Following decades of the free market, the global financial crisis was a major setback. Economic recession in the West has since led many governments to strengthen their grip over informal economic activities, such as transnational tax evasion.

While finding initial purchase in the ILO's development paradigm, the concept of the informal economy has also drawn growing attention from the policy circle in recent years. The Organisation for Economic Co-operation and Development (OECD) (2009) acknowledges the informal economy as a large and growing part of the broader economy in the contemporary world. In the realms of cultural policy and intellectual property, international agencies have also started to engage with the concept of the informal economy. UNESCO (2013), for example, regards the connection between the informal and the formal economy as crucial to informed creative economy policy development. The World Intellectual Property Organization has commissioned research to gain a better understanding of innovation occurring in the informal economy, and its relationship to intellectual property (de Beer *et al.*, 2013). While the challenge of measuring the size of the informal economy persists, policy advisers have called for the need to measure innovation in the informal economy (Charmes *et al.*, 2016). Overall, understanding the complexity of informality and the dynamics between the formal and the informal is indeed crucial to policy development.

The informal media economy and the rise of digital platforms

The evolution of media and new modes of production, consumption and distribution has made informality increasingly visible. In the words of Lobato and Thomas (2015):

> Many informal systems are thoroughly modern in the sense that they take full advantage of – and are enabled by – changes in digital technology, patterns of economic integration and leading-edge consumer behaviours. Formal and informal media economies dance together under the sign of technological modernity.
>
> (p. 29)

Nigeria's movie industry, or Nollywood, is perhaps one of the most notably present informal media economies on the global stage. The now booming industry had its inception in the 1990s, characterised by quick productions on a shoestring budget and straight-to-video distribution. Produced by and for Nigerians, these productions have opened up space for popular creativity and travel via distribution networks relying on pirate infrastructure (Haynes, 1995; Jedlowski, 2012). The rapid growth of Nollywood saw it surpassing Hollywood in 2009 as the world's second largest movie industry by volume, second only to India's Bollywood (Bright, 2015). Its enormous size has led to more measurement initiatives and regulatory gaze. Industry players and regulatory agencies have started to consider how to formalise the space and rectify what they believe to be severe revenue bleed. Meanwhile, the industry is evolving, witnessing more theatrical and televisual exhibition. Formalisation of the industry is expected to bring profit not only to domestic industry players but also to global heavyweights in digital distribution. Netflix, for example, has already inked distribution deals for Nollywood productions to expand their reach across the world. This sketch of Nollywood shows circuits of the informal media economy and its interaction with the formal in its development trajectory. It also shows how informality is perceived by some people as efficient, productive and energetic and is regarded by others as a problem to be rectified.

Apart from this paradigmatic example, various forms of informality have captured scholarly interest in media and cultural studies. These include research on media production, distribution and consumption in VCR markets (O'Regan, 1991, 2012), pirate cultures (Pang, 2006; Athique, 2008), geoblocking circumvention (Lobato and Meese, 2016), amateur media and their coevolution with formal media systems (Burgess, 2012; Lobato *et al.*, 2011; Seijdel and Melis, 2008; Cunningham, 2012), and labour organisation (Qiu *et al.*, 2014; Gregg, 2011; Rosenblat and Stark, 2016; Scholz, 2016; Ross, 2009; Banks, 2007; Hesmondhalgh and Baker, 2011; Gill and Pratt, 2008). Notably, Lobato and Thomas (2015) have produced a book-length study by approaching media industries with the spectrum of formality along multiple dimensions such as taxation, capital intensity, centralisation, state oversight, labour, ease of entry and quality control. By tracing the interaction between the formal and informal in terms of functions, effects and controls, the authors provide rich insights into how the informal media economy is driving media industry transformation in multiple dimensions such as entrepreneurship, labour and regulation.

In the past decade, the proliferation of digital platforms has been a notable development globally. From social media platforms relying heavily on user-generated content to on-demand service platforms connecting individual labourers and customers, these platforms have taken a prominent role in cultural production, distribution, consumption and labour utilisation. As internet industries are increasingly adopting platform strategies in market competition, digital platforms continue to penetrate our society. Meanwhile, key infrastructures such as those for urban transport and financial transactions are being platformised, offering alternatives to government provision. These two parallel developments are conceptualised as the 'infrastructualisation of platforms' and 'platformisation of infrastructures' (Plantin *et al.*, 2016).

As the term 'platform' has become a buzzword, Gillespie's pioneering work (2010) has critically investigated the discursive work that goes into digital media firms' adoption of the term in the context of financial, cultural and regulatory demands. Specifically, digital media corporations exploit the computational, architectural, figurative and political meanings of the term 'platform' to position themselves strategically in relation to multiple actors including users, developers, advertisers and policymakers. In the words of economists (Rochet and Tirole, 2003), platforms operate in what economists call a multi-sided market, where they enable interactions between two or more distinct parties. By enabling different user groups to interact, platforms thrive on network effects, cross-subsidisation and data extraction from users (Srnicek, 2016).

While platforms are often credited with cutting out the middleman, they are not neutral intermediaries. As Van Dijck (2013) compellingly argues, 'a platform is a mediator rather than an intermediary', because it shapes human interactions instead of merely facilitating them:

> Technically speaking, platforms are the providers of software, (sometimes) hardware, and services that help code social activities into a computational architecture; they process (meta)data through algorithms and formatted protocols before presenting their interpreted logic in the form of user-friendly interfaces with default settings that reflect the platform owner's strategic choices.
> (p. 29)

Helmond (2015) conceptualises 'platformisation' as 'the rise of the platform as the dominant infrastructural and economic model of the social web and its consequences', and analyses how the web has transformed into interconnected platforms through application programming interfaces (APIs). Going beyond the technical and economic dimensions, Van Dijck, Poell and de Waal (2016) further point out the need to understand platforms from sociocultural, techno-economic and political perspectives.

This book approaches digital platforms as techno-economic structures and cultural artefacts where politics play out among various actors. It applies a lens of informality to the analysis and situates digital platforms in the dynamics of formalisation and informalisation. As digital platforms reformat the web, they exhibit various forms of informality in the circuits of production, distribution and consumption of media goods and services. These informal circuits raise governance challenges, and in some cases, the legality and legitimacy of the platforms provoke significant debates. Moreover, both formal and informal circuits, as well as their interactions, are closely bound up with the logic of digital platforms. As such, it is crucial to understand how digital platforms navigate between the formal and the informal economy, on both operational and discursive levels; how these processes transform cultural production, distribution, consumption and labour utilisation; how they negotiate with multiple modes of governance; and what social and cultural consequences they produce.

Informal media economy in digital China

In China, the informal media economy has a massive presence. The spread of satellite dishes (Severin, 1994; Fung and Ma, 2002) and pirate DVDs (Pang, 2006; S. Wang, 2003), for example, is only a small part of the broader 'unofficial entertainment undercurrent' (Wilson, 2013). Unlicensed Net bars, second-hand mobile phones and used computers reveal the connection between informal economies and working-class culture and politics among whom Qiu (2009) includes 'the information have-less'. Informality also exists in the circuits of production. These circuits are evident in fan communities who produce subtitle translations and facilitate overseas video circulation (Hu, 2005; Zhang and Mao, 2013); users who produce media stories to construct unofficial time/space (Yu, 2009); the toiling gold farmers of the online gaming culture (Castronova, 2007; Dibbel, 2007; Heeks, 2010); and manufacturing iSlaves on the assembly line (Qiu, 2016). These studies have laid important groundwork for analysing the informal media economy in China and its interactions with the formal.

In recent years, digital platforms have penetrated Chinese society and changed the rubrics of media industries. Examples include smartphones with customised operating systems based on Android, various unofficial Apple and Android app markets, video streaming platforms characterised by weak copyright enforcement and user-generated content, an online literature market relying on amateur creative production, ride-hailing apps matching drivers and passengers. The list can go on. Entrepreneurs and users participate in the informal economy for various reasons, including seeking profits, accessing otherwise unavailable content, performing fandom or looking for the next gig.

Various informal circuits of production, consumption and distribution and labour utilisation travel through the platform-centred digital media ecology. In their discursive work, platforms have featured some informalities prominently while eliding or whitewashing others. Some platforms have stayed in the grey area for a long time before attaining legality. Others benefit from a favourable policy wind and have actively enlisted informality for productivity and innovation. Many informal circuits in the platform economy are linked to extant circuits of informality including those in non-digital spaces. Many intersect and coevolve with formal circuits. And many travel across borders.

The development trajectory of digital platforms is as much about negotiating with multiple parties as it is about navigating between the formal and informal.

It is therefore crucial to understand the diverse forms and functions of informal circuits, the discursive work on the informal, the shifting boundaries and dynamic interactions between the formal and informal, the causes and consequences of such dynamics. Before addressing these questions, it is important to understand the broader context where digital platforms in China operate. This requires us to consider the cultural shift in the fluid boundaries between production and consumption, and the state's multi-pronged approach to the internet, as well as governance beyond the state.

From masses to audience to (prod)users

The rise of digital platforms coincides with the increasing commercialisation of the internet. In China, the process has popularised the notion of 'users' (*yonghu*), which is very different from 'audience' (*guanzhong*, *tingzhong* or *shouzhong*) or 'masses' (*qunzhong*). 'Masses' is a highly politicised notion. The adoption of the term is rooted in an ideology where media are instruments for the party-state to dispense a controlled flow of information to achieve domination over people. The notion of 'masses' gradually gave way to 'audience', an imported term, in the reform and opening era. As Zhang (2000) explains, the term 'audience' gained currency owing to its capacity to depoliticise the media–masses relationship and to place the media in the emerging market-oriented system. The ideational change has opened up space for changing media practices of actors who treat the audience as commodities to be sold to advertisers while still toeing the party line (Zhao, 1998). Moreover, the replacement of 'masses' with 'audience' recognises people's creativity in interpreting mass media messages, although it still implies a sense of passivity in media production (Ang, 1996).

While the terms 'masses' and 'audience' have a longer history and are still in use, the term 'users' carries very different connotations. It suggests more creativity and micro-productivity in consuming, and increasingly, in producing media. The evolving role of users has given rise to the hybrid term 'produsers' (Bruns, 2008). In fact, Toffler (1980) created the term 'prosumer' almost three decades ago to predict the collapsing boundary between production and consumption. The advent of the internet has facilitated the growth of diverse forms of user participation in media production. Tinkering with digital devices, accessing blocked content, writing codes, creating spoofs and authoring internet literature, digital media users are breaking the boundaries between production and consumption, professional and amateur.

Existing studies reveal both optimistic and critical perspectives on the evolving role of users. While earlier celebratory accounts focus on the democratic and participative potential (Jenkins, 2005; Benkler and Nissenbaum, 2006; Tapscott and Williams, 2006), sceptics critique the exploitation of user labour (Fuchs, 2015; Andrejevic, 2007, 2009; Terranova, 2000; Scholz, 2016). There has also been a populist critique of the amateur media for its detrimental effects on mainstream media, copyright, the public trust (Keen, 2007), and the implications of the collective ethos in the digital space for diminishing the importance and uniqueness of the individual voice (Lanier, 2010). Going beyond a dichotomy of empowerment versus exploitation, and professional versus amateur, a more reconciling yet still critical approach has emerged, which proposes the notion of co-creation, and considers amateurs as entrepreneurs (Banks and Deuze, 2009; Burgess and Green, 2009; Burgess, 2009; Fish and Srinivasan, 2012).

Although not every user creates content, all users of digital platforms constantly produce data. Digital platforms render into data what has never been quantified before, including profiles, footprints, preferences, behaviour and even relationships (Mayer-Schoenberger and Cukier, 2013). As a key logic of digital platforms, datafication is intimately bound up with value production (Van Dijck and Poell, 2013). In this light, Dallas Smythe's (1977, 1981) notion of the audience commodity has gained new relevance in the debate on digital labour. As Van Dijck (2009) compellingly argues, in addition to their role in cultural participation, it is crucial to understand the economic meaning of users as producers, consumers and data providers, as well as their volatile position in the labour market.

The diversified forms of labour in the context of collapsing boundaries between production and consumption have led researchers to build on existing conceptual frameworks with a lens of informality. While user-generated content (UGC) is often associated with informality, Lobato, Thomas and Hunter (2011) maintain that UGC moves between the formal and informal over time, and different components of particular UGC platforms and content exhibit differing degrees of formality at any one time. This highlights the inherent diversity of UGC and the various ways in which it interacts with other media systems. Such a recursive trajectory across the formal and informal is influenced by technological innovations, business models, policy frameworks and social circumstances. Similarly, Cunningham (2012) adopts a dynamic perspective on UGC, and explains how innovation emerges from the coevolution of the formal and informal media economies with reference to audio-visual production and distribution in developed economies. Moving beyond UGC, Qiu, Gregg and Crawford (2014) have built on the existing work on the diverse range of digital labour and highlighted both formal and informal circuits in their model of 'circuits of labour'. The formal circuits are characterised by hierarchical domination imposed by capital over the body of labour, which is protected by contracts and intellectual property rights regimes. The informal circuits connect social or communicative capital and the creative or reproductive body. Both the formal and informal circuits can absorb productive energy from their counterparts, as in the case of 'playbour' and 'survival labour'.

In China's digital space, user creativity abounds in content production, distribution and consumption. Undeniably, the idea of creativity is a problematic one for the state (Wang, 2004). While the creative industries discourse has found its way to China, authorities have turned it into economic development projects in which creativity is harmonised (Keane, 2013). Thus user creativity is located in a contested site. Keane (2009) believes creative communities in China are undertapped, representing the most potentially innovative stage in what he proposes as 'the cultural innovation timeline' (pp. 70–96). While often informal in nature and left out of statistics, creative communities are sites of hidden innovation. When innovative potential is recognised, grassroots experimentation can serve as an informal and unofficial incubator for the market (Keane and Zhao, 2012). Meanwhile, it is important to acknowledge that some users are more entrepreneurial than others, seeking to turn passion into profit. This in turn effects changes in the market. Montgomery (2010) for example explains how the rise of entrepreneurial consumers propels the evolution of new business models in the context of media marketisation and weak copyright enforcement. As digital platforms open up space for entrepreneurial attempts, how creative users move along the spectrum of formality and how they coevolve with platforms calls for further research.

Apart from platforms facilitating content creation, the emergence of on-demand labour platforms has given rise to new forms of labour organisation. This constitutes a growing domain of informal employment. Informal employment is certainly not new in the era of platformisation in China. Writing in 2009, economist Philip Huang (2009) called for more research on this neglected part of the economy. The massive rise of an informal economy in China dates back to the 1980s, when China embarked on the road of reform and opening up. Since then, peasant workers (*nongminggong*) have flooded to cities to seek better livelihoods, and workers displaced from state-owned enterprises (SOEs) around the turn of the century have come to constitute a large part of the informal economy. Moreover, 'dispatch workers' (or temporary, supplementary and substitute workers) have remained predominantly in informal employment despite attaining legal status (Huang, 2017). Overall, informal employment as a flexible labour strategy has been growing in China (Brown, 2016; Huang, 2013; Lee, 2016; Wu, 2017). As users engage in platform-based cultural production and service provision, how informal employment has been reconfigured remains significantly under-researched.

Given diverse forms of user participation in cultural production, consumption, distribution and labour utilisation, it is crucial to understand users from multiple perspectives. This book employs the lens of formality and informality to analyse various forms of labour in platform-based cultural production and service provision. It reveals multiple roles played by users in the rise of digital platforms, their positions and movement in the spectrum of formality, their coevolution with platforms and their various social and cultural consequences.

China's multi-pronged approach to the internet and governance beyond the state

The rise of home-grown digital platforms and their navigation between the formal and the informal cannot be fully understood without considering the state's multi-pronged approach to the internet. The combined approach of embracing and adjusting to the inevitable changes brought by digital communications are characterised by MacKinnon (2011) as 'networked authoritarianism'. Specifically, China's relentless push to develop the internet as a new engine of growth paradoxically parallels its tight grip over the internet and persistent attempt to block global internet players. Among other factors, economic growth, techno-nationalism, ideological concerns and national security coalesce as China hones its approaches to the internet, an integral part of its national strategy.

The role of the internet and ICT more broadly in promoting productivity and innovation and facilitating economic restructuring features prominently in state policies. The initial development of the internet in China was situated in the context of the state elevating the role of the ICT industry as a pillar of the Chinese economy based on a foreign direct investment (FDI)-driven, export-oriented model (Hong, 2011). The vulnerabilities of this model has since prompted the state to chart out the vision of building an 'innovation-oriented nation' (*chuangxinxing guojia*), a pledge made by then-President Hu Jintao at the National Science and Technology Conference in 2006. The vision highlighted the significance of encouraging indigenous technological innovation and in doing so moving up the value chain and transforming the negative image associated with 'Made in China' and 'copycat China'. Since 2011, the state has designated a prominent place for the internet industry in economic restructuring, first outlined in the 12th Five-Year Plan. In 2014, President Xi stressed the need to build China into a strong cyber power (*wangluo qiangguo*), which involved working towards the goal of strengthening innovation capacity, developing digital economy and enhancing cybersecurity (*Xinhua News*, 2014). A more recent manifestation of the crucial place of the internet industry in China's economy is the 'Internet Plus' agenda, raised by Premier Li Keqiang in 2015. As a prescription for the ailing economy, the plan carries the hope of economic restructuring by integrating the internet and various sectors, from manufacturing to the creative and cultural industries. The State Council emphasises the need to advance the integrated development of the 'Internet Plus' and 'Made in China 2025' initiatives to drive economic restructuring and increase the competitiveness of the 'Made in China' brand. Moreover, the internet is also expected to propel the development of media industries, and cultural and creative industries more broadly. This connects to the earlier call for 'convergence of technological innovation and cultural creativity' (*keji chuangxin yu wenhua chuangyi ronghe*), a policy theme prominent in media system reform.

While the internet carries hopes of economic revitalisation and innovation for the state, at the same time it provokes concerns over disruption. This has led the state to take measures to reduce the perceived threat. Crucially, this is a matter of not only control but also utilisation and appropriation. Recent years have seen the state escalating content regulation on the internet. In 2011, the State Internet Information Office (SIIO) was established under the State Council Information Office, with the purpose of consolidating internet content regulation, which had previously involved multiple state agencies. In 2014, the SIIO transformed into the Cyberspace Administration of China (CAC), also known as the Central Cyberspace Affairs Commission (CCAC). As a top-level internet governance apparatus under the direct leadership of Xi Jinping, CAC aims to 'make the positions of the Party the strongest voices in the online space' and 'distribute positive energy online' (People.com.cn, 2016). As Oakes (2017) points out, the boundary between official media and informal media can be fuzzy in China in the context of content entrepreneurship on social media, and the state has been relatively savvy in exploiting the fuzziness in its own interest. Meanwhile, the state has continued to block Silicon Valley heavyweights such as Google, Twitter, YouTube and Facebook in China. This provides a convenient shield for home-grown digital platforms from head-on competition with global internet giants in China while fending off inconvenient content from afar. Home-grown platforms share similarities with their global counterparts, and yet at the same time assume distinct Chinese characteristics and operate in a different context. In Yang's (2012) words, '[T]he Internet in China has become domesticated to the extent that it is now possible, even necessary, to talk about the Chinese Internet, as opposed to the Internet in China' (p. 49). In order to defend and advocate its approach to internet governance, China continues to promote the principle of cyber sovereignty, which is an important part of building a strong cyber power (*Xinhua News*, 2014). While the cyber sovereignty model advocated by China is often contrasted with 'multi-stakeholderism' championed by the US, it obscures the complexities and contingencies of China's approach (Shen, 2016).

Indeed, complicating the regulatory landscape is much informality, ambiguity and uncertainty in policy development and enforcement. As Wu Si, a journalist-turned-historian in China, writes: 'Outside the formal regulations of every kind of system in Chinese society, and behind every clear statement, there are unwritten rules that are widely recognised' (Wu, 2001: Preface). These informal rules complement, bypass or twist the operation of formal regulations. Breznitz and Murphree (2011) insightfully point out that any account of China must take into consideration 'structured uncertainty', 'an agreement to disagree about the goals and methods of policy' (p. 38). The political system of decentralised centralisation manifested in the dynamics between the state and local governments, and the tensions between overlapping and sometimes competing bureaucratic authorities, are the main causes of structured uncertainty. Existing literature has revealed the intricate institutional configuration of China's policy formulation process in various fields, including telecommunications (Xia, 2012a, 2012b) and network convergence (Zhao, 2017).

A further complication lies in the dual role of the state. Specifically, the state functions not only as regulator but also as participant in a market increasingly integrated in global digital capitalism. From the telecom to the broadcasting sector, the state has nurtured state-owned and -controlled enterprises and urged them towards corporatisation to enhance competitiveness. Moreover, China's increasing integration in the global capitalism complicates state–market dynamics (Curtin, 2017; Zhao, 2003; Zhao and Schiller, 2001). These factors call into question the state capacity to re-regulate the digital economy, especially the liberalised and quasi-liberalised sections (Hong, 2017).

Meanwhile, governance exists beyond the state. In other words, governance involves multiple actors, operating from top down, bottom up and sideways. As

Braman (2004, 2006) writes, while government refers to the formal institutions, rules and practices of the state, governance refers to the formal and informal institutions, rules and practices of both the state and non-state actors. The involvement of non-state actors, including corporations and civil society, is often connected to the notion of internet governance (Brown and Marsden, 2013). Similarly, Lessig (1999) points out that internet regulation exists in different modalities: laws, markets, code and norms. As different actors participate in a diverse range of regulatory structures, regulation manifests varying degrees of formality, with different results (Lobato and Thomas, 2015). While digital platforms are subject to state regulation, they also deploy self-regulation. Moreover, user communities have assumed visible roles in less formal multi-stakeholder governance (Benkler 2006; Brown and Marsden, 2013). Further, digital platforms command governance power in the form of software code and architectural design as well as protocols such as terms of service (Beer, 2009; Van Dijck and Poell, 2013; Gillespie, 2017).

In China, Yang (2009) observes the extension of governance beyond the government in the development of the internet since the early 2000s. As well as the state at various levels, in different regulatory authorities and assuming dual roles, corporate actors have shaped the evolution of the internet in various aspects such as standard setting and content regulation (Tsui, 2003; Weber and Lu, 2007; Qiu, 2010; Zhao, 2010; Sullivan, 2012). Just as the state is not a unitary entity, corporate actors are not monolithic. As China reintegrates into the world, the geopolitics of the internet (Schiller, 2011; Zhao, 2010) further complicates state–market interactions. Moreover, internet users are part of the fledging digital civil society, which coincides with the shift towards governance (Yang, 2009). In such a context, interactions between the state and the market take various shapes, involving conflicts, comprises and collusion.

Taking into consideration the above context, this book goes beyond the simplistic state–market dichotomy in approaching informal circuits in China's digital media economy. It investigates how the state and the market have coevolved, with informal and formal circuits interacting in multiple dimensions, and with what consequences. It discusses a range of governance approaches to informal circuits, their rationale and effects. It reveals both converging and diverging interests between the state and market. The analysis contributes to ongoing discussions on contingent and complex state–market interactions as China undergoes rapid digital transformation.

Chapter outline

Consisting of seven chapters, this book reveals informal circuits in digital China, their multiple causes and various social and cultural consequences. By adopting a dynamic and historical perspective, the book analyses interactions between the formal and informal media economies in the broader context of the rise of digital platforms, the multiple roles of users in cultural production, distribution, consumption and labour utilisation, and the contingent and complicated state–market interactions. The book offers a series of case studies around digital platforms for open source smartphone production, mobile app distribution, online literature production, video streaming and sharing, and on-demand ride hailing. I draw on a variety of data sources including participant observation in digital platforms, online discussion forums and blogs, interviews with participants, and publicly available documents such as government regulations, press coverage and corporate reports. Each subsequent chapter focuses on one case, and is set out as follows.

Chapter 2 addresses the understudied phenomenon of open source smartphone production in China with reference to the case of Xiaomi, particularly the co-creative process of its Android-based MIUI operating system. It explains how the platform repackages informality for value production, and how the contested process triggers informal governance. The chapter opens with two important contexts. First, the development of *shanzhaiji* in a market with high entry barriers, which led to market deregulation and the state initiative to rebrand 'Made in China'. Second, open source software cultures and the rise of Android in the smartphone era. Following this, I analyse how Xiaomi navigates between the formal and the informal at operational and discursive levels. Specifically, I show how the platform draws on informal energy among users in product development; how it attempts to craft a distinctive brand identity by both aligning with the state rebranding project and capitalising on open source software cultures; how it shares a certain *shanzhai* ethos yet strategically distances itself from the negative connotations of *shanzhai*. Further, I interrogate the complexity of openness, highlight the tension in the conjunction of control, value and ownership, and reveal the power of informal norm-based governance as the brand navigates between the formal and informal.

In Chapter 3 I focus on mobile app distribution in China. I start with an overview of the duopoly of Apple and Google in the mobile app economy in most parts of the world and the cultures of adaptation in smartphone and app consumption, evident in the cultures of jailbreaking, rooting, ROM flashing and sideloading. Then it analyses the China syndrome encountered by Apple and Google, which results from the legacy of informal market and inter-capitalist rivalries as China reintegrated itself into the global economy. It then focuses on the case of 91 Wireless, a local intermediary that has filled the market gap and evolved into a dominant mobile app distribution platform. It analyses how the capacity to manoeuvre between the boundaries of the formal and informal, and across national boundaries, enables the platform to constitute value networks and drive user adoption. Following that it examines the platform's legitimacy-seeking strategies, the challenges it encounters as it attempts to shed its informal skin, and its impact on the culture of app development and distribution. In doing so, the chapter reveals the complexities of app distribution as a site where multiple actors across formal and informal boundaries participate, interact and coevolve.

Chapter 4 turns to the rapidly evolving online video space. I start with a discussion of the cultural contradictions of piracy and UGC, the twin circuits of informality in the one-time wilderness of online video market. Then I discuss how the informal has triggered state action, which reset industry boundaries and strengthened copyright enforcement. I analyse how the state action reflected intertwining economic, political and cultural logics and the dual role of the state as market participant and regulator in internet governance, and media governance more broadly. Moreover, I reveal how digital platforms well-funded by venture capital have found a converged interest with relevant authorities in a formalising market, and have shifted their strategic pendulums. Specifically, many platforms have started to adopt a copyright-as-capital approach in content licensing and to engage in industry self-regulation, which has propelled the formalisation of the market. Following this, I analyse how platforms have started to build context matrix beyond licensing, by developing original programming and rebooting UGC, and discuss their cultural implications.

In Chapter 5 I consider the online literature market in China. I begin by tracing back to the inception of online literature sites as a non-commercial, grassroots alternative to state-controlled publishing businesses. Then I analyse multiple dimensions of formalisation of the space, reflected in the rise of online literature platforms based on the 'freemium' business model and with the influx of capital, growing institutional recognition and increasing state oversight. Following this, I proceed to examine the often-neglected precarious experience of aspiring writers in the platform-driven online literature market. Then I focus on the self-organised secondary market of ghost writing and examine its economic and sociocultural impacts. The analyses reveal new forms of surplus value production and capital–labour relations as digital platforms refashion amateur creative labour in the context of increasing state oversight. As internet literature writers navigate the formal–informal boundaries, aspirations, precarity and agency are registered and negotiated in multiple ways.

Chapter 6 investigates ride-hailing platforms, which have provoked heated debates around their legality and raised significant governance challenges. I reveal multiple forms of entrenched informality that ride-hailing platforms, best represented by Didi, exploit in order to expand the market. These include recruiting taxi drivers as early adopters owing to their perceived advantage over the persistent informality and precarity in the oligopolistic taxi industry; exploiting labour dispatch to expand platform labour in the private car hailing service; and consolidating the existing informal urban market where *heiche* (unlicensed taxis) have played a key role in addressing unmet demand. I then examine the lengthy legalisation process with its many twists and turns, which is imbricated with departmental interests and central–local dynamics in government regulation. I analyse the impacts of government regulation and explain how social inequalities have resurfaced in the digital economy. Following this, I emphasise the need to examine both government regulation and platform governance. I turn a critical eye on algorithm-driven platform regulation, which is closely bound up with the value production regime of digital platforms.

Finally, Chapter 7 summarises the discussions in the previous chapters and points towards future research possibilities. Throughout this book I endeavour to articulate the various ways the informal intersects and interacts with the formal, and to contextualise these dynamics within the broader context of state–market interactions, the rise of digital platforms and the transformative role of media users in China. I hope that, using such an approach, the book has demonstrated how we can capture the complexity and nuance of digital transformation in China.

References

Andrejevic, M. (2007). *iSpy: Surveillance and power in the interactive era*, University Press of Kansas, Lawrence, KS.

Andrejevic, M. (2009). Exploiting YouTube: Contradictions of user-generated labor, in *The YouTube Reader*, eds P. Snickars and P. Vonderau, Mediehistoriskt, Stockholm, pp. 406–423.

Ang, I. (1996). *Living room wars: Rethinking media audiences for a postmodern world*, Routledge, London; New York, NY.

Athique, A. (2008). The global dynamics of Indian media piracy: Export markets, playback media and the informal economy. *Media, Culture & Society*, *30*(5), 699–717.

Banks, J. and Deuze, M. (2009). Co-creative labour. *International Journal of Cultural Studies*, *12*, 419–431.

Banks, M. (2007). *The politics of cultural work*, Palgrave, Basingstoke.

Beer, D. (2009). Power through the algorithm? Participatory web cultures and the technological unconsciousness. *New Media & Society*, *11*(6), 985–1002.

Benkler, Y. (2006). *The wealth of networks: How social production transforms markets and freedom*, Yale University Press, New Haven, CT.

Benkler, Y. and Nissenbaum, H. (2006). Commons-based peer production and virtue. *Journal of Political Philosophy*, *14*(4), 394–419.

Braman, S. (2004). The emergent global information policy regime, in *The emergent global information policy regime*, ed. S. Braman, Palgrave Macmillan, Houndmills, UK, pp. 12–37.

Braman, S. (2006). *Change of state: Information, policy and power*, MIT Press, Cambridge, MA.

Breznitz, D. and Murphree, M. (2011). *Run of the red queen: Government, innovation, globalization, and economic growth in China*, Yale University Press, New Haven, CT.

Bright, J. (2015). Meet 'Nollywood': The second largest movie industry in the world. Retrieved 6 June 2016 from http://fortune.com/2015/06/24/nollywood-movie-industry/.

Brown, R. (2016). Chinese 'workers without benefits'. *Richmond Journal of Global Law & Business*, *15*(1), 20–53.

Brown, I. and Marsden, C. T. (2013). *Regulating code: Good governance and better regulation in the information age*, MIT Press, Cambridge, MA.

Bruns, A. (2008). *Blogs, Wikipedia, second life, and beyond: From production to produsage*, Peter Lang, New York, NY.

Burgess, J. (2009). *YouTube: Online video and participatory culture*, Polity, Cambridge and Malden, MA.

Burgess, J. (2012). YouTube and the formalisation of amateur media, in *Amateur media: Social, cultural and legal perspectives*, eds D. Hunter, R. Lobato, M. Richardson and J. Thomas, Routledge, Oxon, pp. 53–58.

Burgess, J. and Green, J. (2009). The entrepreneurial vlogger: Participatory culture beyond the professional–amateur divide, in *The YouTube reader*, eds P. Snickars and P. Vonderau, Mediehistoriskt, Stockholm, Sweden, pp. 89–107.

Castells, M. and Portes, A. (1989). World underneath: The origins, dynamics, and effects of the informal economy, in *The informal economy: Studies in advanced and less developed countries*, eds A. Portes, M. Castells and L. A. Benton, Johns Hopkins University Press, Baltimore, MD, pp. 11–40.

Castronova, E. (2007). *Exodus to the virtual world: How online fun is changing reality*, Palgrave Macmillan, New York, NY.

Charmes, J., Gault, F. and Wunsch-Vincent, S. (2016). Measuring innovation in the informal economy – Formulating an agenda: OECD.

Cunningham, S. (2012). Emergent innovation through the co-evolution of informal and formal media economies. *Television and New Media, 13*(5), 415–430.

Curtin, M. (2017). Between the state and capital: Asia's media revolution in the age of neoliberal globalization. *International Journal of Communication, 11*, 1378–1396.

De Beer, J., Fu, K. and Wunsch-Vincent, S. (2013). The informal economy, innovation and intellectual property – concepts, metrics and policy considerations. WIPO Economic Research Working Paper No. 10. Geneva: World Intellectual Property Organization.

Dibbel, J. (2007). The life of the Chinese gold farmer. Retrieved 6 June 2014 from www.nytimes.com/2007/06/17/magazine/17lootfarmers-t.html?_r=0.

Fish, A. and Srinivasan, R. (2012). Digital labor is the new killer app. *New Media & Society, 14*(1), 137–152.

Fuchs, C. (2015). *Digital labour and Karl Marx*, Routledge, New York, NY.

Fung, A. and Ma, E. (2002). Satellite modernity: Four modes of televisual imagination in the disjunctive socio-mediascape of Guangzhou, in *Media in China: Consumption, content and crisis*, eds S. H. Donald, M. Keane and H. Yin, RoutledgeCurzon, London; New York, pp. 67–79.

Gill, R. and Pratt, A. (2008). Precarity and cultural work in the social factory? Immaterial labour, precariousness and cultural work. *Theory, Culture & Society, 25*(7–8), 1–30.

Gillespie, T. (2010). The politics of 'platforms'. *New Media & Society, 12*(3), 347–364.

Gillespie, T. (2017). Regulation of and by platforms, in *The Sage handbook of social media*, eds J. Burgess, T. Poell and A. Marwick, Sage, Los Angeles, pp. 254–278.

Gregg, M. (2011). The doublespeak of the gig economy. *The Atlantic*. Retrieved 6 June 2016 from www.theatlantic.com/business/archive/2015/09/gig-economy-doublespeak-new-labor/404779/.

Hart, K. (1973). Informal income opportunities and urban employment in Ghana. *Journal of Modern African Studies, 11*(1), 61–89.

Hart, K. (1990). The idea of the economy: Six modern dissenters, in *Beyond the marketplace: Rethinking economy and society*, eds R. Friedland and A. F. Robertson, Aldine de Gruyter, New York, pp. 137–160.

Hart, K. (2002). The informal economy goes mainstream. *Informal Economy Symposium*. Retrieved 6 June, 2016 from https://vimeo.com/52372732.

Hart, K. (2009). On the informal economy: The political history of an ethnographic concept. *CEB Working Paper No. 09/042*.

Hart, K. (2010). Informal economy, in *The human economy*, eds K. Hart, J. Laville and A. Cattani, Polity, Cambridge, pp. 142–154.

Haynes, J. (1995). Nigerian cinema: Structural adjustments. *Research in African Literatures, 26*(3), 97–119.

Heeks, R. (2010). Understanding 'gold farming' and real-money trading as the intersection of real and virtual economies. *Journal of Virtual Worlds Research, 2*(4), 4–27.

Helmond, A. (2015). The platformization of the web: Making web data platform ready. *Social Media + Society, 1*(2), 1–11.

Hesmondhalgh, D. and Baker, S. (2011). *Creative labour: Media work in three cultural industries*, Routledge, Oxon.

Hong, Y. (2011). *Labour, class information and China's informationized policy of economic development*. Lexington Books, Lanham, MD.

Hong, Y. (2017). Pivot to Internet Plus: Molding China's digital economy for economic restructuring. *International Journal of Communication, 11*, 1486–1506.

Hu, K. (2005). The power of circulation: Digital technologies and the online Chinese fans of Japanese TV drama. *Inter-Asia Cultural Studies, 6*(2), 171–186.

Huang, P. C. C. (2009). China's neglected informal economy: Reality and theory. *Modern China, 35*(4), 405–438.

Huang, P. C. C. (2013). Misleading Chinese legal and statistical categories: Labor, individual entities, and private enterprises. *Modern China, 39*(4), 347–379.

Huang, P. C. C. (2017). Dispatch work in China: A study from case records, part I. *Modern China, 43*(3), 247–287.

Jedlowski, A. (2012). Small screen cinema: Informality and remediation in Nollywood. *Television and New Media, 13*(5), 431–446.

Jenkins, H. (2005). *Convergence culture: Where old and new media intersect*, New York University Press, New York, NY.

Jia, L. R. and Winseck, D. (2018). The political economy of Chinese internet companies: Financialization, concentration, and capitalization. *International Communication Gazette, 80*(1): 30–59.

Keane, M. (2009). Creative industries in China: Four perspectives on social transformation. *International Journal of Cultural Policy, 15*(4), 431–434.

Keane, M. (2013). *Creative industries in China: Art, design and media*, Polity, London.

Keane, M. and Zhao, E. J. (2012). Renegades on the frontier of innovation: The shanzhai grassroots communities of shenzhen in China's creative economy. *Eurasian Geography and Economics, 53*(2), 216–230.

Keen, A. (2007). *The cult of the amateur: How today's internet is killing our culture*, Doubleday, New York, NY.

Lanier, J. (2010). *You are not a gadget: A manifesto*, Alfred A. Knopf, New York, NY.

Lee, C. K. (2016). Precarization or empowerment? Reflections on recent labor unrest in China. *Journal of Asian Studies, 75*(2), 317–333.

Lessig, L. (1999). *Code and other laws of Cyberspace*, Basic Books, New York, NY.

Lobato, R. and Meese, J. (eds). (2016). *Geoblocking and global video culture*, Institute of Network Cultures, Amsterdam.

Lobato, R. and Thomas, J. (2015). *The informal media economy*, Polity Press, Cambridge.

Lobato, R., Thomas, J. and Hunter, D. (2011). Histories of user-generated content: Between formal and informal media economies. *International Journal of Communication, 5*, 899–914.

Mackinnon, R. (2011). Networked authoritarianism in China and beyond: Implications for global internet freedom. *Journal of Democracy, 2*, 32–46.

Mayer-Schoenberger, V. and Cukier, K. (2013). *Big data: A revolution that will transform how we live, work and think*, John Murray Publishers, London.

Montgomery, L. (2010). *China's creative industries: Copyright, social network markets and the business of culture in a digital age*, Edward Elgar, Cheltenham.

Oakes, T. (2017). Mediating Asia: Information, democracy, and the state in and before the digital age, *International Journal of Communication, 11*, 1284–1294.

O'Regan, T. (1991). From piracy to sovereignty: International VCR trends. *Continuum, 4*(2), 112–135.

O'Regan, T. (2012). Remembering video: Reflections on the first explosion of informal media markets through the VCR. *Television and New Media, 13*(5), 383–398.

OECD (2009). Is informal normal? Towards more and better jobs in developing countries. Paris: Organisation for Economic Co-operation and Development.

Pang, L. (2006). *Cultural control and globalization in Asia: Copyright, piracy, and cinema*, Routledge, Abingdon.

People.com.cn (2016). The National Internet propaganda work meeting: Make the views of the Party the strongest voice in the cyberspace. Retrieved 6 January 2017 from http://paper.people.com.cn/rmrb/html/2016-01/07/nw.D110000renmrb_20160107_6-04.htm.

Plantin, J.-C., Lagoze, C., Edwards, P. N. and Sandvig, C. (2016). Infrastructure studies meet platform studies in the age of Google and Facebook. *New Media & Society, 20*(1), 293–310.

Portes, A. and Haller, W. (2005). The informal economy, in *Handbook of economic sociology*, eds N. Smelser and R. Swedberg, Princeton University Press, Princeton, NJ, pp. 403–428.

Portes, A., Castells, M. and Benton, L. A. (eds) (1989). *The informal economy: Studies in advanced and less developed countries*, Johns Hopkins University Press, Baltimore, MD.

Qiu, J. L. (2009). *Working-class network society: Communication technology and the information have-less in urban China*, MIT Press, Cambridge.

Qiu, J. L. (2010). Chinese techno-nationalism and global WiFi policy, in *Reorienting global communication: Indian and Chinese media beyond borders*, eds M. Curtin and H. Shah, University of Illinois Press, Urbana, IL, pp. 289–303.

Qiu, J. L. (2016). *Goodbye iSlave: A manifesto for digital abolition*, University of Illinois Press, Urbana, Chicago, Springfield.

Qiu, J. L., Gregg, M. and Crawford, K. (2014). Circuits of labour: A labour theory of the iPhone era. *TripleC: Communication, Capitalism, Critique, 12*(2), 486–563.

Rochet, J.-C. and Tirole, J. (2003). Platform competition in two-sided market. *Journal of European Economic Association, 1*(4), 990–1029.

Rosenblat, A. and Stark, L. (2016). Algorithmic labor and information asymmetries: A case study of Uber's drivers. *International Journal of Communication, 10*, 3758–3784.

Ross, A. (2009). *Nice work if you can get it: Life and labour in precarious times*, New York University Press, New York, NY.

Sassen-Koob, S. (1989). New York City's informal economy, in *The informal economy: Studies in advanced and less developed countries*, eds A. Portes, M. Castells and L. A. Benton, Johns Hopkins University Press, Baltimore, MD, pp. 60–77.

Schiller, D. (2011). Geopolitical-economic conflict and network infrastructures. *Chinese Journal of Communication, 4*(1), 90–107.

Scholz, T. (2016). *Uberworked and underpaid: How workers are disrupting the digital economy*, Polity, Cambridge.

Seijdel, J. and Melis, L. (2008). *The rise of the informal media*, SKOR/NAi Publishers, Amsterdam.

Severin, W. J. (1994). The new cultural revolution: The spread of satellite dishes in China. *International journal of Public Opinion Research, 94*(6), 72–76.

Shen, H. (2016). China and global internet governance: Toward an alternative analytical framework, *Chinese Journal of Communication, 9*(3), 304–324.

Smythe, D. W. (1977). Communications: Blindspot of Western Marxism. *Canadian Journal of Political and Social Theory, 1*(3), 1–27.

Smythe, D. W. (1981). *Dependency road*, Ablex, Norwood, NJ.

Srnicek, N. (2016). *Platform capitalism*, Polity, Cambridge, UK; Malden, MA.
Stepick, A. (1989). Miami's two informal sectors, in *The informal economy: Studies in advanced and less developed countries*, eds A. Portes, M. Castells and L. A. Benton, Johns Hopkins University Press, Baltimore, MD, pp. 111–134.
Suchman, M. C. (1995). Managing legitimacy: Strategic and institutional approaches. *Academy of Management Review*, *20*(3), 571–610.
Sullivan, J. (2012). A tale of two microblogs in China. *Media, Culture & Society*, *34*(6), 773–783.
Tapscott, D. and Williams, A. D. (2006). *Wikinomics: How mass collaboration changes everything*, Portfolio, New York, NY.
Terranova, T. (2000). Free Labor: Producing culture for the digital economy. *Social Text*, *6*(18), 33–58.
Toffler, A. (1980). *The third wave*. New York: Bantam Books.
Tsui, L. (2003). The panopticon as the antithesis of a space of freedom: Control and regulation of the Internet in China. *China Information*, *17*(2), 65–82.
UNESCO (2013). Creative economy report 2013 special edition: Widening local development pathways. UNESCO and United Nations Development Programme, Paris and New York, NY.
Van Dijck, J. (2009). Users like you? Theorizing agency in user-generated content. *Media, Culture & Society*, *31*(1), 41–58.
Van Dijck, J. (2013). *The culture of connectivity: A critical history of social media*, Oxford University Press, Oxford.
Van Dijck, J. and Poell, T. (2013). Understanding social media logic. *Media and Communication*, *1*(1), 2–14.
Van Dijck, J., Poell, T. and de Waal, M. (2016). *De platformsamenleving: Strijd om publieke waarden in een online wereld*, Amsterdam University Press, Amsterdam.
Wang, J. (2004). The global reach of a new discourse: How far can 'creative industries' travel? *International Journal of Cultural Studies*, *7*(1), 9–19.
Wang, S. (2003). *Framing piracy: Globalization and film distribution in Greater China*, Rowman & Littlefield, Lanham, MD.
Weber, I. and Lu, J. (2007). Internet and self-regulation in China: The cultural logic of controlled commodification. *Media, Culture & Society*, *29*(5), 772–789.
Wilson, M. (2013). Didactic escapism: New viewing practices among China's digital generation, in *Asian popular culture in transition*, eds L. Fitzsimmons and J. A. Lent, Routledge, London; New York, pp. 77–96.
Wu, J. (2017). Migrant citizenship regimes in globalized China: A historical-institutional comparison. *Rural China*, *14*(1), 128–154.
Wu, S. (2001). *Qian guize: Zhongguo lishi de zhenshi youxi* [*Informal rules: The real games of Chinese history*], Yunnan People's Press, Kunming.
Xia, J. (2012a). China's telecommunications industry in the era of 3G and beyond: Market, technology, and institutions. *Telecommunications Policy*, *36*(10), 793–797.
Xia, J. (2012b). Competition and regulation in China's 3G/4G mobile communications industry: Institutions, governance, and telecom SOEs. *Telecommunications Policy*, *36*(10), 798–816.
Xinhua News (2014). Xi Jinping: Build China into a strong internet power. Retrieved 6 June 2014 from www.xinhuanet.com/politics/2014-02/27/c_119538788.htm.
Xinhua News (2017). China's digital economy accounts for 30% of 2016 GDP: Report. Retrieved 5 December 2017 from www.chinadaily.com.cn/business/4thwic/2017-12/04/content_35202779.htm.

Yang, G. (2009). *The power of the internet in China: Citizen activism online*, Columbia University Press, New York.
Yang, G. (2012). A Chinese Internet? History, practice, and globalization. *Chinese Journal of Communication*, *5*(1), 49–54.
Yu, H. (2009). *Media and cultural transformation in China*, Routledge, London; New York, NY.
Zhang, W. and Mao, C. (2013). Fan activism sustained and challenged: Participatory culture in Chinese online translation communities. *Chinese Journal of Communication*, *6*(1), 45–61.
Zhang, Y. (2000). From masses to audience: Changing media ideologies and practices in reform China. *Journalism Studies*, *1*(4), 617–635.
Zhao, E. (2017). The bumpy road towards network convergence in China: The case of over-the-top streaming services. *Global Media and China*, 2(1), 28–42.
Zhao, Y. (1998). *Media, market, and democracy in China: Between the party line and the bottom line*, University of Illinois Press, Urbana, IL.
Zhao, Y. (2003). Transnational capital, the Chinese state, and China's communication industries in a fractured society. *Javnost – The Public*, *10*(4), 53–74.
Zhao, Y. (2008). *Communication in China: Political economy, power and conflict*, Rowman & Littlefield, Lanham, MD.
Zhao, Y. (2010). China's pursuit of indigenous innovations in information technology developments: Hopes, follies and uncertainties. *Chinese Journal of Communication*, 3(3), 266–289.
Zhao, Y. and Schiller, D. (2001). Dances with wolves? China's integration into digital capitalism. *Info*, *3*(2), 137–151.

2 Repackaged informality and norm-based governance

From *shanzhaiji* to open source-powered smartphones

'How a nation of tech copycats transformed into a hub for innovation' (*Wired*, 2015). This is the title of an article published in the December 2015 edition of *Wired* magazine. The story features a diverse range of technology entrepreneurship in China. While many scholars and China observers have yet to be convinced about its innovation capacity, China has had a long-standing reputation for the *shanzhai* culture. *Shanzhai* is one of the ten words that Chinese writer Yu Hua (2012) chooses to capture contemporary China. Often associated with copycats or counterfeit production, *shanzhai* carries a distinctive social and cultural significance. Dating back to the popular Ming dynasty novel *Outlaws of the Marsh* (*Shuihu zhuan*), the word *shanzhai* literally means a mountain village where a brotherhood of renegade bandits would gather. In the early 2000s, *shanzhai* became associated with informal enterprises in the Special Economic Zone of Shenzhen, Guangdong Province, as well as their products. Underlying this association are the characteristics of escaping from authority, rising up against social injustice, and developing a set of rules parallel to those of the government (Keane and Zhao, 2012). Over time, *shanzhai* has become further popularised, referring to the cultural phenomenon of parodies and *e'gao* in the age of UGC and social media (Yang, 2016). Essentially, *shanzhai* is located in a space where copying, re-use and innovation are not mutually exclusive, and the line between the formal and informal is not clear-cut (Lindtner and Dourish, 2011; Keane and Zhao, 2012; Wong, 2014; Zhang and Fung, 2013).

Once well known for *shanzhai* products, the mobile phone industry in China has witnessed a home-grown brand rising to the pinnacle of the global smartphone scene in recent years. Established in 2010, Beijing Xiaomi Technology Co. Ltd launched its first smartphone product in 2011. The company has received venture capitalist funding from investors such as IDG Capital, Temasek Holdings, Qualcomm Inc., All-Stars Investment, Yuri Milner's DST, GIC, Hopu Fund and Yunfeng Capital (Forbes, 2014). Xiaomi is known for developing its Android-based MIUI operating system and selling high-specification products at narrow margins. By the end of 2014 it had leapfrogged Lenovo and LG to become the third largest smartphone manufacturer in the world behind Samsung and Apple (Gibbs, 2014). Xiaomi's CEO and founder Lei Jun attributes the success largely to the ability to spot historic opportunities. According to him,

'Even a pig can fly if it stands at the centre of a whirlwind' (*Wall Street Journal*, 2015). While such statement seems humble, the state project of rebranding 'Made in China' and open source software cultures in the smartphone age have indeed afforded Xiaomi significant opportunities.

This chapter focuses on Xiaomi's initial success in the smartphone market with its Android-based MIUI operating system, and explains how the platform repackages informality for value production, and how the contested process triggers informal governance. The chapter begins with an overview of relevant contexts: first, the development of *shanzhaiji* (*shanzhai* electronic devices, most notably mobile phones) in a tightly regulated market, which eventually triggered industry deregulation and the state's attempt to subsume the informal and rebrand 'Made in China'; and second, open source software cultures and the rise of Android in the smartphone era. It then considers the case of Xiaomi. Based on in-depth interviews conducted between November 2014 and January 2015 with users, amateur developers and corporate employees, and observation of online communities and secondary sources, this chapter analyses how the brand navigates between the formal and informal at operational and discursive levels. Specifically, how the platform draws on informal energy among users in product development; how it attempts to craft a distinctive brand identity by both aligning with the state rebranding project and capitalising on open source software cultures; how it shares a certain *shanzhai* ethos yet strategically distances itself from the negative connotations of *shanzhai*. Moreover, I interrogate the complexity of openness, highlight the tension in the conjunction of control, value and ownership, and reveal the power of norm-based governance as the platform navigates between the formal and informal.

Collapsed boundaries in industry deregulation and national rebranding of 'Made in China'

Mobile phone manufacturing was once a sector with high entry barriers in China. Back in 1998, the then Ministry of Information Industry (MII) and the State Planning Commission (SPC) introduced a strict licensing regime in the emerging sector then dominated by Motorola, Nokia and Ericsson (Office of State Council of PRC, 1998). Along with the licensing scheme, the regulatory authorities stipulated that 60 per cent of mobile phones produced in foreign-owned factories must be exported. The purpose, evidently, was to nurture national champions, or large state-owned enterprises (SOEs), a strategy often used in the Chinese version of the development state. Such an intention further manifested itself in the state's move to identify information industries as pillar industries in the Tenth Five-Year Plan released in 2001.

Unsurprisingly, the licensing regulation pushed many private enterprises into the informal arena. Known as *shanzhai* producers, these unlicensed enterprises evaded tax and skipped after-sales service to cut costs. Many traders employed cash-based transactions to avoid being traceable by regulators. By utilising the integrated chip solution developed by the Taiwanese company MediaTek in

2003, these producers were able to significantly reduce production cycles and respond agilely to local needs. While often associated with copycat or counterfeit products of inferior quality, *shanzhai* producers have their innovative side. Zhu and Shi (2010) describe *shanzhai* as 'grassroots innovation' in contrast to the officially sanctioned 'indigenous innovation', as the former takes place outside the purview of state control. Crucially, the *shanzhai* mobile industry has developed innovation networks that are more open than the brand name manufacturers, which are constrained by corporate secrecy and exclusive deals with telecom operators (Wallis and Qiu, 2012). *Shanzhai* producers never design anything from scratch. They always build on the best of existing products, and there are rules in the community that they should share as much information as they can to make it easy for others to add value and also act responsibly within the supply chain (Jeffrey, 2011). Thus, *shanzhai* producers can be conceptualised as embodying adaptive creativity (Tatsuno, 1990), and second-generation innovation (Breznitz and Murphree, 2011). The practice of sharing has contributed to an emergent regional innovation system (Keane and Zhao, 2012). As such, creativity takes on a networked character. This is distinct from the individual-based conception of creativity in the Western context, which serves as the foundation of intellectual property law (Pang, 2012).

Moreover, *shanzhai* has its cultural potency. *Shanzhai* mobile phones not only appealed to the working class owing to their affordable prices and pragmatic features such as dual SIM cards and extended battery life, but also became adopted by artsy, 'cool' youth in major cities because of the embodiment of a rebellious spirit as well as their kitsch designs, lower price and functional innovations (Wallis and Qiu, 2012). The dissemination of *shanzhai* phenomenon into popular cultural production further manifests its cultural resonance in the wider society (Keane and Zhao, 2012). In the words of Zhang and Fung (2013), *shanzhai* combines 'the traditional Chinese metaphor of grassroots anti-establishment heroism with modern rhetoric of technology-empowered bottom-up democracy' (p. 402).

The development of *shanzhaiji* eventually collapsed licensing regulation, and by extension, the boundaries between the formal and informal market. The state started to lower the entry threshold in 2005, and completely lifted the licensing regulation two years later. The relaxing and ultimate abolishment of the licensing regulation is attributable to two factors. First, authorities were divided in their attitudes towards *shanzhai*, and the increasing number of *shanzhaiji* manufacturers increased enforcement costs to a prohibitively high level (Liao and Chen, 2011). While a large number of SOEs suffered staggering losses as a result of the influx of *shanzhai* devices, both local governments and telecom operators had few incentives to assist MII in policing the informal market. Local governments regarded it as a contributor to local GDP and job opportunities, and telecom operators benefited from the network consumption on *shanzhai* devices. Second, *shanzhaiji* producers took the initiative to earn a place in the formal economy. As Zhang and Fung (2013) explains, while *shanzhai* producers derive cultural potency from being alternative to the establishment, some paradoxically harbour aspirations to join the ranks of the mainstream. Breaking into the formal economy is not only an economic process of securing buyers and consumers; it involves the social processes of building and enhancing legitimacy, via its emphasis on fairness and justice, to challenge institutional pressures (Lee and Hung, 2014).

Industry deregulation effectively allowed informal enterprises a gateway to the formal economy. This is closely connected to the state's intention to selectively relocate the *shanzhai* energy to the formal economy. Soon after deregulation, the state media China Central Television (CCTV) portrayed *shanzhai* with a nuanced approach in 2008 and 2009. On one hand, it questioned the mixed quality of *shanzhaiji* and highlighted the need to protect consumer rights. On the other hand, it acknowledged the market success of *shanzhai*. Indeed, some *shanzhaiji* enterprises have unexpectedly achieved what China hoped the state-supported national champions to accomplish, both at home and abroad (Wallis and Qiu, 2012). The state media linked the success of *shanzhai* to people's wisdom, but meanwhile deemed *shanzhaiji* producers to be harmful to domestic industries and to the 'Made in China' brand, which therefore needed to be upgraded. As Yang (2016) insightfully points out, the state media attempted to appropriate the *shanzhai* discourse to realign the state with 'the people', who needs to be 'protected' from 'fake' products, and thereby subsume the *shanzhai* energy and create the nation's own IPR-legible brands.

This attempt is closely connected to the national rebranding project of revamping the image of 'Made in China'. Indeed, the state has found itself facing an urgent need to appropriate a global discourse on 'Made in China' by constructing a national imaginary, targeting both domestic and overseas consumers (Yang, 2015). Previous state-initiated communication campaigns, such as a week-long special program, 'Believe in Made in China', aired on the state media CCTV in 2007, and the 30-second 'Made in China, Made with the World' commercial aired on CNN in 2009, aimed to shake off the tag of inferior quality associated with 'Made in China'. The result has however perpetuated the stereotypical image of China as the world's factory (Shambaugh, 2013). Another relevant state developmental project on a broader scale revolved around the notion of propelling a shift 'from made in China to created in China' (Keane, 2007). Here creativity becomes 'reified as intellectual property which the rights holders own and can benefit from' (Pang, 2012, p. 3). The 'Created in China' discourse departs from the previous attempts in that it conveys a shifted focus from tangible manufacturing to intangible values arising from brands. The attempted move upward along the value chain indicates the effect of the Intellectual Property Rights (IPR) regime on China especially after its entry into the World Trade Organization (WTO). Such attempts involve distilling the creative elements of the *shanzhai* economy and repackaging them into the new promotional discourse and value production process. In other words, the negative connotations of the informal have to be muted as the informal is subsumed into the formal.

However, it was not long before *shanzhaiji* enterprises began to witness a bleak market scenario. The entry of new players into the formal market has intensified market competition and significantly driven down profit margins.

Sales grew at a slower rate in 2010 and started to slip in 2011 (Jiao, 2011). The once bustling Huaqiangbei market in Shenzhen saw a growing number of resellers in the electronics malls packing up and quitting the *shanzhaiji* business (Ho, 2013). This can be attributed to several factors. Notably, MTK was slow to offer a turn-key solution for smartphones, hence preventing *shanzhaiji* manufacturers with little research and development capability to compete in the market as they were able to do earlier. Moreover, competitive pricing and operator subsidies have made smartphones more appealing to some consumers. While the *shanzhaiji* market has declined, some of the *shanzhai* ethos has found new life in the era of smartphone and open source culture.

The era of smartphone and open source culture

The launch of the iPhone in 2007 and the App Store in the following year opened up the smartphone chapter. This marked a significant moment of technological and media convergence between the mobile and the computer (Burgess, 2012). The highly closed nature of the iPhone in the early days has drawn criticism, most notably perhaps from Zittrain (2008), who called it a 'tethered appliance' characterised by networks of control. While Zittrain perceived the mobile as a contrast to the generative possibilities of the internet, Goggin (2009) points to the fact that the iPhone has become more open through a process of adaptation over time, allowing better access for developers and facilitating a thriving user culture.

Following iPhone, the unveiling of the Android platform in 2007 has opened up further space for innovation. Although its open nature is relative (Goggin, 2012; Spreeuwenberg and Poell, 2012), the Android Open Source Project (AOSP) allows third parties to access and tweak the Android source code and create custom operating systems and applications. The open source approach has made it a commercially appealing choice, leading many device manufacturers to pump out Android mobile phones. Consequently, Android has gained a growing market share in the mobile OS market and has become a significant competitor of iOS. According to Sawhney (2009), open source mobile phone projects have offered the potential to create 'arenas of innovation'.

The open source software movement has inherited the ethos of the commons of software code from the free software movement, which had its roots in a culture linked with an ethic of individual liberty and technical prowess (Himanen, 2001a). Richard Stallman, who launched the GNU Project in 1983, and with it the free software movement, emphasised the need to provide users with four kinds of freedoms:

Software Freedom 0.

> The freedom to run the program for any purpose.

Software Freedom 1.

> The freedom to study how the program works, and change it to make it to do what you wish. Access to the source code is precondition to this.

Software Freedom 2.

> The freedom to redistribute copies to help your neighbours.

Software Freedom 3.

> The freedom to improve the program and release your improvements (and modified versions in general) to the public, so that the whole community benefits. Access to the source code is a precondition to this (Stallman, 1999).

Such freedoms constitute the foundation of the GNU Public Licence (GPL) for free software, developed by Stallman in 1989. As an attempt to codify the practices of free software development, GPL requires all codes created under the licence to maintain the terms of the licence and themselves remain free, with the source code released to a publicly accessible repository (Stallman, 1999).

While the open source software production popularised by Eric Raymond has inherited the idea of the commons of software code of free software movement and the two are often conflated into FOSS (Free and Open Source Software), the former does not require all code be subsequently available for free. Stallman criticises open source in that it misses the point of free software. According to Stallman (2015), as a splinter-off from the free software community, open source has become associated with philosophical views based on the practical values of code quality, which is quite different from those of the free software movement stressing users' essential freedoms. The rhetoric of open source software with a focus on practical value has unsurprisingly convinced many businesses and individuals to use and develop free software. Among the more recent beneficiaries of open source software movement is Android, which has challenged the iOS in the marketplace.

Apart from significant cost savings, the advantages of open source software lie in several aspects. First, an open source community will be likely to contain more talented programmers than the development teams at proprietary software firms, resulting in a quick fix of bugs, and diversified approaches to problems leading to the best being adopted, and ultimately more robust products (Raymond, 2001). Apart from that, making source code available to the public means the software can be modified, upgraded or improved without the need to 'reinvent the wheel' (Kettell, 2008). Further, open source software can meet the demands of minority users even when there is little prospect for mass adoption, which proprietary software firms typically avoid doing (Benkler, 2002). Moreover, users can benefit from open source projects and avoid the proprietary lock-in.

For Benkler (2003), FOSS is the most visible part of a new economy of commons-based peer production of information, knowledge and culture, which is different from the property- and contract-based models of firms and markets. Benkler (2006) considers peer production as contributing to a transformation in the structure of value creation, where the logic of contribution replaces the logic of scarcity. The total reward of participating in commons-based peer production consists not only of a monetary reward, but also an intrinsic hedonic reward and a social-psychological reward. Such practices introduce new forms of labour relations, as amateur programmers contribute to source codes that are used within the software industry (Weber, 2004). For Terranova (2004), the open source movement demonstrates the over-reliance of the digital economy on free labour, free in the sense both of not financially rewarded and of willingly given. This illustrates the interconnection of the formal and informal, and also raises questions of how they interact with each other.

The case of Xiaomi

Co-creative process across formal and informal boundaries

Taking advantage of the programmability and generativity of the open source Android, Xiaomi launched its customised version of Android named MIUI in 2010, one year earlier than the launch of the first Xiaomi mobile. While the brand is well known for smartphones, its operating system played a significant role in building up a fan base prior to launching the mobile phone. This distinguished Xiaomi significantly from other Android phone producers at the time.

The development process of MIUI exemplifies the redeployment of elements originating in the informal economy in the formal market (Lobato and Thomas, 2015). As well as an in-house research and development team, Xiaomi enlists users as product managers, developers and testers from outside the organisational boundary. Users contributing informally to product development with relevant expertise are labelled the 'honorary development team'. Active users on the MIUI online forum who are enthusiastic about product improvement, and the wider user community who seek top product performance, also contribute to product development. They report bugs, suggest improvements, make comments and vote on different ideas. The diversity of the contributing users allows them to work through problems collaboratively while each contributing in their own way. Rapid prototyping and networked production thus characterised the development of MIUI system.

While there is no monetary reward in the commons-based production, users are motivated by various intrinsic and extrinsic rewards. Interviews with co-creators for Xiaomi reveal various motivations. For some, participating in product development informally is intrinsically rewarding (Personal Interview, 2014, 2015). Others find sufficient incentive in getting the first peek of the product in development, or shaping better products in various ways (Personal Interview, 2014, 2015). Indeed, the bug list on the online forum of MIUI has been the most active part of the online forum. Further, interviewees who self-crown as hard-core Mi fans often follow developers' microblog accounts and have a clear idea of who is responsible for certain features. This allows them to notify appropriate developers of any bugs they find. Users with more technological expertise often aim to develop their proficiency in tweaking the system. Many among them mentioned that they valued peer recognition of their technological expertise (Personal Interview, 2014, 2015). Over time, active participation on the Xiaomi forum has become an identity label for mobile enthusiasts. As one interviewee put it:

> You simply can't claim yourself as a mobile phone tinkerer if you have not posted any suggestions for improvement at Xiaomi forum.
>
> (Personal Interview, November 2014)

The vitality of the online community further facilitates the evolution of users' motivations to participate in co-creation activities. As some users become more technologically sophisticated, they hope to reciprocate after benefiting from the community. As one user recounted:

> I went to the forum for the first time when I had to solve a problem with my Xiaomi. People were very helpful there and I got my problem solved. Then I became more involved in the forum. Gradually I have become a sophisticated player and want to help new users in the forum. It makes me feel great.
>
> (Personal Interview, November 2014)

A user with more sophisticated technological expertise echoed:

> I've answered many questions on the forum. Those people I help may never be able to answer my question, but someone else might be.
>
> (Personal Interview, November 2014)

This speaks to the gift culture associated with the open source community (Raymond, 2001). This gift culture is intimately bound up with a shared belief in the public ownership of intellectual property.

In-house developer teams at Xiaomi are organised around modules and thus become more nimble. Two or three developers form a team and follow one module's development process, and different teams work in parallel and follow common protocols (Personal Interview, January 2015). Modularisation is a key aspect of modern software design that allows the management of complex systems by dividing software architecture into smaller components (Baldwin and Clark, 2000; Gehl, 2012). According to Helmond (2015), modularisation constitutes a key dimension of the platformisation of the web. The modularisation of software production has gained prominence with the emergence of a free and open source movement (Raymond, 2001). This allows module designers to experiment with different options, with each module developing incrementally on its own semi-independent trajectory while subject to a coordinating framework of design rules. In the case of Xiaomi, developers interact with enthusiastic fans constantly so as to continuously improve the design. These module-based developer groups have decision-making power based on their own interactions with users, which motivates them to solicit and respond to user feedback (Personal Interview, January 2015). Moreover, the short development and update cycle means developers can afford to make mistakes, which can be corrected very quickly.

Individual in-house developers are required go to the online forum on a daily basis to learn about user feedback for continuous product improvement. Initially this expectation encountered a lack of understanding from some senior developers, as they considered it a customer service representative's job (Personal Interview, January 2015). Gradually they have come to see the point of this practice. As one developer says:

> They are our treasures. The most valuable treasures are the honorary development team. They are a group of frenetic geeks. They are willing to try out new features even though there might be bugs and the system might not run smoothly. They will also answer questions from other users, help them solve problems and collect feedback from them.
>
> (Personal Interview, January 2015)

Thus in-house developers take the additional task of online community facilitation by directly interacting with end-users day in and day out to elicit user feedback, discover user expectations, spot problems and explain design rationale. Ordinary fans act as sounding boards as they evaluate the product and initiate the feedback loop, which then informs the development process further. As the user base grows beyond the capacity for in-house developers to engage with it directly, the developers have the assistance of more sophisticated users and hardcore fans, who leverage their technological expertise to act as boundary spanners to facilitate communications between in-house developers and ordinary users.

As a result of the interactions between developers and user communities, the organisation releases updates to the operating system every Friday by incorporating suggestions and feedback from users. This allows Xiaomi to continuously improve the product based on rapid prototyping. Such rapidness is a means rather than an end, as it facilitates further improvement of the product by engaging users. While the 'release early, release often' approach in commercial settings allows developers to experiment with immature ideas and continuously improve products, it is important to note the countervailing force in user expectations (Weber, 2000). To accommodate users who may not like buggy releases and even less the process of updating or installing new releases on a frequent basis, Xiaomi has a stable version for them to use, which does not load updates as frequently. This proves to be an effective strategy addressing different user needs. In fact, while some users expressed enthusiasm and excitement over the weekly updates, which allow them to get a fresh taste of new features, others acknowledged their preference for the more stable version with a longer update cycle (Personal Interview, 2014, 2015). The difference in product release approaches here speaks to the need for a platform to attend to multiple publics with different needs (Gillespie, 2010).

For the organisation, acknowledging user contributions and respect for users are important in nurturing the relationship with them. As the organisation incorporates user input in the product development process, contributing users receive acknowledgement in the release of the updated version. Many users including amateur developers discussed how they felt about being respected. As one interviewee commented on this practice, 'Xiaomi keeps its ears open and respects us users. This is a big reason why I support Xiaomi' (Personal Interview, January 2015). Respect for users and acknowledgement of their contributions further result in a word-of-mouth effect. One moderator of the online forum discussed this common mentality among users during the interview. As he recalled, he was 'honoured' when his suggestion was adopted by Xiaomi and he did not hesitate to share the news with his family and friends and also in online communities (Personal Interview, January 2015). As Lei Jun outlines his vision, 'Every user becomes your R&D, every user becomes your sales, every user becomes your friend, that's the company we want to make' (quoted in Kan, 2013). Therefore, as Xiaomi engages users in the co-creation process, it not only facilitates product development but also gains branding currency through user advocacy.

As Lobato and Thomas (2015) point out, 'the brand's power exists in its mobility, which can include the capacity to move between formal and informal economies' (p. 140). As the enterprise channels informal creative energy into product development and knowledge production, actors from outside corporate boundaries contribute with varying levels of interest and resource endowments of time and expertise. As Stark (2009) observes, the boundaries of the unit of action, the unit of innovation and the unit of entrepreneurship are not those of the legally bounded firm; it is more distributed networks that span organisational boundaries. In Xiaomi's case, such distributed networks comprise employees, hard-core fans and 'ordinary' users who participate in the development process and collaborate with each other in order to shape better products while meeting various socio-psychological needs. As the formal and informal interact with each other in co-creating products, knowledge and value, respect for the community is essential in facilitating its growth and maintaining its vitality.

Cultivation of a distinctive brand identity

As Xiaomi navigates the formal/informal boundaries in product development, it has carefully crafted its brand mission, values and commitment. As stated on the official website, its mission of 'innovation for everyone' is underpinned by the belief that 'high-quality products built with cutting-edge technology should be made accessible to everyone', and its commitment to 'creat[ing] remarkable hardware, software, and Internet services for and with the help of our Mi fans'. Evidently, Xiaomi wishes to develop a brand identity based on high quality, technological innovation, a co-creative culture and affordable pricing that distinguishes itself from competitors, including national brands and *shanzhaiji.*

The emphasis on networked production leading to high quality and innovation is closely linked to an open source culture. This relies to a large extent on directing creative energies in informal space to the formal market. As Xiaomi mobilises potential contributors from outside the corporate boundary, its discursive work around brand positioning supports its operational logic. As Xiaomi's founder and CEO Lei Jun put it, 'We're building a toy for our fans' (quoted in Watkins, 2013), or 'We do not sell mobile phones; we sell a sense of participation' (quoted in Kan, 2013). Moreover, as reflected in the slogan 'born for enthusiasts' (*wei fashao er sheng*), the brand-targeted mobile enthusiasts are its initial fan base, including those who pursue high product performance and tinkerers who seek playability and customisability of smartphones. The brand narrative on participatory culture as a selling point and prioritisation of fans and enthusiasts in its brand positioning rides on the cultural imaginary of the internet as a playground where digital labour activities do not 'feel, look, or smell like labour at all' (Scholz, 2012, p. 2).

The promotional discourse further enhances the connection with co-creative users by highlighting the organisation's recognition of user contributions. A salient example is a micro-movie titled *One Hundred Dream Sponsors* produced by Xiaomi in 2013. The micro-movie tells the story of a carwash worker, who owns a low-end Volkswagen Jetta, realising his dream of becoming a racing driver and winning the race with the support of a group of people. Here the organisation pays tribute to the first 100 user testers who helped to improve MIUI, and addresses them as sponsors of Xiaomi's dreams. The micro-movie was first released at Mi Fans Festival in 2013 and then distributed on various online streaming platforms. Users recognised the organisation's respect for them, although some were quick to point out that it was a good advertising strategy (Personal Interview, November 2014). Others expressed their hope for the organisation to maintain its respect for users in future (Personal Interview, November 2014).

Further, the brand narrative shows the organisation's attempt to establish differentiation from *shanzhai* on one hand and highlight its alignment with the interest of the state on the other. First, Xiaomi's attempt to draw a clear line between *shanzhaiji* and itself is perhaps best illustrated by a statement often iterated by Lei Jun. For Lei, one of Xiaomi's greatest achievement is to have defeated many *shanzhaiji* manufacturers in China (Sina.com, 2017). This statement alludes to the difference between Xiaomi and *shanzhaiji* producers. The distinction however is not as clear-cut as it seems. First of all, while the term *shanzhaiji* often conjures up the image of inferiority, many products in fact do not pale in comparison to their 'genuine' counterparts and have achieved market success despite not having a legitimate, state-defined status. Some *shanzhaiji* enterprises have unexpectedly achieved market success both at home and abroad (Wallis and Qiu, 2012). Second, while Xiaomi operates as a legal brand and many *shanzhai* producers have a history of operating in the grey or black economy, the two share similarities in production mode. By cultivating fan communities and engaging them in co-creative production based on open source software, Xiaomi has to some extent inherited the *shanzhai* ethos of decentralised innovation through sharing, rapid prototyping and iterative design. While *shanzhaiji* enterprises operate in defiance of IPR, Xiaomi rides on the alternative copyright regime represented by open source software. Such a regime reverses the dominant meaning of private intellectual property as a right of exclusion and propagates software freedom. By involving users in product development, the brand adopts a more inclusive approach to innovation, expanding from the networked model and focusing more on industry partners in the *shanzhai* model. The boundary between the formal and informal is contingent in both Xiaomi and *shanzhai* producers. However, the brand strategically negates similarity with *shanzhai*, as reflected in its co-creative production process. The muted informalities however underlie Xiaomi's innovative capacity and value production.

While eliding its similarities with *shanzhai* in production mode, Xiaomi further differentiates itself from *shanzhai* by aligning with the state interest. In connection with the message of high quality resulting from networked production, Lei Jun established the association between the brand vision and the state project to revamp the 'Made in China' image on multiple occasions. As Lei said, Xiaomi will 'produce new national products with better product quality than overseas brands, and by so doing to redefine "Made in China", which has so far been associated with inferior quality' (quoted in Sun, 2016). Therefore, unlike anti-establishment *shanzhai* enterprises, Xiaomi attempts to align with the state cause by taking on the mission of improving the national image. By blending the brand vision and value with the state discourse on nation rebranding, it reflects a growing trend of commercial nationalism, where 'commercial institutions take on an increasingly important role in framing issues of national identity and promulgating branded forms of nationalisms and nationalist brand identities' (Volčič and Andrejevic, 2018, p. 612).

Crucially, the connection between the brand narrative and the state project of revamping the 'Made in China' brand has only become possible owing to Xiaomi's status as a formal, IPR-eligible brand. By contrast, *shanzhai* enterprises situated in the shadow economy prior to industry deregulation have not had the capacity to create such an alliance even when they crossed the quality threshold. Their defiance of IPR inherently contradicts the state mission, especially in the post-WTO era. As Zhang and Fung (2013) explain, *shanzhai* represents a new subjectivity – the 'digital trickster who thrives on the instrumental marriage among commercial self-branding/promotion, playful irreverence, and populist anarchism' (p. 408). The informal economy of *shanzhai* thus exists outside the aura of the state rebranding project.

Contested co-creation and norm-based governance

While the organisation can conveniently link co-creation to the imaginary of user empowerment, the site of co-creation can be a contested terrain. Indeed, the celebratory discourse of the internet's democratic potential, or the myth of the 'digital sublime' (Mosco, 2004), is confronted with tensions and contradictions. While the brand derives value from open source culture and co-creative users, brand narratives and legitimacy could face serious challenges when the complexity of openness emerges and organisational practice is misaligned with accepted community norms.

The co-creative process involves integrating different kinds of knowledge and authority. Mansell (2013) discusses how collaboration across formal and informal boundaries could involve conflicts between the values and norms associated with the production of different forms of knowledge and authority. These include 'constituted authority' characterised by hierarchical relations based on the formal norms of science and its institutions; and 'adaptive authority', referring to loose, bottom-up, often informal, forms of authority that are frequently associated with information activities of many loosely connected online groups (p. 256). The distinction between forms of authority highlights different aims: whereas constituted authority is concerned with the valorisation of certain forms of knowledge and control over access to them, adaptive authority aims to generate information for timely sharing and immediate application. As the formal comes into contact with the informal in knowledge production, tensions may arise. Such tensions have become particularly evident when the formal adopts discourses and norms that resemble those typical of the informal, but its social technology remains that of constituted authority.

In the context of FOSS practices, tensions arise as multiple actors work across formal and informal boundaries. Earlier research on the FOSS movement tended to focus on how its connection to hacker culture has produced shared norms based on shared values and ethics (Mansell, 2013). Of paramount significance are norms of software freedom, which governs free software and supposedly contributes to the maintenance of commons-based knowledge, including open source knowledge (Himanen, 2001b). However, treating free and open source communities as a unified entity sharing uniform values is simplistic and reductive. It runs the risk of considering the free/open character of these communities as something given and undifferentiated where no conflict takes place (de Paoli *et al.*, 2008).

In fact, the complex configurations of techno-legal specifications and political economic strategies in free and open source communities exhibit what Coleman and Golub (2008) call a 'mosaic of ethical positions' (p. 271). Similarly, as Powell (2012) points out, the historical links between hacker culture, the free software movement and the emergence of open source software production illustrate 'the unstable and unresolved dialectic between marginal forms of knowledge and governance, and hegemonic ones' (p. 696). With the development of the movement, various licences have been developed to operationalise the governance of different practices. As a fundamental part of free and software communities, licences manifest heterogeneity and contingency, which give rise to controversies and conflicts (Powell, 2012). As different licences grant different levels of freedom, interlocking layers of information infrastructure add to the complexity of free and open source cultures. In the context of coexisting yet competing philosophies and interlocking layers of code, organisations riding on the wave of free and open source cultures face challenges in navigating the space.

This is a thorny situation faced by Xiaomi, which attempts to build its own platform based on a tweaked version of Linux-based Android. Android is released under Apache 2.0 Licence, a permissive free software licence that does not require derivative works or modifications to the original to be distributed using the same licence. This means development based on works using the Apache licence may not remain free and can become completely proprietary. However, the Linux kernel that Android uses is software under GNU General Public Licence (GPLv2). Unlike proprietary software that deprives users of freedom, GNU GPL is a copyleft licence that uses copyright to guarantee their freedom. Specifically, copyleft licences are 'a legal instrument that gives everyone the rights to use, modify, and redistribute the program's code, or any program derived from it, but only if the distribution terms are unchanged' (de Paoli *et al.*, 2008). The intention of requiring all derivative software also to be licensed under the GPL is to facilitate the growth of free software and fend off the enclosure caused by proprietary software. As the GNU GPL embodies a moral stance against proprietary software, it clashes with the pragmatic view of many programmers and imposes constraints on them, since they want to combine proprietary code and free code simply to deliver better solutions (gnu.org, 2014). Therefore Android has shunned the GNU GPL licence and embraced Apache 2.0 licence so as to accommodate the interests of large corporate partners, OEMs (original equipment manufacturers) and telecoms.

As a platform building on platforms, Xiaomi's MIUI is embroiled in interlocking levels of code, and more importantly, the different values they carry. While Android allows its derivatives to become proprietary, Xiaomi's use and modification of the Linux kernel in developing MIUI means that it must comply with the GPLv2 licence and release the source code of the modifications. However, Xiaomi has restricted access to its kernel modifications. This clearly did not comply with the regime of reciprocal sharing imposed by the GPL-based licence. Such non-compliance with the licence that nurtured Android in the first place sparked controversy among users, especially amateur developer communities. Many developers posted on the official MIUI forum to urge Xiaomi to release its kernel source code. One post read:

> I do not ask for version 4.1 or version 5. I only want the kernel source code, and capable developers can come up with good stuff for us. Why can't you just release it? This is Android, not iOS.
>
> (Sunrise paused, 2012)

In a similar vein, another post challenged Xiaomi on its slogan:

> Xiaomi's router software is obviously not quite there yet. Why not release the kernel source code and relevant drivers to allow resourceful developers to make it better? How can the current scenario be anything near 'born for geeks/enthusiasts'?
>
> (lvxj126, 2014)

During the interviews, many users echoed such responses. Some interviewees regarded Xiaomi's non-disclosure of the kernel source code as an indication of lack of respect for users, as it violated the notion of public ownership imposed by the licence. As one user expressed his disappointment:

> I have always thought Xiaomi respects its users and take user experience as its priority. Yet, without disclosing its kernel modifications for Mi3, we Mi fans who love the fun of rooting our devices and trying different ROMs really suffer. There is no third-party ROM as of yet.
>
> (Personal Interview, January, 2015)

Another user explicitly contrasted Xiaomi's transgression with its earlier efforts to show its respect for users through the micro-movie:

> It's simply not enough to acknowledge user contributions in their marketing material. If they really respect users, they should also respect the values of the community.
>
> (Personal Interview, January 2015)

Xiaomi's enclosure approach obviously led users to question its practice in three aspects. First, users questioned its ethics in relation to non-compliance with the licence on which it was built. Second, users questioned the gap between its practice and the brand promise of servicing mobile enthusiasts, many of whom hold dear the importance of adhering to licensing terms. Third, its transgression and the resultant constraints on innovations hurt user experience, therefore showing the organisation's disregard for its users.

Such challenges also came from the international community of developers and users, as the open source mode of production is distributed and autonomous. One notable example is the online petition 'OpenMIUI', which pressured Xiaomi to comply with the GPLv2 licence and make kernel modifications public. Another example is an international unofficial MIUI ROM support site, MIUIAndroid, which published a letter to its online community of users and developers, citing the fact that they were pressuring Xiaomi to open up the kernel source code (MIUIAndroid.com, 2013). Moreover, Xiaomi's transgression has resulted in online posts on the international developer forum XDA, criticising Xiaomi for its non-compliance with the GPLv2 licence and urging the organisation to release the kernel source code in early 2015. The posts emphasised amateur developers' rights to access the source code, the lack of which may result in a more limited opportunity for better software from both developers' and ordinary users' perspectives:

> This transgression is not only morally and legally wrong, but it prevents our developers from modifying key aspects of Xiaomi's phones to make our software visions come true. Moreover, this can potentially concern users wary of security backdoors and other kinds of spyware.
>
> (Serrafero, 2015)

Under ongoing pressure from the developer and user communities both at home and abroad, Xiaomi finally released its kernel source code on Github in March 2015, although it is still not quite up to date with all versions.

This incident highlights the tensions in co-creation where ownership and control of the product and knowledge production process is negotiated between the brand and relevant users. The online protest and petition reveal that amateur developers have a strong sense of ownership of the kernel source code based on the open source software. These developers are willing to take the initiative to solve problems and produce better products for various and evolving needs. While the promotional discourse of the brand employs the notion of the internet as playground and refers to its products as toys, the non-disclosure or delayed release of its kernel source code deprives amateur developers of the right to play. As the brand provides strong disincentives to contributors, who uphold the values and norms behind codes of practice associated with different licences in the complex space of openness, the transgression can pose a serious threat to the continued vitality of the developer community. Moreover, it reduces the opportunity for better products to emerge from collaborative production based on information commons. Interestingly, users do not necessarily put their hope in Xiaomi to develop better products based on the kernel source code. By contrast, users think highly of the broader developer community. Therefore, Xiaomi's non-compliance with the licence has not only diluted its brand value, but more importantly, it has prohibited open innovation on a wider scale. Consequently, brand legitimacy has encountered challenges from users including developer communities, whom the platform relies upon heavily for value production.

As the formal meets the informal, property relations have re-emerged in business models organised around 'open' innovation, instituted new modalities of control over both production and consumption and extended commodification processes rather than curtailed them (Barron, 2013). According to Barron (2013), this highlights how free and open software production is intimately connected, though in complex and ambiguous ways, with the dynamics of contemporary capitalism. While free software projects emerged from a resistance to proprietary control of digital architectures, they have been made to serve as 'laboratories for the development of organisational and managerial techniques tailored to a project-based capitalist economy' (p. 599). Focusing on the role of amateur contributors in the informal sphere, Mansell (2013) critiques their positioning as data sources, rather than collaborators and the resulting power asymmetry. The attempted enclosure of what is categorised as public property based on licensing terms speaks to these arguments. Similarly, Powell (2016) suggests that the focus on authority and legitimacy through the participation process as a means rather than as an end may limit openness in knowledge production. In Xiaomi's case, the conflation of means and ends leads to the threat to brand legitimacy and the dilution of brand value. Moreover, this undermines the organisation's attempt to construct its own platform as it attends to multiple publics, including amateur developers and users.

As the meeting place of the formal and informal becomes a contested site, informal and norm-based governance assumes a significant role. In contrast to formal regulation, informal approaches 'operate through manners, convention and example and tend to co-exist with top-down regulation' (Lobato and Thomas, 2015, p. 117). While in principle the GPL could be enforced through legal remedies, the extent of enforceability remains unclear (McGowan, 2001). Networked developer communities and 'ordinary' users have thus become crucial actors conferring or challenging organisational legitimacy and enforcing informal regulation. Xiaomi's partial compromise with both domestic and transnational developer and user communities who become increasingly vocal online demonstrates the power of an informal approach to copyright enforcement based on norms. Norm-based enforcement includes 'everything from informal gossip and disdain to formal exclusion from the group governed by the norms' (Rai, 1999, p. 81). Within the open source community, informal sanctioning mechanisms are often practised, which include 'flaming' and 'shunning' – public condemnation of those who breach the norm, and refusal to cooperate with these people (Rai, 1999). In Xiaomi's case, such norm-based enforcement is visible in both user and developer communities. This involves individual developers leaving extensive comments on both official forums and non-official developer forums complaining about Xiaomi, mobilising users on the matter, pressuring and negotiating with Xiaomi. As users and developers internalise the norms associated with free and open source cultures, the informal regulation of knowledge production process plays a vital role despite the absence of formal enforcement. As tensions arise from power asymmetry, the fragmentation of ethical positions and the incommensurability of standards for data curation, the meeting point of the formal and informal thus becomes a site where legitimacy is contested in relation to ownership, control and value.

Conclusions

From *shanzhaiji* to open source smartphones, the mobile phone industry in China has witnessed interesting intersections and coevolution of the formal and informal. *Shanzhaiji* production as an informal practice came into being as a result of the strict licensing regulation by the state, on the back of technologies developed in the formal sector and the ethos of anti-establishment heroism and bottom-up democracy. While located outside the formal sphere, some *shanzhaiji* manufacturers were innovative despite the common association with copyright infringement. Its development not only disrupted the formal market but also nullified the licensing regulation.

As the deregulated market paralleled the development of an open source culture, the market witnessed the rise of a new generation of smartphone makers, most notably represented by Xiaomi. By capitalising on the Android platform and open source culture, Xiaomi has developed its Android-based operating system, a crucial platform for its market expansion. The operation's logic has resided in redirecting informal energy among users to the formal sphere. Meanwhile, the organisation has attempted to craft a distinctive brand identity focusing on high quality, technological innovation and a co-creative culture. Crucially, promotional discourse involves establishing differentiation from *shanzhai* by accentuating the latter's connotations of inferior quality and informal status, and eliding similarity with *shanzhai* in production mode. While the brand narrative employs the celebratory discourse on the internet as a playground and stresses fun and empowerment in its co-creative culture, it deliberately obscures the fact that the brand inherits, or appropriates, the *shanzhai* ethos of openness and networked knowledge production. The appropriation is evident in its informal enlisting of users as a crucial part of co-creating product, and more importantly, knowledge and value. Further, while funded by transnational capital, the organisation has attempted to craft a brand identity by closely aligning with the state interest. This involves packaging the brand as a digital champion for the national rebranding project to bolster the reputation of the 'Made in China' label. This approach constitutes a sharp contrast with that of *shanzhai*, which involved gaining social legitimacy with the connotation of anti-establishment grassroots. Crucially, an alliance with the national rebranding project in terms of quality and innovation is a privilege exclusive to formal brands.

As the formal and the informal interact with each other in the co-creative culture, challenges arise at the conjunction of control, value and ownership. Although the licensing regulation that used to cast a shadow on *shanzhai* is no longer in place, attempts to derive legitimacy from the institutional context including the alliance with the national branding project prove to be insufficient to deliver the crafted brand identity. As open source software culture facilitates innovations across the formal and informal spheres, incongruities between different licences and their associated norms and cultures, as well as the multilayered nature of information infrastructure, set the boundaries for organisations. Indeed, internet regulation takes many forms, from laws, markets and code to norms (Lessig, 1999). Situated in the complexity of openness in the FOSS movement, the brand's transgression in the form of licence violation has triggered challenges from multiple users of the platform. Essentially, it deprives developers the right to tinker and derive fun from further adaptations, and denies users the opportunity to benefit from customised and promisingly better versions. Furthermore, it hurts the possibilities of democratic production, innovation and cultural generativity on a wider scope. All this runs counter to the brand promise, which employs a discourse on the internet as playground and digital democracy. Just as *shanzhai*, as informal brands in the shadow economy, can gain legitimacy and challenge state regulation for access to the formal economy, community-defined legitimacy holds significant power for brands that have gained an alliance with the state and capitalised on informal energies. Indeed, the power of informal, norm-based governance should not be ignored.

As dispersed users with varying skills and motivations interact with organisations, the overlapping area between the formal and the informal becomes at once a site of promise and contestation. The promise of knowledge and value production is entwined with tensions in the negotiation of control and legitimacy, which results from power asymmetry, and a fragmentation of ethical positions as well as incommensurability of standards for data curation. As digital platforms increasingly operate at the intersection of the formal and the informal, how brand meanings, values and legitimacy are developed and negotiated have become central to debates about digital futures. In China, the state's move towards a stronger IPR regime in the post-WTO era and its growing adoption of open source culture provides an interesting context in which to trace the formal–informal dynamic as it intersects with state–market interactions. For transnationally funded enterprises such as Xiaomi, the strength and longevity of the alliance with the state remains a question. After all, relying on Android to build a second-level platform betrays the flimsy nature of 'Made in China' rhetoric in the age of platformisation.

References

Baldwin, C. Y. and Clark, K. B. (2000). *Design rules: The power of modularity*, MIT Press, Cambridge, MA.

Barron, A. (2013). Free software production as critical social practice. *Economy and Society*, *42*(4), 597–625.

Benkler, Y. (2002). Coase's Penguin, or, Linux and the nature of the firm. *Yale Law Journal*, *112*(3), 369–376.

Benkler, Y. (2003). Freedom in the commons: Towards a political economy of information. *Duke Law Journal*, *52*(6), 1245–1276.

Benkler, Y. (2006). *The wealth of networks: How social production transforms markets and freedom*, Yale University Press, New Haven, CT.

Breznitz, D. and Murphree, M. (2011). *Run of the Red Queen: Government, innovation, globalization, and economic growth in China*, Yale University Press, New Haven, CT.

Burgess, J. (2012). The iPhone moment, the Apple brand, and the creative consumer: From 'hackability and usability' to cultural generativity, in *Studying mobile media: Cultural technologies, mobile communication, and the iPhone*, eds L. Hjorth, J. Burgess and I. Richardson, Routledge, New York; London, pp. 28–42.

Coleman, E. G. and Golub, A. (2008). Hacker practice: Moral genres and the cultural articulation of liberalism. *Anthropological Theory*, *8*(3), 255–277.

De Paoli, S., Teli, M. and D'Andrea, V. (2008). Free and open source licenses in community life: Two empirical cases. *First Monday*, *13*(10).

Forbes (2014). Xiaomi raises $1.1 billion at $45 billion valuation. Retrieved 6 January 2015 from www.forbes.com/sites/parmyolson/2014/12/29/xiaomi-raises-1-1-billion-at-45-billion-valuation/#33465f3334a3.

Gehl, R. (2012). Real (software) abstractions on the rise of Facebook and the fall of MySpace. *Social Text*, *30*, 99–119.

Gibbs, S. (2014). China rising: Xiaomi becomes world's third biggest smartphone manufacturer. *Guardian*. Retrieved from www.theguardian.com/technology/2014/oct/30/china-xiaomi-third-biggest-smartphone.

Gillespie, T. (2010). The politics of 'platforms'. *New Media & Society*, *12*(3), 347–364.

gnu.org (2014). What is copyleft? Retrieved 3 March 2015 from www.gnu.org/copyleft/copyleft.html.

Goggin, G. (2009). Adapting the mobile phone: The iPhone and its consumption. *Journal of Media & Cultural Studies*, *23*(2), 231–244.

Goggin, G. (2012). Google phone rising: The Android and the politics of open source. *Continuum*, *26*(5), 741–752.

Helmond, A. (2015). The platformization of the web: Making web data platform ready. *Social Media + Society*, *1*(2), 1–11.

Himanen, P. (2001a). *The hacker ethic and the spirit of capitalism*, Random House, New York, NY.

Himanen, P. (2001b). *The hacker ethic: A radical approach to the philosophy of business*, Random House, New York, NY.

Ho, V. (2013). Shenzhen's Huaqiangbei sellers are struggling as phones get cheaper. Retrieved 8 March 2014 from http://techcrunch.com/2013/05/02/shenzhens-huaqiangbei-sellers-are-struggling-as-phones-get-cheaper/.

Jeffrey, L. (2011). Innovation spaces of the future: Research notes on China's shanzhai meeting the makers. Retrieved 12 February 2012 from www.iftf.org/node/3943.

Jiao, L. (2011). Winter comes for shanzhai mobile phones, possible transitions ahead. Retrieved 6 June 2014 from http://media.people.com.cn/GB/40758/15244971.html.

Kan, M. (2013). Xiaomi takes crowdsourced phone development model abroad. Retrieved 8 May 2015 from www.pcworld.com/article/2038184/chinas-xiaomi-takes-crowdsourced-phone-development-model-abroad.html.

Keane, M. (2007). *Created in China: The great new leap forward*, New York, Routledge.

Keane, M. and Zhao, E. J. (2012). Renegades on the frontier of innovation: The shanzhai grassroots communities of shenzhen in China's creative economy. *Eurasian Geography and Economics*, *53*(2), 216–230.

Kettell, S. (2008). The political economy of open-source software in the United Kingdom. *Bulletin of Science, Technology & Society*, *28*(4), 306–315.

Lee, C.-K. and Hung, S.-C. (2014). Institutional entrepreneurship pin the informal economy: China's shanzhai mobile phone. *Strategic Entrepreneurship Journal*, *8*, 16–36.

Lessig, L. (1999). *Code and other laws of Cyberspace*, Basic Books, New York, NY.

Liao, Z. and Chen, X. (2011). Why the entry regulation of mobile phone manufacturing in China collapsed: The impact of technological innovation. *Journal of Law and Economics*, *54*(4), S207–S228.

Lindtner, S. and Dourish, P. (2011). The promise of play: A new approach to productive play. *Games and Culture*, *6*(5), 453–478.

Lobato, R. and Thomas, J. (2015). *The informal media economy*, Polity Press, Cambridge.

lvxj126 (2014, 30 April). Strong suggestion to Xiaomi: Release the kernel source code and relevant drivers for Mi Router. Retrieved 3 March 2015 from http://bbs.xiaomi.cn/t-9796298.

Mansell, R. (2013). Employing digital crowdsourced information resources: Managing the emerging information commons. *International Journal of the Commons*, *7*(2), 255–277.

McGowan, D. (2001). Legal implications of open-source software. *University of Illinois Review*, *241*(1), 241–304.

MIUIAndroid.com (2013). Exclusive: Xiaomi device kernel will be open sourced. Retrieved 8 March 2015 from http://miuiandroid.com/2013/09/17/exclusive-xiaomi-mi-device-kernel-will-open-sourced/.

Mosco, V. (2004). *The digital sublime: Myth, power, and cyberspace*, MIT Press, Cambridge, MA; London.

Office of State Council of PRC (1998). Opinions concerning the accelerating the development of the mobile telecommunication industry. Retrieved 26 October 2014, from http://iep.clemson.edu/wp-content/uploads/2012/04/Coase-Centennial-Conf.-LiaoChen_2_.pdf.

Pang, L. (2012). *Creativity and its discontents: China's creative industries and intellectual property rights offenses*, Duke University Press, Durham, NC.

Powell, A. (2012). Democratizing production through open source knowledge: From open software to open hardware. *Media, Culture and Society*, *34*(6), 691–708.

Powell, A. (2016). Hacking in the public interest: Authority, legitimacy, means, and ends. *New Media & Society*, *18*(4), 600–616.

Rai, A. K. (1999). Regulating scientific research: Intellectual property rights and the norms of science. *Northwestern University Law Review*, *94*(1), 77–152.

Raymond, E. S. (2001). *The cathedral and the bazaar: Musings on Linux and open source by an accidental revolutionary*, O'Reilly Media, Sebastopol, CA.

Sawhney, H. (2009). Innovations at the edge: The impact of mobile technologies on the character of the Internet, in *Mobile technology: From telecommunications to media*, eds G. Gerard and H. Larissa, Routledge, New York, pp. 105–117.

Scholz, T. (2012). *Digital labor: The internet as playground and factory*, Routledge, New York; London.

Serrafero, M. T. (2015). Xiaomi finally releases kernel sources. Retrieved 4 April 2015 from www.xda-developers.com/xiaomi-finally-releases-kernel-sources/.

Shambaugh, D. (2013). *China goes global: The partial power*, Oxford University Press, Oxford.

Sina.com (2017). Lei Jun: Xiaomi defeats almost all shanzhaiji. Retrieved 1 September 2017 from http://tech.sina.com.cn/mobile/n/n/2017-09-01/doc-ifykpysa2406231.shtml.

Spreeuwenberg, K. and Poell, T. (2012). Android and the political economy of the mobile internet: A renewal of open source critique. *First Monday*, *17*(7). Retrieved 1 April, 2014 from http://firstmonday.org/ojs/index.php/fm/article/view/4050/3271.

Stallman, R. (1999). The GNU operating system and the open source revolution, in *Open sources – Voices from the open source revolution*, eds C. DiBona, S. Ockman and M. Stone, O'Reilly and Associates, London, pp. 53–70.

Stallman, R. (2015). Why open source misses the point of free software. Retrieved 9 March 2015 from www.gnu.org/philosophy/open-source-misses-the-point.html.

Stark, D. (2009). *The sense of dissonance: Accounts of worth in economic life*, Princeton University, Princeton, NJ.

Sun, B. (2016). Xiaomi CEO Lei Jun: We aim to produce new national products that beat foreign brands. Retrieved 20 March 2016 from www.xinhuanet.com/fortune/2016-03/15/c_128800801.htm.

Sunrise paused (2012). Release the source code and we can do the rest. Retrieved 10 October 2015 from www.miui.com/thread-860180-1-1.html.

Tatsuno, S. (1990). *Created in Japan: From imitators to world-class innovators*, Harper & Row, New York, NY.

Terranova, T. (2004). *Network culture: Politics for the information age*, Pluto, London.

Volčič, Z. and Andrejevic, M. (2018). Nation branding in the era of commercial nationalism. *International Journal of Communication*, *5*, 598–618.

Wallis, C. and Qiu, J. L. (2012). Shanzhaiji and the transformation of the local mediascape in Shenzhen, in *Mapping Media in China*, eds W. Sun and J. Chio, Routledge, London, pp. 109–125.

Wall Street Journal (2015). Xiaomi, China's new phone giant, takes aim at world. Retrieved 7 July 2015 from www.wsj.com/articles/xiaomi-chinas-new-phone-giant-takes-aim-at-world-1433731461.

Watkins, N. (2013). Xiaomi phones: A co-created phenomenon. Retrieved 20 March 2014 from www.innovativechina.com/2013/06/xiaomi-phones-a-co-created-phenomenon/.

Weber, S. (2000). The political economy of open source software. Retrieved 6 February 2015 from http://brie.berkeley.edu/publications/wp140.pdf.

Weber, S. (2004). *The success of open source*, Harvard University, Cambridge, MA.

Wired (2015). How a nation of tech copycats transformed into a hub for innovation. Retrieved 30 December 2015 from www.wired.com/2015/12/tech-innovation-in-china/.

Wong, W. W. Y. (2014). *Van Gogh on demand: China and the readymade*, University of Chicago Press, Chicago and London.

Yang, F. (2015). *Faked in China: Nation branding, counterfeit culture and globalization*, Indiana University Press, Bloomington and Indianapolis.

Yang, F. (2016). From bandit cell phones to branding the nation: Three moments of shanzhai in WTO-era China. *Positions*, *24*(3), 589–619.

Yu, H. (2012). *China in ten words* (trans. A. H. Barr), Pantheon Books, New York, NY.

Zhang, L. and Fung, A. (2013). The myth of 'shanzhai' culture and the paradox of digital democracy in China. *Inter-Asia Cultural Studies*, *14*(3), 401–416.

Zhu, S. and Shi, Y. (2010). Shanzhai manufacturing – an alternative innovation phenomenon in China: Its value chain and implications for Chinese science and technology policies. *Journal of Science and Technology Policy in China*, *1*(1), 29–49.

Zittrain, J. (2008). *The future of the Internet – and how to stop it*, Yale University Press, New Haven, CT.

3 In and out of shadows

Negotiating boundaries and legitimacy in mobile app distribution

Within a decade of the launch of the Apple App Store, the app economy had witnessed considerable growth worldwide. According to the market researcher App Annie (2016), the global app economy is projected to double in size to $101 billion by 2020. As 'a platform for, and creature of, its applications', the iPhone with its iOS operating system opened the chapter of adapting the mobile for the internet (Goggin, 2009, p. 233). As discussed in the previous chapter, this soon provoked an answer from a group of technology companies led by Google, which launched the Android Operating System (OS) through the Open Handset Alliance (OHA), by strategically adopting particular open source practices (Spreeuwenberg and Poell, 2012). It marked a gradual shift from value chains controlled by telecom operators and device manufacturers to value networks centring on OSs and apps (Goggin, 2011; Goldsmith, 2014).

While 'app economy' becomes popular parlance, the economic production is inextricably intertwined with a cultural process. As Lash and Lury (2007) suggest, 'Culture, which was previously a question of representation, becomes thingified. In classical cultural industry, mediation was a question of representation, in global culture industry it is a mediation of things' (p. 4). More than economic drivers, apps have exerted profound influence on the evolution of internet cultures. As Goggin (2011) contends, apps constitute a significant area of cultural development and innovation. This results from the entrance of computer and internet production, user cultures and movement into mobile media. How apps operate as new circuits for culture, what terms of access and power relations exist, and how the politics of openness play out call for further research (Goggin, 2011).

Informal circuits are unquestionably part of this thriving economic and cultural development. As well as creative users, who assume a significant role in decentralised innovation in the digital media economy (Von Hippel, 2005; Stoneman, 2010), digital platforms have emerged to facilitate the hacking, repurposing and subversion of technologies and the unofficial circulation of apps. On a global level, this is particularly relevant when considering the nonlinear process of globalisation as transnational media corporations expand their footprint to various parts of the world through synergistic approaches (Arsenault and Castells, 2008; Chalaby, 2005). As brands cross borders, creative brand engagements emerge in the form of 'appropriation, resignification, negation, and indifference that trouble, and often undo, the very ontology of the brand' (Nakassis, 2013, p. 123). Indeed, while Apple and Google have successfully established a duopoly in the mobile app economy in most parts of the world, the picture looks very different in China.

The present chapter turns a critical eye on mobile app distribution in China, focusing on intermediaries that cater to local users by manoeuvring between the formal and informal. It starts with an overview of the duopoly of Apple and Google in the mobile app economy in most parts of the world and the cultures of adaptation in smartphone and app consumption. It then analyses the China syndrome encountered by Apple and Google, which results from both inter-capitalist rivalries, as China reintegrates itself into the global economy, and the legacy of informal market. Following this, I take up the case of 91 Wireless, which has evolved from an amateur project into a major local platform in China by filling the market gap and has subsequently been acquired by the internet giant Baidu. The analysis draws on data from interviews with a diverse range of participants in the formal and informal markets, observations on marketplaces and publicly available documents. Respondents to interviews conducted in November and December 2014 included relevant publics such as parallel dealers, rooting and jailbreaking service providers, corporate employees and independent developers. I analyse how the capacity to manoeuvre between the boundaries of the formal and the informal, and across national boundaries, enables the platform to constitute value networks and drive user adoption. Following that I examine the platform's rhetorical strategies and governance approaches in its attempt to seek legitimacy and shed its informal skins. Finally I reveal the contradictory, and sometimes ambivalent, opinions of developers on the platform's navigation across formal/informal boundaries, which reflects asymmetrical power on the digital platform and the complexity of coercive empowerment. By tracking the evolution of the platform, this chapter explains how the rhetoric of the informal as heroic or democratic could be tenuous, how a polemic perception of the informal could be risky and how the lens of formal/informal interactions can add to our understanding of the nature and politics of digital platforms.

The duopoly in the rising app economy and their discontents

In the battle of mobile platforms, Apple and Google take different approaches. Apple has maintained an overtly tight grip over the iOS for the purpose of maintaining quality control, and equally if not more importantly, ecosystem dominance. The App Store has a lower reach but a higher-end customer base, enabling app developers to more easily monetise their content and services (App Annie and IDC, 2015). By contrast, Google employs a relatively more open strategy and attracts developers with a large user base, while relying more on digital advertising than Android for monetisation. In the Android ecology, device manufacturers can develop a customised OS, which is then tied to particular hardware. By signing up to OHA, manufacturers have to pass the compatibility test defined by Google and therefore cede a lot of control to the latter. Their insistence on compatibility within the ecosystem makes practical sense as an attempt to prevent incompatibility, the main weakness of open source projects (Weber, 2004). Apart from that, it makes economic sense to Google. As the platform establishes the principles of compatibility, Google pushes its own services and steers hardware development. Android manufacturers have to sign an Anti-Fragmentation Agreement (AFA) if they want to put Google's Play Services and Play Store on their devices. This stops the manufacturer from building a competing fork of Android. Moreover, the Mobile Application Distribution Agreement (MADA) that Google signs with Android phone manufacturers requires the latter to pre-install Google Search and Chrome and set Google Search as the default search service on their devices as a condition to license certain Google proprietary apps. This intricate technical, legal and political economic manoeuvring has allowed Google to establish its dominant position in the mobile internet market (Spreeuwenberg and Poell, 2012). Google's use of open source in a delimited way is consistent with a new social imaginary of openness in digital technology and culture, which ultimately 'underpins an enclosure of mobile media platforms, and a relentless extraction of value from these for the benefit of well-entrenched and more recently formed media and communications corporations' (Goggin, 2012, p. 742).

Despite the duopoly status of Apple and Google, the evolution of their mobile ecosystems has witnessed informal practices attempting to escape corporate confines. Thanks to enthusiastic hackers and the rapid dissemination of hacking tools, iPhone jailbreaking has become a site of 'cultural politics of modification', where battles over code, commons and architecture are playing out (Goggin, 2009, p. 243). A jailbroken iPhone allows its user to use it with a different carrier than the one it is configured with, to change its default browser, mail client or to install third-party apps from outside the App Store. Cydia, for example, is an app store emerging with and catering to the jailbreak community. Named after an apple worm and alluding to the disruptive effects on Apple, Cydia (2014) hosts many apps that are turned away at the door owing to restrictions that Apple places on developers. Initially, jailbreaking was shrouded in the fog of its legal uncertainty, which generated wide and fierce debates (Wolk, 2010). Since the practice allows users to break the boundaries set by Apple, jailbreaking has attracted vocal criticism from the brand. The firm explicitly referred to jailbreaking as a case of violating the Digital Millennium Copyright Act, a law that makes it illegal to circumvent technology restrictions on copyrighted works (Apple Inc., 2008). The Electronic Frontier Foundation (EFF), a non-profit organisation in the United States that supports civil liberties, is a major proponent of jailbreaking, claiming it as a fair use of Apple's iOS. In 2010, the US Library of Congress declared iPhone jailbreaking legal over Apple's objections, although for a limited timeframe and to be reviewed every three years. Since 2015, the US regulators have further legalised jailbreaking tablets and smart TV.

In the case of Android, while it comes with flexibility and customisation, manufacturers, distributors and carriers have managed to lock down interface features and preloaded software that users have not asked for. Like jailbreaking an iOS device, rooting enables users to gain privileged control over the OS so that they can perform various tweaks. For example, users can fully uninstall unwanted apps to free up storage capacity for apps they really want. Without rooting the device, users can merely disable unwanted apps, which still eat into storage capacity. Another practice often associated with rooting for Android users is flashing a custom ROM (read-only memory), that is, replacing the stock OS with a third-party ROM. While rooting is usually not required to run applications outside Google Play, Android users often find third-party ROMs better alternatives in catering to their needs. Vendors who build on the Android Open Source Project (AOSP), yet do not sign up to OHA, are emerging as a force to be reckoned with. These Android forks skip all Google add-ons such as Gmail, Google Maps and YouTube, and build their own ecosystems. Most notable cases include Amazon's Fire OS, Alibaba's Yun OS and Xiaomi's MIUI, discussed in the previous chapter. Third-party Android app stores have also become more readily available. This has exacerbated fragmentation in the Android market, where independent app developers have created a proliferating range of apps for different OS forks and devices.

Jailbreaking and rooting cultures are closely associated with the practice of sideloading, meaning downloading apps without going through the official App Store or Google Play Store. From Cydia to stores associated with Android forks, third-party services allow uses to circumvent the boundaries imposed by the official stores. Moreover, installation packages in the form of IPA files for iOS and APK files for Android are widely available online. Users often find unapproved apps including the tempting choices of pirate games and music on such alternative platforms. These venues also host development versions of software as developers beta-test them prior to formal release in official stores. For iOS users, sideloading was initially only possible for jailbroken devices, but has become more readily available for people with an Apple ID, Apple's developer tool Xcode 7, and an iOS version of 9 or above. For Android users hoping to sideload apps, Android app managers have come to their assistance. While rooting is not necessary for Android users, users often install custom ROMs on rooting, and shop apps from platforms associated with Android forks as well as other unofficial stores.

The cultural practice of tinkering and adaptation has witnessed widespread adoption by users. Through jailbreaking, rooting, ROM flashing and app sideloading, users have taken on a new character as what Campbell (2005) calls the craft consumer. A craft consumer is 'a person who typically takes any number of mass-produced products and employs these as the "raw materials" for the creation of a new "product", one that is typically intended for self-consumption' (Campbell, 2005, pp. 27–28). As well as users, new intermediaries have also engaged in these cultural adaptation projects. Alternative distribution platforms as well as OS forks, jailbreak and rooting service providers are exemplary cases here. Once often referring to a hobby of technological elites, the term hacking has become polysemic, encompassing a wide set of meanings and practices (Gunkel, 2005). Such practices can often become lucrative businesses.

Clearly, the growing app economy involves an array of formal and informal actors. As Lobato and Thomas (2014) point out, mobile media is a particularly interesting case in which to analyse relationships between elements in the economy that take place within and across formal/informal divides because of the unstable combination of formal and informal elements. While some formal players are heavily capitalised and regulated, a diversified model of the mobile media economy includes various institutions and infrastructures outside or at the margins of this system. In the case of mobile app distribution, despite the duopoly of Apple and Google, informal practices epitomised by jailbreaking, rooting, ROM flashing and sideloading are intimately connected with alternative modes of app distribution. App distribution therefore constitutes a site where the cultural politics of openness and enclosure are closely entwined with the dynamics between the formal and the informal. This is particularly interesting when the story unfolds in China, where app distribution is much less dominated by Apple and Google and perceptions of copyright regimes exhibit ambiguities and contradictions among diverse users.

The China syndrome

In China, currently the world's largest smartphone market, alternative app distribution is closely associated with parallel imports in the device market. For a long time, it has been the grey and black market that has kept Chinese consumers' strong appetite for the iPhone fed. As well as the US, Hong Kong, as the world's leading tax haven, is an important source of parallel imports. Scalpers hire local residents with identity cards to preorder iPhones, which are then smuggled to wholesalers in Guangdong, and from there shipped to different parts of China. It was not until 2009 that iPhone entered China formally via a deal with China Unicom, the country's second largest mobile operator at the time, with no WiFi and priced at about 25 per cent more than what it was sold for in Hong Kong. The crippled version resulted from the state government ban on WiFi and promotion of WAPI (WLAN Authentication and Privacy Infrastructure), the Chinese national standard for WLAN (local area network). As China reintegrates itself into the global economy, especially in the ICT sector, the state has invested heavily in research and development in indigenous and proprietary technologies in order to reduce its reliance on overseas technology and move up the industry in the global economy (Y. Zhao, 2010). As well as economic necessity, techno-nationalism also drives the pursuit of technological prowess (Qiu, 2010). Official iPhones on offer in China have only become WiFi-enabled since 2010, when Apple complied with the state mandate, and started supporting both WiFi and China's home-grown WAPI protocol. In its early foray into mainland China, the iPhone was released with a delay relative to other markets, often because of the lengthy process involved in getting permits from the Ministry of Industry and Information Technology (MIIT). The deprioritisation of mainland China in product release schedule, the strong market demand for WiFi-enabled devices and the potentially less inhibiting price tags of smuggled devices thus fuelled the informal market. As well as the highly coveted iPhones, Android-based devices, most notably Samsung, also feature prominently in parallel imports into China and have witnessed various adaptations such as rooting and ROM flashing.

While Apple and Android devices are in high demand in China, mobile app distribution is much less dominated by the two behemoths. The late entry of Apple into China and the absence of Google services including Google Play has left a gap in the app distribution market. The gap has quickly been filled by many third-party platforms. While Apple can negotiate some structural obstacles in its foray into China, as its frictions with the Chinese party-state and wireless carriers are more of an inter-capitalist rivalry (Y. Zhao, 2008), adaptation cultures in smartphone and app consumption have frustrated Apple further. Consumers can obtain devices from the informal market, jailbreak them, connect them to local operators, and access 'a democratic mobile platform open to free software and entertainment' beyond Apple's official scheme (Shi, 2011, p. 13). Moreover, the inconvenience of accessing App Store alienated local users further. For example, it was not until 2011 that Apple started to accept payment in local currencies to allow customers of over 20 Chinese banks to make payments to sign up for an App Store account to purchase apps. Unofficial adoption and creative appropriation of the iPhone transgress corporate confines, although this paradoxically reinforces Apple's brand name and cultural influence in China (Shi, 2011). The problem in China is not unique to Apple. Google also faces structural obstacles in its attempted expansion into the country, which has experienced a more dramatic turn. Google partially exited the mainland Chinese market in 2010 following a high-profile dispute with the state government regarding internet censorship and a hacking incident originating in China. Like Apple's challenges in China, the standoff between Google and China illustrates the changing dynamics of the US-led transnational capitalism as China reintegrates itself with the global economies and the two negotiate the terms of capitalist development (Yeo, 2016). Despite its claiming the moral high ground in its 'withdrawal' from mainland China in protest about Chinese censorship, Google still expects to capitalise on the growth of Android OS and mobile advertising in China (Yeo, 2016). However, internet users are not hesitant in turning to the abundant pool of forked Android OS and third-party Android stores, which have replaced Google services with local alternatives.

Moreover, pre-installation during ROM flashing plays a vital role in promoting the discoverability of Android apps. As flashing allows apps to be written into the ROM and users cannot delete them without flashing the device again, pre-installed apps are perceived as having a higher chance of user retention. Given this, from mobile device dealers to telecom operators, retail stores to carrier stores, ROM flashing and app sideloading modify mobile devices time and again. As an industry informant disclosed:

> While mobile devices are preloaded with various sorts of apps, they undergo several times of flashing as they are dispatched from warehouse to warehouse, warehouse to retailer, and retailer to end user.
>
> (Personal Interview, 2014)

In another interviewee's words, the apps in mobile devices are 'washed' multiple times before they reach end-users (Personal Interview, 2014). Thus this is a continuous process of writing, un-writing and rewriting in the hope of acquiring users. These intermediaries receive commissions from app developers, who have to compete for users' attention in a crowded market. Therefore, before a mobile device is sold, the device manufacturer or the distributor has already recouped part of their costs through app pre-installation.

China thus constitutes a glaring exception to the global market dominance of App Store and Google Play in mobile app distribution. This has resulted from the legacy of the grey and black market, cultures of tinkering and adaptation, and inter-capitalist rivalry as China reintegrates itself with global capitalism. Meanwhile, unofficial platforms have come to command the mobile app distribution market in China. This has put Apple and Google in a difficult position for capturing value from the booming app economy in the country.

The rise of a local distribution platform: networked approach across the formal/informal

In what is now a crowded landscape of mobile app distribution in China, 91 Wireless is an intriguing case that has evolved by crossing the boundaries between the formal and the informal. While it now operates 91 Assistant, a mobile app distribution service catering to users of Android, iOS and Symbian, its history should be traced back to its predecessor, which was dedicated to managing iPhones. The trajectory of the platform began with an amateur developer named Xiong Jun in 2007, one year before Apple launched its App Store. A fan of the iPhone, Xiong bought the first-generation iPhone in 2007. However, he found managing software on iPhone a painful experience. This led the accounting-trained Xiong to develop programs in his spare time to improve the user experience. He then shared these programs on www.weiphone.com (later renamed as www.feng.com), one of the earliest online forums dedicated to the iPhone in China. When Xiong found these programs well received by early adopters of iPhones in the forum, he consolidated them and developed a tool named 'iPhone PC Suite'. Within a month, it acquired over 200,000 users. As an alternative to iTunes, the iPhone PC Suite allowed users to manage iPhones on desktop computers with ease. This was crucial in driving its adoption in a market where users of Apple's music and media organising software iTunes were few, and these few users often faced barriers such as the lack of a local currency payment option till 2011.

The popularity of the iPhone PC Suite attracted the attention of the Hong Kong-listed NetDragon Websoft Inc., a leading online game developer and operator in China. Very soon, NetDragon bought the iPhone PC Suite for RMB100,000 and invited Xiong to join the company. Thus the amateur project became integrated into an industry incumbent. Based on iPhone PC Suite, Xiong continued to develop 91 Assistant and incorporated more in-house developed software such as a caller location tracker and a mobile reading app. This allowed

91 Assistant to build its user base among early adopters of iPhones in China, who obtained jailbroken devices through unofficial channels. Thus elements of informality lingered following the incorporation into the formal incumbent. In a sense, it created a market that was secondary to the informal device market by meeting user demands for content and service.

The connection between 91 Assistant and informalities became more evident after Apple released the Software Development Kit (SDK) and launched the App Store in July 2008. As the licensing and retailing function of the App Store formalised a market for low-cost or free software, it facilitated app distribution for low-end developers (Lobato and Thomas, 2014). Consequently, a rapidly growing pool of apps became available to users. However, apps circulated beyond the official App Store, through informal circuits. A large quantity of cracked iPhone apps began to circulate in online forums. A notable forum in China is www.weiphone.com mentioned earlier. In this context, 91 Assistant turned into a site aggregating and categorising cracked iPhone apps distributed in various online forums, and allowed users to download these apps for free. In a sense, it built up its app library by relying on hackers and enthusiastic users who cracked and circulated apps within their community. The formalising features of archiving, sorting and categorisation improved the visibility and discoverability of apps, adding value to their unofficial, networked circulation. This allowed the platform to grow its user base and assist users to transit to the app culture in the early days of smartphone adoption.

As well as capitalising on hackers and building up its app library, 91 Assistant approached key players in the informal market to drive its adoption through pre-installation. By distributing software discs of its installation files to parallel traders for free, 91 Assistant allowed them to attract potential buyers with enhanced iPhones featuring access to cracked apps (Personal Interview, 2014). To assist parallel dealers to optimise operational efficiency, the software has a function that processes multiple devices at once (Personal Interview, 2014). Further, geographic clustering of parallel dealers in electronics markets such as Zhongguancun in Beijing, Buyecheng in Shanghai and Dalijia in Fuzhou further facilitated the adoption of 91 Assistant among distributors, which then trickled down to the user level. As one informant put it, pre-installing 91 Assistant on jailbroken devices became at one time almost a 'standard reconfiguration' for iPhone parallel dealers to attract users (Personal Interview, 2014). The wide spread of this informal practice can be deemed as knowledge diffusion occurring within dense social networks of players in the informal economy as they agglomerate in certain geographic areas (Lee and Hung, 2014).

Actors in the informal market continued to play their role when 91 Wireless started developing the Android market through its distribution platform HiMarket in 2009. Meanwhile, its approach to the Android market is characterised by capitalising on the opportunity afforded by open source, the key feature of Android OS. The Chinese-language custom ROM launched by 91 Wireless addressed the market demand at a time when local users did not show much interest in Google Android due to its English interface. Apart from that, the

ROM also included popular apps such as smart dialling to enhance its appeal to Chinese users. The custom ROM with the distribution platform became pre-installed at scale on Android devices circulating in the informal market, especially on unlocked HTC smartphones. This allowed 91 Wireless to gain rapid traction in the Android app distribution market. As several informants mentioned, grey-market Android devices pre-installed with the custom ROM incorporating HiMarket were more popular than official Android mobile phones in China (Personal Interview, 2014). The first Android mobile phone G1, which entered the Chinese market via parallel imports, evidenced the popularity of the custom ROM. While the industry expected a price drop due to its unfriendly interface for Chinese users, the version pre-installed with the custom ROM came with a higher price tag on the shadow market (Personal Interview, 2014).

As well as parallel dealers, online Android communities also played a role in driving the adoption of HiMarket: 91 Wireless distributed the custom ROM widely in online Android forums. Among these, www.hiapk.com is particularly worth mentioning. Established by NetDragon in April 2009 to cultivate a community of Android developers and users, it significantly drove the adoption of HiMarket by both developers and users. While the online forum contributed to building up the developer community mainly in China, 91 Wireless attempted to direct the energy of distributed developers overseas to its own platform. According to a former employee, the team at 91 Wireless contacted app developers working for Android Market (later known as Google Play) and encouraged them to put their apps on HiMarket (Personal Interview, 2014). These apps were to be localised into Chinese and available for free, and developers could benefit from the advertising-supported model in the Chinese market. While Apple touted its capacity to generate revenue for developers through paid apps, Google Android is known for the difficulty to monetise from such apps with the same approach (Salz and InMobi, 2014). The majority of Android apps are free, and developers derive income from in-app advertising provided by Google's Admob group. By promoting HiMarket among overseas developers and extending the advertising-based revenue model to China, 91 Wireless was able to build up its Android app library.

Thus 91 Wireless has built its initial success on its capacity to reconfigure the official OS for local users, its redirection of informal energy of developers from the official platforms and onto its own and its engagement with key players in the shadow economy. Its user base witnessed a sharp increase from 0.8 million in June 2008 to over two million at the end of 2009, and crossed the three million mark in 2010 (*Southern Metropolis Daily*, 2011). Multiple actors in the informal economy including hackers, parallel dealers, jailbreaking and rooting service providers and app developers have contributed to its growth trajectory. The partners specialising in hardware, software and content have come together to deliver the integrated service package to users. Together, they constitute an alternative app distribution space. This is similar to the strategies adopted by *shanzhai* mobile phone entrepreneurs, where multiple actors formulate a network based on division of labour across design, integration and production, and seek technological expertise and promotional channels in their partners (Lee and Hung, 2014). At a time when App Store remained an unactivated icon on many users' iPhones and Google Play simply did not exist in China, the network approach of 91 Wireless highlighted localised media and cultural practices in the context of 'disjunctures between industry and users' in smartphone cultures (Watkins, Hjorth and Koskinen, 2012, p. 666).

This however does not mean a decisive separation between the official and the unofficial. In fact, 91 Wireless did not hesitate to venture beyond the underground device market. When China Unicom started to sell the iPhone in 2012, customers would often find people standing close to the counters in the operator shops to help them jailbreak devices they purchased and pre-install the 91 Assistant. These people claimed they were China Unicom staff but they did not wear official uniforms as staff members did. Such proximity of the formal and informal is similar to the telco's inclusive approach towards users' shadow market devices when it started to sell the iPhone. At a time when China Unicom was competing with the other two major carriers for 3G users, the operator publicly announced the plan to greenlight the connection of smuggled iPhones to its network. While it was technically feasible to block these devices out of its 3G network, China Unicom embraced users of these devices with open arms in order to gain market share. Similarly, China Unicom turned a blind eye to the informal app distributor, which developed in close connection with the shadow device market. For the telecom operator, high-value customers in data consumption were crucial in achieving a sustainable growth in revenue from data usage in the smartphone age. The pre-installed app distribution software became a bonus for potential customers and created value for the telecom operator. According to data from the China Internet Network Information Centre (CNNIC, 2013), mobile phones had become the top device accessing the internet in China by June 2012, with 388 million mobile internet users out of the 538 million internet users in total. While network operators used to control most aspects of mobile service delivery, the growing mobile app economy has introduced shifting power dynamics where platform providers command a stronghold over content and service distribution (Basole and Jarla, 2012). The aggressive move to cater for official iPhone users in China continued to fuel the growth of the app distributor. By July 2012, the number of its users crossed the one million mark (Netease News, 2012).

The rapid growth of 91 Wireless culminated in its acquisition by Baidu for US$1.9 billion in 2013, at the time the most expensive acquisition in the history of China's internet (Baidu Inc., 2013). According to industry observers, as one of the three internet giants collectively known as BAT, Baidu intended to secure its position in the mobile internet market through acquisition (Personal Interview, 2014). Prior to this deal, the other two leading internet giants in China, namely Tencent and Alibaba, had already secured their place in the mobile internet. Tencent had reaped success from its mobile messaging app WeChat, and Alibaba had invested in the microblogging service Weibo, the mobile internet browser UC, and the mobile map app Gaode. For Baidu, as one interviewee put it, 91 Wireless as a mobile distribution platform carried the hope of 'securing a ticket to the mobile internet economy' (Personal Interview, 2014). As well as its distribution capacity, the existing developer community on 91 Wireless was also expected to provide value to Baidu, as the latter hoped to build a vibrant developer community around it. Therefore, both the telecom operator's inclusive approach and Baidu's acquisition of 91 Wireless reflect the contingent boundaries between the formal and informal, where the informal becomes tied up with strategies of value creation in the formal sphere (Lobato and Thomas, 2014).

The quest for legitimacy

Rhetorical strategies

Despite increasing capital intensity and growing interaction with organisations in the formal economy, the legitimacy of 91 Wireless remains a nebulous issue. Suchman (1995) defines organisational legitimacy as the 'generalized perception or assumption that the actions of an entity are desirable, proper, or appropriate within some socially constructed system of norms, values, beliefs, and definitions' (p. 574). Compared to pragmatic legitimacy, which rests on audience self-interest, moral legitimacy is more elusive to obtain and more difficult to manipulate (Suchman, 1995). For 91 Wireless, while certain informal elements gained legal status, such as the US government's legalisation of iPhone jailbreaking over Apple's objections in 2010, other forms of informality continue to cloud the app distribution platform. As well as the association of 91 Wireless with the grey device market, the facilitated, unauthorised circulation of cracked apps remains a persistent form of informality that threatens its legitimacy. The need to shed its informal skins became crucial to gain legitimacy for sustainable development. In order to do so, the venture has adopted strategic metaphors as rhetorical strategies.

As a rhetorical device, metaphor 'allows us to comprehend one aspect of a concept in terms of another ... which will necessarily hide other aspects of the concept' (Lakoff and Johnson, 1980, p. 10). For Van Dijck (1998), the strategic use of metaphor is an important part of 'the process of image construction' (p. 4). Similarly, Steen (2008) emphasises that metaphor 'does not only manifest a linguistic form and a conceptual structure, but also a communicative function' (p. 221). Deliberate metaphors involve 'a distinct rhetorical strategy that senders utilise to achieve a specific discourse function by means of a metaphorical comparison' (Steen, 2008, p. 224). As well as increasing the accessibility of an unfamiliar, abstract or complex concept, a major communicative purpose of deliberate metaphors is 'to produce an alternative perspective on a particular reference or topic' (Steen, 2008, p. 231). Metaphors have played a vital role of not only informing but also shaping popular and critical understanding of the internet (Adams, 1997; Graham, 1998; Wilken, 2007), mobile media (Aguado and Martínez, 2008; Hjorth, 2005; Wilken, 2013), intellectual property (Loughlan, 2006; Patry, 2009), and digital platforms (Gillespie, 2010).

The strategic use of metaphor by 91 Wireless is best illustrated by the remarks of its CEO Hu Zemin during a media interview with the *Global Entrepreneur* magazine. In Hu's words, the 91 Assistant platform has provided 'underground customer service for Apple' (quoted in Zeng, 2012). Evidently, recasting the unofficial distribution of cracked apps in the light of customer service was an attempt to create an alternative perspective, more specifically, to create a normative consensus among users on the legitimacy of the platform. The term 'underground customer service' served the purpose of reminding users of the context where the official was absent, insufficient or inconvenient. It was culturally grounded in a society where informal circuits have played a vital role in addressing people's demand for cultural consumption (Lu, 2010; Wang, 2003; E. J. Zhao, 2017). Thus the metaphor served to evoke legitimacy and solicit support for the service provider in the shadows. This approach has a historical precedent. Most notably, as discussed in the previous chapter, unlicensed mobile phone manufacturers in China also employed rhetorical strategy in seeking legitimacy. These enterprises adopted the term *shanzhai* as a self-referential metaphor, establishing an association between the informal market entrepreneurs and rebellious heroes depicted in the Chinese classical novel *Water Margin*. This enabled *shanzhai* entrepreneurs to offer a justification for their business and to receive endorsement from sympathetic advocates, media and the general public, and ultimately to find their way into the formal economy (Lee and Hung, 2014). For 91 Assistant, the emphasis was on its role in facilitating the informal circulation of apps and thereby addressing the market gap and servicing local users.

Moreover, the metaphor hinted at the role of the app distributor in promoting the adoption of iPhones for Apple in China. While Apple started to highlight its surging internet services revenue, hardware product lines accounted for over 80 per cent of the company's annual revenue eight years after the launch of the App Store (Apple Inc., 2016). In this light, the rhetorical manoeuvring not only appealed to local users' desire for the brand but also played to the tune of Apple's strategy of using software to promote the appeal of its hardware. The relationship between piracy and network effects has had the ear of leading multinational market players in the information technology industry. For example, Bill Gates has referred repeatedly to the role of piracy in securing Microsoft's market share and undercutting Linux adoption in China (Karaganis, 2011). The rhetorical strategy thus constituted an effort to recast the character of the platform as serving both consumers and the authentic brand.

Further, the metaphor worked together with the clarification of its role in media, emphasising it was 'collecting' rather than 'producing' cracked paid apps as a distribution platform (Zeng, 2012). This specified one aspect of the positioning of the 'platform', an often-used metaphor for strategic positioning in the digital domain to address multiple publics (Gillespie, 2010). The popularity of the term lies in its broad appeal to multiple audiences, while eliding the tensions (Gillespie, 2010). By emphasising its role of collecting apps, the platform distanced itself from the greyer area of the production process, which involved hacking into the paid apps and making them free. Yet such an emphasis revealed a contradiction. On one hand, while it presented itself as a customer service provider for the authentic brand by providing content and service in an informal manner, it evoked images of networked sharing for social good. On the other hand, however, it downplayed the networked dimension in its approach of working together with informal market players to build up its market share. As Warnick (2004) points out, 'technological metaphors are critiqued with regard to their potential to hide certain aspects of technology as a result of metaphor choice while making others appear natural' (p. 269). Similarly, Wilken (2013) notes that technological metaphors are 'never innocent' (p. 642), especially when deployed as part of deliberate rhetorical strategies.

Governance by platform with a self-serving logic

As well as rhetorical strategies, 91 Wireless started to adopt governance approaches to retain and grow its developer community. Indeed, digital platforms command governance power in various forms such as protocols, architectural design and software code, some more visible than others (Beer, 2009; Van Dijck and Poell, 2013; Gillespie, 2017). In the case of 91 Wireless, copyright enforcement was of paramount importance in its quest for legitimacy and in its attempt to attract developers as a platform. Yet its approach was only partial. As its CEO Hu Zemin explained, for developers who were advertisers, the platform took the initiative of taking down cracked versions of apps that were promoted on the platform (quoted in Zeng, 2012). For non-advertisers, however, the platform took a more passive approach by taking down unauthentic versions when requested and the process could be prohibiting (Personal Interview, 2014). Clearly the platform treated advertiser-developers as priority publics over other developers in copyright enforcement. Such differentiated approaches served the economic logic of the platform, which was based on the advertising-supported business model. In fact, revenue from app promotion contributed to over 60 per cent of the platform's total revenue (Zeng, 2012). As several developers revealed, quotation for a spot in the recommended section was continuously on the rise, yet this did not stop some developers from investing in such capital-intensive promotions (Personal Interview, 2014).

According to Gillespie (2010), platforms have to 'present themselves strategically to each of these audiences, carve out a role and a set of expectations that is acceptable to each and also serves their own financial interests, while resolving or at least eliding the contradictions between them' (p. 7). However, the copyright enforcement approach of 91 Wireless not only departed from the neutrality suggested by the 'platform' rhetoric (Gillespie, 2010), but also accentuated the tension between different developers, specifically between those who spent money on the platform to promote apps and those who did not. The differentiated approaches to copyright enforcement were designed to steer developers towards app promotion to generate profit for the platform. In other words, it was bound up with platform's economic logic. Underlying this logic was the severe challenge of discoverability despite the lower barrier to publishing in the mobile app economy (Holzer and Ondrus, 2011; Nieborg, 2016; E. J. Zhao, 2017). As internet giants, small-scale enterprises and independent developers competed for exposure on the same platform, those with fewer financial resources thus had to face higher risks.

Further, in response to public challenges especially those from developers in relation to copyright issues, 91 Wireless steered iOS developers towards publishing free apps. The message from CEO Hu to developers was clear: 'If you want to profit from paid downloads, go to App Store. If you want to attract more users, come to us' (quoted in Zeng, 2012). The value of its platform, according to Hu's remarks, was its large user base, which was not necessarily linked to commercialisation through paid apps. For developers, the recommended strategy was to release free apps to build up a user base and seek commercialisation through other means. Alternative revenue models other than upfront purchase have indeed attracted academic and popular attention. For example, Lessig (2008) proposes the concept of a hybrid economy, where the profit motives of traditional business blends with the non-market ethos of a sharing economy. Anderson (2009) discusses various incarnations of 'freeconomics' in an age of abundance. The abundantly clear message from 91 Wireless followed a similar line. What raises questions here is the role of the platform in steering developer practice in self-serving ways through informal governance. In other words, although the recommended approach was not enforced as a protocol, the platform attempted to establish 'rule of thumb' agreements with developers to serve its economic logic. As means of circulation become the locus of control in the app economy (Nieborg, 2016), the platform can exert its influence not only on app distribution but also on modalities of app development and monetisation. In the words of Van Dijck (2013), 'a platform is a mediator rather than an intermediary' (p. 29), because it shapes cultural practice. To understand the governance approaches to the platform, they should be considered together with its economic logic.

Ambivalence and contradiction in developers' attitudes

While the app distribution platform employs strategic metaphors and governance approaches to pursue legitimacy, ambivalence and contradiction have characterised developers' attitudes towards it. Some downright despise its unauthorised collection and distribution of cracked apps for commercial purposes. During the interviews, my mention of 91 Wireless immediately triggered responses pointing to its history of distributing cracked apps. Some developers manifested their 'zero tolerance' for piracy (Personal Interview, 2014). One developer put a rhetorical question to the request for his comments: 'What comments would a person have towards thieves when their belongings have been stolen?' (Personal Interview, 2014). This is a typical case where those who do not support the user of the strategic metaphor adopt their own metaphor as a form of opposition. Indeed, the thief metaphor is widely used in the discourse on intellectual property. This selection of metaphor reflects a wider phenomenon where the negative associations of lawlessness favours intellectual property owners and lends legitimacy to enforcement taken against thieves (Loughlan, 2006). The underlying ideology of this metaphor obviously runs counter to what is embedded in the metaphor of the 'commons', 'an image of property, especially land, held in common by all and used by all for their own *and* for the common benefit', evocative of an earlier time of community and non-alienated labour (Loughlan, 2006). The notion bears similarity with Chinese traditions of sharing and copying for the common good, which have come under pressure as the country has begun to embrace a more Western, individualised and property-based notion of culture and copyright. As Montgomery and Fitzgerald (2006) point out, as a new generation of creators emerge in China, more stringent copyright protection would appeal to them. The 'zero tolerance for piracy' of some developers speaks to such a trend. It also reflects the 'politics of metaphor' (Hellsten, 2002), where the choice of metaphors becomes a contested field among different parties with their own purposes.

Yet such opposition has met with a harsh reality check. During the interviews, many developers pointed to the difficulty and high cost of protecting their intellectual property. Without organisational support or collective action, individuals cannot afford to engage in prolonged and resource-consuming lawsuits (Personal Interview, 2014). Indeed, this is what distinguishes individual app developers from multinational music labels, film studios or internet giants. Many of these organisations have continued to spend significant resources on anti-piracy lobbying and enforcement efforts, with low returns on investment (Wang, 2003). In the mobile media domain, corporations are embroiled in intellectual property infringement suits, which are tied to their projects of enclosing and controlling media platforms (Goggin, 2012). Individual app developers however face the challenge of limited resources if they intend to adopt similar approaches in the context of asymmetric power on digital platforms.

While some developers who despised 91 Wireless for its circulation of cracked apps, they recognised the power of the platform in the app distribution market. One developer raised the example of the digital giant Tencent's use of 91 Assistant to distribute new versions of its messaging app QQ in 2009 despite divided opinions within the organisation over the legitimacy of the platform (Personal Interview, 2014). This testifies to the significant reach of the platform in the mobile app distribution market, and is yet another typical example of the formal using the informal to create value for itself (Lobato and Thomas, 2014). Given this, individual developers are caught in a dilemma, where they have to weigh the perceived benefits of publishing on the platform against the risks associated with unauthorised app distribution. To some developers, the former may outweigh the latter. Or so they hope. The fact is, market concentration means that choices are limited.

Moreover, the platform's attempt to promote the development of free apps has further engendered divided views from developers. Some developers agreed that the recommended approach was the way to go. For them, securing a mass market could lead to alternative revenues in future, such as those from advertising or in-app purchases (Personal Interview, 2014). These developers pointed to the fact that revenue models based on freemium culture or advertising are well embraced by content and service providers, most notably in the gaming industry (Personal Interview, 2014). Whether such potential can come to fruition however remains a question. Others perceived the approach as a whitewashing strategy considering the platform's practice of collecting and distributing cracked iOS apps in building up its inventory (Personal Interview, 2014). In its attempt to influence the revenue model of app development, the platform intended to avoid being embroiled in possible copyright disputes and claims over lost revenue from developers of paid apps. Indeed, app development is constrained by structural limitations in an asymmetric power space (Mosemghvdlishvili and Jansz, 2013). Such constraints have resulted from the need for an app distribution platform that is largely associated with informality to seek legitimacy and sustainability.

Conclusion

This chapter carries the discussion of the connection and dynamics between the formal and informal into the territory of mobile app distribution. As the mobile internet becomes increasingly app-centric, app distribution has become a site where multiple actors negotiate terms of access and power relations. The app distribution market in China has its distinctiveness, whereas the duopoly of the mobile app economy in many markets is much diluted as a result of the unmet needs of local users, the legacy of the informal device market and inter-capitalist rivalries as China reintegrates itself with global capitalism. Platforms facilitating informal app distribution have quickly come to fill the gap, capitalising on cultures of jailbreaking, rooting and ROM flashing.

The development trajectory of 91 Wireless reveals a value network approach, initially working with black- and grey-market players including parallel dealers, hackers and developers both at home and abroad, before gradually connecting with formal players such as telecom operators and internet giants as they find a converged interest. The increasing intimacy between the app distribution platform and legacy heavyweights has coevolved with the mobile media, where app distribution becomes a strategic gateway to the mobile internet. Thus the platform derives its power from the capacity to formulate value networks comprising actors from both formal and informal economies and across geographic boundaries as the technological and cultural environment evolves.

For a platform that has developed by absorbing informal energy with questionable approaches, it is crucial to build legitimacy and achieve sustainability. This legitimacy-building process highlights a contested field where multiple publics participate in the negotiation of meanings, values and ethics. For the platform, this involves presenting itself strategically to its various audiences, articulating its position and value to them, and aligning their expectations with its own business model. While the rhetorical manoeuvring may purchase some legitimacy by highlighting the benefits to local users and lessen the threat of litigation from the authentic brand, the emergence and use of competing metaphors among developers prove the process a continuing challenge. As well as the rhetorical strategies, the partial approach to cleansing the informal element of copyright infringement prioritises the key publics of advertiser-developers in the context of poor app discoverability and an advertising-based revenue model. Further, the platform's legitimacy-seeking strategy involves shaping app development practices, when free apps are encouraged to align with user expectations but more importantly to reduce the risks associated with copyright infringement of paid apps. Thus incoherence in logics is evident not only in the contradiction between its claim as a platform 'collecting' apps and the its impact on 'production' cultures, but also between the neutrality suggested by the 'platform' rhetoric (Gillespie, 2010) and the biased approach to key publics. The formalising trajectory of the platform thus is closely entwined with the power asymmetry in the mobile app economy.

Just as the formal and informal interact in various ways, developers' attitudes towards the platform's navigation between the boundaries are more complicated than a simple dichotomy suggests. Underlying developers' seemingly polemic attitudes are ambivalence and paradoxes. This reflects the ongoing transformation in a weak copyright environment, where some among the new generation of content creators become more copyright-conscious. More importantly, this reveals the coercive power of the platform, as developers become beholden to platform logics of maximising profits and minimising risks in a market where app discoverability remains an ongoing concern.

As this chapter has illustrated, it is through the interplay of the formal and informal that the nature and politics of digital platforms emerge. While informality contributes much to facilitating app circulation, enabling user empowerment and a culture of openness in the local context, it would be a hastened conclusion to consider such heroic character as inherent and static. As certain forms of informality linger and others are cleansed or disguised for strategic purposes, it is crucial to understand the process and its implications for cultural production. This requires us to interrogate platform practices at both discursive and operational levels as they move in and out of the shadows while attending to multiple publics in China's digital transformations.

References

Adams, P. C. (1997). Cyberspace and virtual places. *Geographical Review*, *87*(2), 155–171.

Aguado, J. M. and Martínez, I. J. (2008). The construction of the mobile experience: The role of advertising campaigns in the appropriation of mobile phone technologies, in *Mobile phone cultures*, ed. G. Goggin, Routledge, London, pp. 1–12.

Anderson, C. (2009). *Free: The future of a radical price*, Hyperion, New York, NY.

App Annie (2016). App Annie mobile app forecast: The path to $100 billion. Retrieved 1 June 2016 from http://files.appannie.com.s3.amazonaws.com/reports/App-Annie-02-2016-Forecast-EN.pdf?aliId=113453053.

App Annie and IDC (2015). App Annie & IDC mobile app advertising and monetization trends 2013–2018. Retrieved 3 March 2016 from www.appannie.com/insights/mobile-app-advertising-and-monetization-trends-2013-2018/.

Apple Inc. (2008). In the matter of exemption to prohibition on circumvention of copyright protection systems for access control technologies. Retrieved 1 June 2015 from www.copyright.gov/1201/2008/responses/apple-inc-31.pdf.

Apple Inc. (2016). Annual report pursuant to section 13 or 15(d) of the Securities Exchagne Act of 1934. Retrieved 12 December 2016 from http://files.shareholder.com/downloads/AAPL/4030414814x0x913905/66363059-7FB6-4710-B4A5-7ABFA14CF5E6/10-K_2016_9.24.2016_-_as_filed.pdf.

Arsenault, A. H. and Castells, M. (2008). The structure and dynamics of global multimedia business networks. *International Journal of Communication, 2*, 707–748.

Baidu Inc. (2013). Baidu signs memorandum of understanding to acquire 100% interest in NetDragon's subsidiary 91 Wireless. Retrieved 1 June 2015 from http://ir.baidu.com/phoenix.zhtml?c=188488&p=irol-newsArticle&ID=1837836

Basole, R. C. and Jarla, J. (2012). Value transformation in the mobile service ecosystem: A study of app store emergence and growth. *Service Science, 4*(1), 24–41.

Beer, D. (2009). Power through the algorithm? Participatory web cultures and the technological unconsciousness. *New Media & Society, 11*(6), 985–1002.

Campbell, C. (2005). The craft consumer: Culture, craft and consumption in a postmodern society. *Journal of Consumer Culture, 5*(1), 23–42.

Chalaby, J. K. (2005). From internationalization to transnationalization. *Global Media and Communication, 1*(1), 28–33.

CNNIC (2013). 2012 CNNIC Annual Report. Retrieved 1 March 2015 from http://english.cnic.cas.cn/rp/201312/P020131211605484386895.pdf.

Cydia (2014). Cydia AppStore. Retrieved 1 May 2015 from www.cydiaios7.com/cydia-app-store.html.

Gillespie, T. (2010). The politics of 'platforms'. *New Media & Society, 12*(3), 347–364.

Gillespie, T. (2017). Regulation of and by platforms, in *The Sage handbook of social media*, eds J. Burgess, T. Poell and A. Marwick, Sage, Los Angeles, pp. 254–278.

Goggin, G. (2009). Adapting the mobile phone: The iPhone and its consumption. *Continuum, 23*(2), 231–244.

Goggin, G. (2011). Ubiquitous apps: Politics of openness in global mobile cultures. *Digital Creativity, 22*(3), 148–159.

Goggin, G. (2012). Google phone rising: The Android and the politics of open source. *Continuum, 26*(5), 741–752.

Goldsmith, B. (2014). The smartphone app economy and app ecosystem, in *The Routledge companion to mobile media*, eds G. Goggin and L. Hjorth, Routledge, New York, pp. 171–180.

Graham, S. (1998). The end of geography or the explosion of place? Conceptualizing space, place and information technology. *Progress in Human Geography, 22*(2), 165–185.

Gunkel, D. (2005). Editorial: Introduction to hacking and hacktivism. *New Media & Society, 7*(5), 595–597.

Hellsten, I. (2002). *The politics of metaphor: Biotechnology and biodiversity in the media*, Tampere University Press, Tampere.

Hjorth, L. (2005). Locating mobility: Practices of co-presence and the persistence of the postal metaphor in SMS/MMS mobile phone customization in Melbourne. *Fibreculture Journal, 6*.

Holzer, A. and Ondrus, J. (2011). Mobile application market: A developer's perspective. *Telematics and Informatics, 28*(1), 22–31.

Karaganis, J. (ed.). (2011). *Media piracy in emerging economies*, Social Science Research Council, New York, NY.

Lakoff, G. and Johnson, M. (1980). *Metaphors we live by*, University of Chicago, Chicago, IL.

Lash, S. and Lury, C. (2007). *Global culture industry: The mediation of things*. Polity, Cambridge.

Lee, C.-K. and Hung, S.-C. (2014). Institutional entrepreneurship in the informal economy: China's shanzhai mobile phone. *Strategic Entrepreneurship Journal*, *8*(1), 16–36.

Lessig, L. (2008). *Remix: Making art and commerce thrive in the hybrid economy*, Penguin, New York, NY.

Lobato, R. and Thomas, J. (2014). Informal mobile economies, in *The Routledge companion to mobile media*, eds G. Goggin and L. Hjorth, Routledge, New York, pp. 114–122.

Loughlan, P. (2006). Pirates, parasites, reapers, sowers, fruits, foxes…The metaphors of intellectual property. *Sydney Law Review*, *28*(2), 211–226.

Lu, J. (2010). Internet software piracy in China: Technology, culture and patriotism. *Electronic Journal of Communication*, *20*(3 and 4).

Montgomery, L. and Fitzgerald, B. (2006). Copyright and the creative industries in China. *International Journal of Cultural Studies*, *9*(3), 407–418.

Mosemghvdlishvili, L. and Jansz, J. (2013). Negotiability of technology and its limitations. *Information, Communication & Society*, *16*(10), 1596–1618.

Nakassis, C. V. (2013). Brands and their surfeits. *Cultural Anthropology*, *28*(1), 111–126.

Netease News (2012). 91 Wireless users reaching over 100 million with highest monthly revenue of 2 million RMB. Retrieved 1 March 2015 from http://tech.163.com/12/0731/17/87ORF89600094MSB.html.

Nieborg, D. (2016). From premium to freemium: The political economy of the app, in *Social, casual and mobile games: The changing gaming landscapes*, eds W. Michele and T. Leaver, Bloomsbury Academic, London; New York, pp. 225–240.

Patry, W. F. (2009). *Moral panics and the copyright wars*, Oxford University Press, New York, NY.

Qiu, J. L. (2010). Chinese techno-nationalism and global WiFi policy, in *Reorienting global communication: Indian and Chinese media beyond borders*, eds M. Curtin and H. Shah, University of Illinois Press, Urbana, IL, pp. 289–303.

Salz, P. A. and InMobi (2014). Apponomics: The insider's guide to a billion dollar app industry. Retrieved 1 June 2014 from www.inmobi.com/ui/pdfs/apponomics.pdf.

Shi, Y. (2011). iPhones in China: The contradictory stories of media-ICT globalization in the era of media convergence and corporate synergy. *Journal of Communication Inquiry*, *35*(2), 134–156.

Southern Metropolis Daily (2011). The industry chain of jailbreaking for muggled Android phone: The best channel for app development. Retrieved 1 March 2013 from www.cww.net.cn/news/html/2011/10/24/20111024831412936.htm.

Spreeuwenberg, K. and Poell, T. (2012). Android and the political economy of the mobile internet: A renewal of open source critique. *First Monday*, *17*(7). Retrieved 1 June 2014 from http://firstmonday.org/ojs/index.php/fm/article/view/4050/3271.

Steen, G. (2008). The paradox of metaphor: Why we need a three-dimensional model of metaphor. *Metaphor and Symbol*, *23*(4), 213–241.

Stoneman, P. (2010). *Soft innovation: Economics, product aesthetics, and the creative industries*, Oxford University Press, Oxford.

Suchman, M. C. (1995). Managing legitimacy: Strategic and institutional approaches. *Academy of Management Review*, *20*(3), 571–610.

Van Dijck, J. (1998). *Imagenation: Popular images of genetics*, London: Macmillan.

Van Dijck, J. (2013). *The culture of connectivity: A critical history of social media*, Oxford University Press, Oxford.

Van Dijck, J. and Poell, T. (2013). Understanding social media logic. *Media and Communication*, *1*(1), 2–14.

Von Hippel, E. (2005). *Democratizing innovation*, Cambridge, MA: MIT Press.

Wang, S. (2003). *Framing piracy: Globalization and film distribution in Greater China*, Rowman & Littlefield, Lanham, MD.

Warnick, B. R. (2004). Technological metaphors and moral education: The hacker ethic and the computational experience. *Studies in Philosophy and Education*, *23*(4), 265–281.

Watkins, J., Hjorth, L. and Koskinen, I. (2012). Wising up: Revising mobile media in an age of smartphones. *Continuum*, *26*(5), 665–668.

Weber, S. (2004). *The success of open source*, Harvard University Press, Cambridge, MA.

Wilken, R. (2007). The haunting affect of place in the discourse of the virtual. *Ethics, Place and Environment*, *10*(1), 49–63.

Wilken, R. (2013). An exploratory comparative analysis of the use of metaphors in writing on the Internet and mobile phones. *Social Semiotics*, *23*(5), 632–647.

Wolk, M. H. (2010). The iPhone jailbreaking exemption and the issue of openness. *Cornell Journal of Law and Public Policy*, *19*(3), 795–828.

Yeo, S. (2016). Geopolitics of search: Google versus China? *Media, Culture & Society*, *38*(4), 591–605.

Zeng, H. (2012). Hu Zemin: Commanding the gateway to the mobile internet. *Global Entrepreneur*, *7*, 62–65.

Zhao, E. J. (2017). Beyond the game of cat and mouse: Challenges of discoverability and piracy in the mobile gaming market, in *Global Game Industries and Cultural Policy*, ed. A. Fung, Palgrave Macmillan, London, pp. 253–270.

Zhao, Y. (2008). *Communication in China: Political economy, power and conflict*, Rowman & Littlefield, Lanham, MD.

Zhao, Y. (2010). China's pursuits of indigenous innovations in information technology developments: Hopes, follies and uncertainties. *Chinese Journal of Communication*, *3*(3), 266–289.

4 Swinging pendulums

From the Wild West to content matrix on online video platforms

The staple of audio-visual content available in formal markets in China has long been characterised by heavy-handed government intervention. Until the mid-1990s, broadcast media were defined as public institutions (*shiye*) by the Chinese government; their content innovation was relatively stagnant and distribution geographically constrained under state control. Many approaches to China's media have focused on the regulatory architecture that governs China's media and frequently hinders it from being competitive (Zhao, 1998, 2008; Lynch, 1999; Lee, 2000; Donald and Keane, 2002; Brady, 2008; Zhu and Berry, 2009). In the context of restrictive censorship, strict import quotas and a weak domestic content industry with dominant players backed by the state, the unauthorised circulation of audio-visual content has played a crucial role in the broadening media diet of Chinese viewers. Meanwhile, counterproductive pricing strategies (Yar, 2005; Karaganis, 2011) have further pushed viewers towards informal media circulation. In terms of legal institutions, although China has brought its intellectual property laws generally to comply with its commitments under the WTO Agreement on Trade-Related Measures on Intellectual Property Rights (TRIPS), enforcement remains problematic (Massey, 2006; Mercurio, 2012; Pang, 2006). Consequently, from peripatetic street vendors to backrooms of legitimate video stores, the informal media economy has grown vibrantly to feed viewers who have long regarded copyright as a public or common good (Lu and Weber, 2008; Pang, 2012). As Wang (2003) points out, these informal market players 'operate through and around formal institutions such as the state, its regulatory and enforcement capacities, and its sovereignty' (pp. 74–75).

The advent of digital platforms has further facilitated content circulation. This is not without constraints. The state has set access boundaries by blocking global players, most notably YouTube, with its technological exclusionist project of the Great Firewall. Although users can circumvent state-led geoblocking, online video platforms in mainland China have grown rapidly as they capitalise on the market gap while being shielded from head-on competition with near-global platforms. To a large extent, video streaming and sharing platforms inherited the informal zone of consumption exploited by their predecessors in the early years. While initially inundated with infringing content, digital platforms have increasingly subscribed to copyright-driven logic in recent years. The evolution towards the more formal end therefore raises questions as to how and why such a process has occurred and with what impact.

Meanwhile, video sharing sites have witnessed user-generated content (UGC) blossoming in various forms such as spoof videos, fan vidding and machinima. While UGC is often portrayed in contrast to professionally produced content, it only offers a partial perspective when framing user creativity as an essentially non-commercial activity. As Lange (2008) reminds us, it is a synchronically laden categorisation to assume that people who post videos on YouTube were, are and always will be 'ordinary' in terms of professional training, aspirations and reputation. While UGC is often associated with informality, Lobato, Thomas and Hunter (2011) maintain that UGC moves between the formal and the informal over time under various influences such as technological innovations, business models, policy frameworks and social circumstances. In China, the role of UGC on the strategic maps of corporate video platforms has experienced ups and downs. This calls for further research on the coevolution between UGC and digital platforms, including how UGC is mobilised to serve the operation logic of the platforms at various times.

This chapter draws on interviews with industry practitioners and online video producers, and secondary sources such as government regulations, newspapers and trade journals to examine the dynamics of formal and informal with reference to the rapidly evolving online video market in China. I start with a discussion of the cultural contradictions of piracy and UGC, the twin circuits in the one-time wilderness of the online video market. Then I consider the state action to formalise the market by resetting industry boundaries and strengthening copyright enforcement. I discuss how state action reflected intertwining economic, political and cultural logics, and the dual role of the state as market participant and regulator in internet governance and media governance more broadly. Moreover, I reveal how digital platforms that are well-funded by venture capital found converged interest with relevant authorities in a formalising market, and shifted their strategic pendulums. Specifically, many platforms started to adopt a copyright-as-capital approach to content licensing and engage in industry self-regulation, which propelled the formalisation of the market. Following this, I analyse how platforms have started to build context matrix beyond licensing, including developing original programming and rebooting UGC, and discuss their cultural implications.

The twin circuits of piracy and UGC and their cultural contradictions

Before the emergence of on-demand streaming platforms, peer-to-peer sharing networks played a significant role in facilitating networked consumption via informal circuits. Major platforms included eDonkey, BTChina, VeryCD and Xunlei, launched in the early 2000s. As well as domestic productions not generally available in formal circulation such as underground films, these sites hosted a large amount of overseas audio-visual content, mostly from America, Europe and Eastern Asian markets such as Japan, Korea, Hong Kong and Taiwan. These platforms, together with well-coordinated and highly efficient fan-subbing groups, have played a major role in popularising overseas audio-visual content through informal flows (Hu, 2012; Meng, 2012; Davis and Yeh, 2017). For young people who were bored with mainland programming with a heavy dose of ideological control, consumption of overseas audio-visual content was a significant source of cultural and social capital. Thus, while these platforms, fan-subbing groups and viewers challenge the control of the state and the copyright regime utilised by the global media industries, they paradoxically extend the reach of overseas productions (Meng, 2012). As Lobato suggests, piracy can be an alternative distribution system for media content, better understood as 'an enabling energy rather than – or as well as – a form of economic parasitism' (2008, p. 33). Recent studies show creative energies among online translation communities transferring to civic engagement (Zhang and Mao, 2013). Further, pirate consumption has not only provided alternative cultural diet for enthusiasts but also nurtured a new generation of creative producers including both professionals and amateurs (Li, 2012).

User creativity attracted much industry interest soon after the launch of YouTube in 2005 and its acquisition by Google one year later. A parallel universe of online video sites emerged in China, and UGC quickly became an industry buzzword. With notable exceptions such as LeTV focusing on licensing professional productions and TV streaming portals such as PPS and PPTV, many platforms, including Tudou.com, Youku.com and 56.com, were modelled on YouTube. Backed up by international venture capital, video sharing sites envisioned a future of a thriving community of amateur creators sharing original videos online, which would later be monetised. Although the term *user* comes with inherent diversity (Lange, 2008), most platforms hoped to attract creators who do not necessarily possess sophisticated production skills.

The low entry barrier in terms of budget, equipment and expertise indeed attracted many grassroots amateurs. From the light-hearted to the more socially and politically critical, many user-generated short videos spread quickly online, and some have become huge internet phenomena in China (Voci, 2010). The lip-synching videos of Back Dorm Boys (*houshe nansheng*), for example, are more light-hearted. One of these is a spoof video of the Beijing 2008 Olympics theme song, expressing Chinese people's disappointment in the national football team. Examples of those with more political thrust include *The Bloody Case That Started from a Steamed Bun (yige mantou yinfa de xue'an)* and *The War of Internet Addiction* (*wangyin zhanzheng*). The former mocks eminent Chinese film director Chen Kaige's 2005 mega-budget film *The Promise* and CCTV's signature pretentiousness in news broadcasting. The latter critiques internet censorship imposed by the state, the profit-driven gaming companies and so-called experts who subjected young 'internet addicts' to electroshock therapy. While some of these videos were created by individuals, others mobilised a large number of users in networked creativity. Taken together, these video sharing sites have decentralised the state-controlled mediascape and provided an alternative cultural space. They did not push peer-to-peer sharing out of fashion, however, mainly because at the time it offered a much wider range of professionally produced films, drama series and variety shows. Moreover, downloaded content often came with high-definition quality, which online video platforms could not then afford to stream owing to limited bandwidth.

While original UGC has witnessed hit titles and manifested sociocultural value, users have also actively shared professional productions on these platforms. Such user-led informal circulation has allowed video sharing platforms to exploit a regulatory loophole and host professional productions without assuming legal liabilities. According to the Regulations for the Protection of the Right of Communication through the Information Network (the State Council, 2006), a service provider will be shielded from legal liability if their claim for safe harbour protection is successful. To receive safe harbour protection, service providers must meet several requirements. Among others, service providers must follow notice-and-takedown procedures. Moreover, service providers must show they have no actual or constructive knowledge of a user's infringement activities, otherwise they can be held for contributory infringement. However, the provisions do not clarify under what circumstances service providers will be deemed to have constructive knowledge. This allows service providers to play edge ball with the provisions and claim they have no such knowledge in order to avoid liabilities while continuing to host infringing content. Another grey area lies in the differentiated requirements for different categories of service providers claiming immunity. For storage services, platforms receiving direct financial benefits from infringing activities are denied safe harbour protection. For linking and search services, platforms can receive safe harbour protection even if they receive direct financial benefits from relevant activities. The definition of direct financial benefits, however, is unclear. Whether pre-roll advertising, for example, constitutes direct financial benefit is a contentious issue (Personal Interview, July 2014). These grey areas in safe harbour provisions have raised challenges to its practical application.

Meanwhile, such regulatory uncertainties have given rise to considerable litigation. Notably, service providers including Tudou and 56 have successfully claimed immunity based on the safe harbour principle in legal disputes. Undeniably, many platforms have exploited the regulatory loophole while amassing a quick fortune based on an advertising-supported business model by hosting infringing content. In a sense, UGC has become a shield for some service providers from liability while hosting infringing content. Overall, although safe harbour provisions are established with a view to balancing the interests of copyright owners, online service providers and information users, their effectiveness is questionable and abuse is prevalent (Wang, 2010).

In this context, the prospect of building a sustainable advertising-supported business model based on UGC soon proved to be a pipe dream. The mixed quality and copyright trespasses apparently reduced its appeal to advertisers. Meanwhile, the numerous uploads created diseconomies of scale, where platforms suffered greater losses when they attracted more viewers because they lacked a viable business model and yet had to bear enormous bandwidth costs. Consequently, initial enthusiasm for UGC gave way to a shared sense of frustration among industry practitioners. Tudou's founder, Wang Wei, notably referred to UGC at an industry conference in 2008 as 'industrial waste water', owing to its low quality, costly bandwidth consumption, infringement risks and hence weak ability to generate a profit despite high-volume traffic.

The strike of the state and reconfiguration of industry boundaries

The informal circuits of piracy, including those carried by UGC in the Wild West of the early online video market, eventually triggered state regulation. The regulatory measures reflected the evolving rationale of internet governance, or media governance more broadly, where economic, political and cultural logics intertwine and become complicated by the duality of the state as market participant and regulator. Most notably, the then industry watchdog the State Administration of Radio, Film and Television (SARFT) and the Ministry of Industry and Information Technology (MIIT) promulgated the Administrative Provisions on Internet Audio-Visual Program Service ('the Provisions') (SARFT and MIIT, 2007), which signalled a watershed moment in the industry. By requiring online video service providers to apply for the Licence for Dissemination of Audio-Visual Programs through Information Network, the Provisions reset the market entry threshold. Together with strengthened enforcement actions, the state action triggered a major industry shakeout. The regulatory approaches here involved a mix of authorisation and restriction strategies. Authorisation typically involves licensing schemes seeking to move the informal to the formal zone, and restriction usually involves enforcement mechanisms to reduce informal activity (Lobato and Thomas, 2015, pp. 35–36).

While international media has long waged copyright battles against China, the state action was more than an attempt to respond to conformist pressure from both domestic and international copyright owners. More importantly, the state intended to protect the economic interests of the state-owned and controlled media and to extend domestic ideological control online. Noticeably, China Central Television issued copyright infringement notices to several online video sites that streamed the Spring Gala in 2007. Following the release of the Provisions, SARFT closed down 341 websites that had not obtained legal licences to operate by 31 March 2009, including many peer-to-peer sharing sites such as BTChina and btbbt where infringing content proliferated (Liao, 2009). The state's crackdown on infringing audio-visual content was a part of a special enforcement campaign dubbed 'Sword Net Action' (*jian wang xingdong*). Jointly initiated in 2005 by National Copyright Administration, the National Internet Information Office, the MIIT and the Ministry of Public Security, the annual campaign marked the state's shifted focus from offline to online piracy in copyright enforcement. For Feng (2017), this reflects the convergence between 'cultural (censorship) and economic (copyright) enforcement' in China's media regulation matrix. The economic logic speaks to the state's intention to invigorate China's cultural sector. This however does not mean loosening ideological control. In Yang's words (2014), a visible ideological thread underwrites an expanding system of internet control in China. In fact, as some content is prohibited form circulation even in the formal market, copyright enforcement often serves the purpose of censorship.

Moreover, the state crackdown on the privately owned infringing sites served the purpose of sanitising and formalising the market to pave the way for state-owned or controlled media to enter the online video market. According to the Provisions, companies applying for internet audio-visual service permits had to be 'legal persons, fully state-owned or state ownership-controlled, with no law breaching records in the prior three years'. The 'state ownership' or the 'state control' requirement applied to video websites launched after the Provisions were released, signalling an exemption for existing privately owned video websites. By December 2008, SARFT (2008) had granted 332 licences to online video service providers, the majority of which were state-owned TV stations, radio stations and news media at national, provincial and local levels. As the regulation established a new entry barrier creating market space for the state-owned or controlled media, it allowed some leeway for incumbents to apply for a licence to continue operations and grow the market.

One notable new entrant into the online video market is CNTV, a streaming platform launched by the state-owned CCTV in December 2009 to capitalise on the formalising market. According to its official statement, CNTV is built from China's largest online video program database (CNTV, 2010), and includes content derived from other terrestrial TV stations at no cost. As well as access to domestic content libraries from CCTV and provincial broadcasters, CNTV has commanded a strategic high ground in much-coveted, exclusive coverage rights to international sports events. Therefore, CNTV is essentially competing against privately owned video sites by establishing a copyright hierarchy and monopoly (Hu, 2014). This is closely connected to the favourable state policy towards the state media. Back in 2000, SARFT issued a Circular for Enhancing the Management of Reporting and Broadcasting Sporting Events ('the Circular'), providing that CCTV should be responsible for negotiating and purchasing the right to broadcast in China significant international sports competitions, including the Olympic Games, the Asia Games, the World Cup and other major sports events, and that no other local TV stations should be allowed to purchase them outright. Since then, CCTV has become the only broadcaster in China to purchase the right to such international sports events, with no competition from local broadcasters. Clearly, the authorities feed the state media with favourable policies to protect it from competition with provincial broadcasters and secure its national monopoly. Such preferential policies have now extended to the digital arm of the state media, affording opportunities for the state media to benefit from the formalising market. Despite these advantages in sports licensing, the state-run CNTV is less motivated to innovate, and is thus generally regarded as lacking appeal to domestic audiences owing to the propaganda-laden and genre-limited programming.

Meanwhile, provincial TV networks have also entered the market in the hope of maintaining their audiences, who are increasingly migrating online. One considerable player is Hunan Satellite TV (HNSTV). Having established itself as a leading provincial network and a strong brand of entertainment programming (Zhang and Fung, 2010), HNSTV determined to expand its reach in the online landscape. Initially, HNSTV profited from licensing its content to online video sites while streaming its programs on its own digital platforms including www.hunantv.com and the mobile portal Mango TV. In 2014, the network integrated its digital platforms under the brand Mango TV, and stopped licensing content to other streaming platforms. Hit shows including *Divas Hit the Road* (*huaer yu shaonian*), *X-change* (*bianxingji*) (Season 8), and *Song of Vengeance* (*changzhanji*) became available only on HNSTV's own online platforms. While the broadcaster had previously received a US$32 (RMB200) million licensing fee from iQiyi for five of its popular shows, the management was confident that advertising revenue and subscription fees from users of their own platform would surpass the revenue loss in copyright licensing (Personal Interview, July 2014). This strategy has attracted a rapidly growing number of users to Mango TV, achieving its target of attracting ten million users half a year ahead of the original plan. Since then, Mango TV has continued to benefit from the copyright policy of Hunan TV and has enriched its content library with exclusive content from the latter. In other words, Mango TV has cemented its position in the online screen market as the exclusive online video portal of Hunan TV, a broadcast network with a solid reputation in in-house production capacity.

Thus, the state's disciplining of the market has moved it closer to the copyright regime dominant under global capitalism. The state action was to a large extent embedded in the context of evolving approaches to internet governance and the dual role of the state, as well as pressures from domestic and international copyright owners. As licensing regulation and copyright enforcement reset market boundaries and formalise the market, it has allowed state and provincial broadcasters to capitalise on their content resources to compete in the growing digital market. For new entrants, approaches to the online market and resulting outcomes are differentiated. While the state-run CNTV relies on rights monopoly and hierarchy in a favourable policy environment and lacks the motivation to innovate, Mango TV's being the digital arm of HNSTV has reaped some success from the latter's strong in-house production capacity and exclusive licensing policy.

Industry self-regulation and its discontents in the context of copyright as capital

As the state action introduced a major industry shakeup, digital platforms, well-funded by transnational venture capital, played a major role in moving the industry towards the formal end. Indeed, it would be premature to conclude that legal and administrative institutions should bear all the credit in reducing infringement (Gu, 2018). As a result of unsustainable business models based on piracy and advertising, as well as UGC's perceived lack of economic value discussed earlier, the industry witnessed a voracious pursuit of licensed professionally produced content in the following years. Copyright became 'a main form of capital' (Lash and Urry, 1994, p. 136), and the financially resourceful platforms bet big. Online video sites jostled for licensed films and television content from not only domestic producers but also East Asia, America and Europe in the hope of raking in advertising dollars. As both international and domestic venture capital fuelled the arms race in licensed content acquisition, the market saw a steep escalation of acquisition costs. Within five years of the emergence of online streaming platforms, the price per episode of TV drama for example rose from 1,000 to one million yuan (Zhang, 2011). Top-tier content costs even more.

As well-resourced industry players respond to the state crackdown on infringing sites by subscribing to the content licensing approach, they have become a major force in the privatisation of governance capacity. A salient example of industry self-regulation is the China Online Video Anti-Piracy Alliance established in 2009, which includes over 110 online video enterprises, rights holders and advertising agencies. Moreover, technological measures such as a video fingerprinting system have also been deployed to detect and take down infringing content (Youku, 2010). As streaming platforms started to license content from rights holders and rely on advertising as a major revenue source, copyright enforcement became important for them to protect and capitalise on the formalising market. Moreover, the imperative to maintain a healthy relationship with content partners has also motivated compliance.

Such privatisation of enforcement has accompanied by a blizzard of suits and countersuits in the industry. Copyright functions not only as a means to protect investment but also a way of conducting politics. Meanwhile, the 'purchase first and sue later' approach further entrenches the copyright-driven operational logic of streaming platforms. Deep-pocketed platforms have found converged interests with state regulators in maintaining the raised entry barriers by employing copyright ideology, with which many of them did not comply earlier yet are able to claim moral high ground with the support of capital in the formalising market.

The great leap in licensing cost as well as increasing copyright enforcement and litigation has caused a continued consolidation of the online video market. While many have simply exited the market, the number of mergers and acquisitions, as well as IPOs (initial public offerings) in the domestic and international stock markets, has grown since 2009. This included Shanda's acquisition of ku6 in 2009 and the subsequent IPO at NASDAQ in 2010; iQiyi's acquisition by Baidu in 2012 and its merger with PPS in 2013; and the merger of Youku and Tudou in 2012, forming Youku Tudou, which was acquired by Alibaba in 2015. Thus, as both state authorities and industry players propelled the market towards the formal end, formalisation is evident not only in the growing adoption of copyright-driven logic as evidenced in content licensing and self-regulation, but also in increasing market concentration.

Evolving content strategies beyond licensing

While the strategic pendulum shifted away from infringing content as streaming platforms were busy inking licensing deals, it was not long before platform owners realised the need to reformulate content strategies. The vigorous pursuit of licensing deals pushed up costs but did not deliver audience loyalty. Viewers switched platforms frequently, depending on which one bought the rights of their preferred hits. Moreover, the emerging trend of broadcasters cutting back on their sales of online streaming rights further pressured independent platforms to reconsider content strategies. Consequently, these digital platforms became motivated to develop a content matrix in which original programming and UGC stand side by side with licensed, professionally produced content.

Original programming

As a measure to offset budgetary pressure from licensing and to build differentiation not only from online peers but also from the unappealing national brand, digital platforms started to experiment with original programming. Youku's initial forays into original productions saw the launch of Youku Originals in 2010. The Bright Eleven and Beautiful 2012 projects under the strategy brought together rising talents and established film directors to experiment with micro-movie production. Tudou closely followed with the 'Orange Box' original production initiative in 2010, pumping out trendy drama series. Examples included *That Love Comes* (*huanying ai guanglin*), directed by Taiwanese director *Ke Hanchen*, and *Utopia Office* (*wutuobang bangongshi*), which was fully planned, written, produced and marketed by an in-house team at Tudou (2011). In the following years, major online video platforms including iQiyi, LeTV and Tencent Video all embarked on the project of original content production.

As streaming platforms started to experiment with original programming, state policy in the broadcasting sector propelled such initiatives further. Notably, the 'One Series, Two Satellites' policy, enacted in 2015 by the State Administration of Press, Publication, Radio, Film and Television (SAPPRFT), pushed collaboration between independent production firms and streaming platforms. Specifically, the state media regulator banned broadcasters from airing the same TV series on more than two channels for the first run, with the intention of creating a market for more content and pushing up the ratings, which were continuously dropping as a result of one series being broadcast on multiple channels (China Media News, 2015). Consequently, the dwindling distribution space on broadcast networks pushed production companies to the online space. These include drama production companies such as Dongyang Flower Film &TV Co., Ltd (acquired by LeTV in 2013), Ciwen Media, Croton Media, Daylight Entertainment, and variety show production firms such as Canxing Productions, 3CMedia, EE-Media, Vision Media and Vivid Media. As these production firms found a converged interest with online video sites, they became important collaborators for streaming platforms in their original programming strategies.

Over the years, original programming has received increasing investment, welcomed more collaborators and delivered an increasingly diversified range of content, particularly in variety shows and drama series. As one interviewee put it, they are no longer 'filler content' (Personal Interview, June 2016). In 2016, over 2,000 episodes of original drama series were produced, consuming a total investment of 27 billion yuan (Chen, 2017). The year saw 111 original variety shows streaming online (Zhang, 2017). Most viewed among the former included debate talent talk show *You Can You Bibi* (*qipashuo*, iQiyi with MeWe Media, since 2014), talk show *Mars Intelligence Agency* (*huoxing qingbaoju*, Youku with Galaxy Entertainment, since 2016), and stand-up-comedy-like show *Roast* (*tucao dahui*, Tencent Video with Fun Factory, since 2017). Over 15 variety shows garnered more than 500 million viewers in 2016 (Zhou and Xiong, 2017). Drama series included sub-genres such as sit-coms, idol drama, suspense, horror, sci-fi drama and fantasy drama. *The Mystic Nine* (*lao jiu men*) and *Grave Robbers' Chronicle* (*daomu biji*), the most viewed series in 2015 and 2016, received over 1 billion and 10 billion views separately. Backed by professional production and proven viewership online, an increasing number of original productions from online video sites have made their way to television broadcasters, with *The Legend of Zu* (*shushan zhanji*) produced by iQiyi in 2015, setting the trend in motion.

Online video platforms have also taken a page from the broadcasters' playbook and adopted the approach of format acquisition and adaptation. Indeed, Chinese broadcasters have employed television format adaptation as an industry development strategy over the past two decades (de Burgh, Zeng and Chen, 2011; Zhang and Fung, 2014; Keane, 2002; Moran and Keane, 2006). Format licensing allows broadcasters to capitalise on proven success with the additional security of having knowledgeable collaborators, therefore they 'pay for the outsourcing of risk' (Chalaby 2016, p. 12). Resulting hit shows in the online space include *Are You Normal?* (*ni zhengchang ma?*), adapted from the quiz show *Are You Normal, America?* by Tencent Video in partnership with the independent production firm Vivid Media in 2014, and *We 15* (*women shiwuge*) produced by Tencent Video, loosely based on Talpa's Utopia in 2015, *I'm Going to School* (*wo qu shangxue la*), and adapted from a South Korean format by iQiyi, Dragon TV and JTBC in 2015.

As a part of the content matrix, original programming has generated more genres, harvested growing viewership and increasingly licensed to broadcasters. Independent production houses have been an important force in pumping out professional-standard content. Such initiatives share some similarity with those implemented by Netflix and Amazon, which according to Cunningham and Craig (2016, pp. 5413) are essentially 'old wine in new bottles' given the continuities in screen production practices. Despite such continuities, original programming of online video platforms in China has demonstrated visible value in experimenting with new genres previously rarely seen on broadcaster networks. The risky side of the story, though, is the state's tightening grip over internet content. SAPPRFT for example has strengthened censorship of online series, bringing them to the same standards applicable to regular TV series (*Xinhua News*, 2016).

Formalisation of amateur media: UGC rebooted

Formalisation as evidenced in investment in professional productions, both through licensing and original programming, does not mean the exclusion of amateur creativity in content production. As Vonderau (2015) writes:

> While current industry discourse often maps the digital world as one marked by linear moves between informal and formal forms of media use, where streaming follows piracy and waste is transformed into gold, it appears rather as a *mise-en-abyme* where infrastructures are infinitely built into each other, creating anomalies that again become part of a system, and so on, driven by a constant tension between a construction of order and its destruction.
>
> (p. 726)

Moreover, as Lobato, Thomas and Hunter (2011) argue, UGC itself sits on a spectrum of formality as different components of UGC exhibit differing degrees of formality and may move between formality and informality over time in terms of regulation, capital intensity, measurement, institutionalisation, rationalisation and labour organisation. According to Cunningham and Craig (2019), professionalising amateurs may constitute a more radical cultural and content challenge to established media than streaming platforms following the approach of licensing, and increasingly producing, content.

In a historical light, amateur production on online video platforms in China has evolved with platform content strategies and state governance. UGC experienced nearly unfettered growth until the state introduced licensing regulation and strengthened copyright infringement, which led to the demise of many video sharing platforms. While UGC seemed to be cast aside when platforms battled fiercely for supremacy in licensed professional content offerings, it has remained a part of the online screen ecology. As original content becomes increasingly important for online platforms to build a competitive advantage, UGC has staged a decisive comeback. This time, online video sites hope to move it towards the formal end.

Noticeably, following the merger between Youku and Tudou,[1] the new venture (NYSE: YOKU) officially launched a 'Sharing Plan' (*fengxiang jihua*) similar to the YouTube Partner Program in 2013. The program supports creators of original content by providing UGC 'partners' with a 30 per cent share of advertising revenue. The revenue-sharing plan marked a significant differentiation from the earlier approach to UGC. In the words of Yang Weidong, President of Tudou, who announced the plan at the Tudou Video Festival, this opened the chapter of 'Tudou 2.0' (Youku Tudou Inc., 2013). To enhance their appeal to advertisers, platforms emphasise the importance of originality in UGC and put in place a vetting process. Moreover, UGC partners receive training, covering cinematography, digital marketing and case study seminars. Other platforms such as iQiyi, Tencent Video and Sohu have also made similar moves.

The move to nurture original content and professionalise UGC manifests itself further in Youku Tudou's rebranding into Heiyi Group in 2015. The name Heiyi, literally meaning harmonious union, conveys the venture's mission to build an ecosystem where content creators, sitting at various points of the amateur–professional spectrum, can take part and generate value. Any registered user can establish a channel (*zipindao*) by uploading a video, which suggests openness and inclusivity in a strategy aiming to build a large pool of creators. As Youku Tudou's Chief Product Officer Gu Sibin explains, *zipindao* is a prime destination for video entrepreneurs, be they amateurs or professionals (China.com.cn, 2015). This echoes the name of the conference where the brand was announced: open ecosystem conference. To accelerate the development of individual channels dedicated to made-for-web original content, the venture announced a ten billion RMB (US$1.6 billion) plan. The plan aims to nurture 100,000 channels with more than 1,000 subscribers; 10,000 channels with a monthly income over 10,000 RMB (US$1,600), and 100 channels with a market value above 100 million RMB (US$16 million).

To facilitate the professionalisation and commercialisation of amateur content, the platforms rate content creators based on average daily viewing time of their videos over 180 days from Tier 1 (under two hours) to Tier 12 (over 50,000) hours. Various features and support mechanisms are on offer, which are tied to different tiers. These include efficiency-oriented features such as the eligibility to upload sizeable videos, to upload content synchronously to both Youku and Tudou, and to receive accelerated approval for publishing. Moreover, various revenue streams can be activated as creators move up the tiers, including receiving 70 per cent of the advertising revenue, receiving contributions from fans, adding an overlay to prompt viewers to purchase products online and receive a 90 per cent share of the revenue, and activating a paid subscription channel. Further, support mechanisms are in place for 'worthy' creators to promote their channels. These include features that enable creators to display channel logos in uploaded videos, receive prioritised placement in search results, and enable bullet screens (*danmu*),[2] where viewers can send comments via text messages to be projected directly on screen (Youku, 2015). Overall, these features afford more opportunities for creators to improve efficiency, diversify revenue streams, enhance fan engagement and strengthen self-promotion.

Thus, professionalisation of UGC involves not only an increased intensity in capital investment and industry regulation against infringing content, but also promotion of entrepreneurial ethos. As Youku Tudou's president Wei Ming explains, *zi* (roughly translated as 'self') can be understood in terms of self-reliance, uniqueness in style and self-promotion (Sina.com, 2015). Indeed, the hope of online video platforms lies in promoting the entrepreneurial ethos so that professionalising amateurs can internalise it, willingly take inherent risks in creative production and engage in continuous learning to generate marketable content. Moreover, self-branding becomes a crucial part of being a content creator. Several video creators report that platforms encourage content creators to add their own logos to the videos and to build their own brands (Personal

Interviews, January 2016). The call on creators to brand themselves is as much about promoting entrepreneurial drive to nurture marketable content as it is about saddling individual creators with the risks inherent in creative production. In the words of Marwick (2013), self-branding in fact encourages people to 'take on the responsibility of economic uncertainty by constructing identities that fit current business trends' (p. 305).

The platform logic in promoting entrepreneurial ethos and professionalising UGC is underpinned by data-driven evaluation working in conjunction with incentive mechanisms. Datafication and algorithms take a central role here (Beer, 2009; Van Dijck and Poell, 2013). For Van Dijck and Poell (2013), the logic of popularity on social media platforms is conditioned by the logic of datafication, programmability associated with algorithmic culture and connectivity through the socio-technical affordance of networked platforms. In tracing the professionalisation of amateur video creators, Cunningham and Craig (2019) characterise the proto-industry of social media entertainment as the volatile, interdependent clash of cultures between Hollywood (entertainment IP-driven content industries) and Silicon Valley IT (iterative tech experimentation). While the former is conventionally characterised by an IP-driven approach, non-scalability, notoriously fickle consumer taste, and content and talent development, the latter is dedicated to scale, automation and iterative tech experimentation.

In assessing value, or more precisely, economic value of content, creators and platforms, a shift in focus has become evident. Specifically, user loyalty, viewing time and average revenue per user (ARPU) have become more important metrics to watch then unique visitors (UVs) and video views (VVs) (Personal Interview, December 2015). Together with other data such as subscription data and comment data, they constitute a set of value indicators. In this context, creators and viewers become quantified, in accordance with platforms' imperative to increase and diversify revenue. The platforms thus facilitate a 'social network market' (Potts *et al.*, 2008), where individual choices are determined by the choice of others in the network. When networked preference is embedded in recommendation algorithms, it results in 'a closed commercial loop in which culture conforms to, more than it confronts, its users' (Hallinan and Striphas, 2016, p. 122). This reflects a broader trend where tech giants are becoming 'the new apostles of culture' (Striphas, 2015, p. 407).

Crucially, as platforms design algorithms to facilitate evaluation and mediate networked consumption, it also steers production. For example, subgenres that are perceived as more commercially viable by platforms receive priority treatment in algorithms. In the case of Youku Tudou, creators producing beauty, cooking and parenting tutorials, music, animation and comedy, and those with large followings and the potential to tap into e-commerce, receive priority. This guides creators' entrepreneurial drive, which has a visible effect on the content library. As several video creators discuss the thumb rules of moving along the tiered system, finding an appropriate genre and sticking to it is crucial. In the words of one creator, 'You must make sure your videos are located in the same category. Games, beauty, or pets…You can select one and you need to stick to it until you are known for it' (Personal Interview, December 2015). This strategy reflects content creators' efforts to 'fit into' predefined or prioritised categories by platform. As platforms capitalise on the 'long tail' (Anderson, 2006) generated by professionalising amateurs, the latter have to navigate the politics of content aggregation (Vonderau, 2015). While corporations reveal some key indicators in their algorithms, the inner workings remain a black box. For creators, they need to constantly tweak and optimise content to garner good-looking indicators generated by algorithms. As professionalising amateurs internalise the commercial logic of the platform, successful attempts only reinforce platform logic, potentially leading to homogenisation in content production.

Moreover, algorithm-driven measurement and ranking mechanisms are closely connected to the resources available to support content creators. Yet the shifting boundaries between privilege and rights raise controversies. One prominent example is the feature of platform certification of originality launched by Youku Tudou. Drawing lessons from earlier development, the platform attempts to reduce the infringement risks associated with UGC and enhance its appeal to advertisers. Moreover, the platform has designed this feature as a value-added service for the creator community. Once certified, creators can benefit from platform-enforced copyright protection enabled by digital fingerprinting technology, where revenue gained from infringing content will be returned to them. Certified creators also receive prioritised treatment in search rankings and content recommendations. However, a platform certification of originality is only available to content creators who have achieved a certain amount of popularity (above Tier 5). While a diverse range of community-building and commercialisation opportunities can be unlocked in a similar fashion, tying copyright governance to the tiered system of creators has met challenges from these creators.

Jessica Ren, who creates beauty videos in the name of Rare Jessie, discussed her dissatisfaction with such terms. As she complained,

> The platform needs to motivate creators, which I understand. However, I found it unreasonable when the button of original creative work was greyed out to me.... This means even if I have spent days working on a video, originality of my work can't get recognised by the platform and my interest as an author cannot be guaranteed in the same way as other creators sitting at the higher end of the tiered system. I simply can't understand this.
>
> (Personal Interview, December 2015)

Interestingly, this perception of copyright is very different from that of creators in the Wild West days of online video space. Rather than seeing creativity as communal property, the creator has internalised the capital logic of copyright as the industry has become formalised, where creativity is an individual asset to be commodified and protected as property (Pang, 2012). Jessica attempted to contact Youku but her point was dismissed. As a result, she decided to migrate to another platform.

Evidently, underlying the purported openness and inclusiveness portrayed by digital platforms is inequality. Selective openness to support resources guided by data-driven metrics bespeaks the uneven nature of the playing field. For creators at the lower end of the tiered system, such differentiated treatment means that the platform is not to be relied on to assert their rights. In other words, author rights in this case are to some extent linked to the algorithm-informed popularity of the work, and thus becomes a privilege than a right. At a time when platforms are distancing themselves from their informal past, copyright governance is paradoxically uneven and porous. Noticeably, some platforms users manifest agency in resisting such algorithm-informed inequality. As Cunningham and Craig (2019) point out, it is important to note Foucault's (1991) distinction between power and domination and to highlight the relational, contingent, unstable and reversible nature of power in algorithmic culture.

As well as data-based evaluation and algorithm-driven steering, platforms also influence content visibility and popularity using 'analogue', institutionalised mechanisms. Yet increasing state oversight of online content has become a crucial influence on platform mediation. For instance, compared to previous initiatives such as the establishment of the 'Independent Spirit Award' (*duli jingshen jiang*) in the Tudou Video Festival in 2011, the potential for independent and experimental work to be promoted has gradually faded. In fact, the Tudou Video Festival was quietly terminated in 2016. Moreover, the formalising industry has witnessed the attenuation of UGC's political potential. Hu Ge's transformation from amateur spoofer to video entrepreneur is an example of the public–private cooperation that takes place on and beyond the Chinese internet (Yu, 2015). This reflects the wider reality in China where private entrepreneurs have been either co-opted by the reigning political authorities or have chosen to incorporate themselves into the dominant political institutions as partners of the ruling party in its economic pursuits (Dickson, 2007).

From the above analysis, it is evident that UGC has staged a strong comeback. For online video platforms, UGC has become a crucial part of the content strategy as they face the challenge of surging licensing costs and the need to enhance viewer loyalty with original content. In analysing YouTube's investment philosophy in relation to UGC, Postigo (2016) likens the platform to 'a bettor at a roulette table who is in the happy position of betting on all the numbers, where the payout in aggregate outweighs what appears to be an otherwise wild investment' (p. 15). The metaphor is also applicable to Youku Tudou and many other platforms in China, as they bet on content creators at different points on the amateur–professional spectrum while at the same time licensing, and increasingly producing, content.

As UGC returns to the strategic map, it is no longer associated only with amateurish practices, but is conceived as a dynamic concept with the potential to move towards the professional end of the spectrum to serve the commercial logic of digital platforms. In other words, UGC is no longer an isolated hinterland of inferior or infringing content, a burden on the bandwidth, or a site that is hard to monetise. Instead, it has become a part of the screen ecology in which platforms spread the risks inherent in creative production while maintaining the benefits of economies of scale and maximising the value of commercially viable content.

The process of formalisation involves increasing capital investment together with incentive mechanisms and support resources, the content vetting process and measurement apparatus. As platforms nurture the entrepreneurial ethos to serve their interests, the process of formalisation is also a process of reconstituting the meaning of value. The prominent role of algorithm-driven measurement, classification and ranking mediate networked preference among viewers and steer production cultures to serve commercial logics of platforms. As support mechanisms are tied to algorithm-driven performance indicators, the prospect of the productive and profitable formalisation of UGC exists alongside the risk of skewed and partial algorithms, and inequality in cultural production. Moreover, platform governance comes with the risk of being co-opted by state regulation.

Conclusion

This chapter has traced how the space of wilderness upon the twin circuits of piracy and UGC has become formalised in multiple dimensions in the online video market. This process has coevolved with the dynamics between the state and the market, as well as the collapsing boundaries between amateurs and professionals. When the lens of the formal and the informal is overlaid onto an analysis of state–market interactions and the professional–amateur spectrum, it aids our understanding of the logic behind formalisation, the diverse participants and their interactions in the process, the multiple dimensions of formalisation and their cultural impacts.

The state, as a major force propelling formalisation, was driven by the imperative to respond to the conformist pressure from both domestic and international copyright owners, to extend domestic ideological control online and to capitalise on the formalising space as market participants. This renders a clearer picture of the role of the state including its overlap with the market in the growing digital economy in China as well as in the post-WTO global context. The state action has shifted market boundaries, witnessing the state-owned or -controlled broadcasters capitalising on their content libraries to gain a foothold in the streaming market. The state media in particular stand to benefit more from copyright monopoly and are less motivated to commit to content innovation. While some broadcasters seek additional revenue by licensing content to independent digital platforms, exclusive licensing to digital arms affiliated with broadcasters has also emerged as a strategy to carve out a position in the formalising market. Meanwhile, as the state has raised the market threshold, it has left some leeway for incumbents to continue operation, and more importantly, to continue growing the market while the national team have come to capitalise on it.

Digital platforms, especially well-resourced ones, find a converged interest in strengthened copyright enforcement and a higher entry barrier to the formalised market. The challenge of monetising UGC, a notion that once promised both cultural participation and commercialisation potential, has driven digital platforms to adopt the logic of copyright as capital. This logic manifests itself not only in the licensing of professional productions but also in an increasing level of industry self-regulation, and growing litigation.

The resulting spiralling cost in licensing, the need to develop competitive advantage and reduce reliance on broadcasters, and the state's tighter grip of the broadcasting industry have seen digital platforms experimenting with alternative strategies beyond licensing. These include original programming and the formalisation of amateur media. The effort to construct a content matrix bespeaks online video platforms' ambition to move upstream while sharing risks with production partners and building up long-term development potential in the evolving screen ecology. Original made-for-web content has thus witnessed growth in investment, genres, viewership, advertising revenue and licensing to broadcasters. The state's move to rein in online content, however, may result in increasing self-censorship by platforms.

Meanwhile, platforms are mobilising UGC as part of a content matrix, with a view to professionalising and commercialising it. By establishing the measurement system and the revenue-sharing mechanism, setting up terms and conditions for platform usage and providing support resources, online video platforms are attempting to reboot UGC and push it towards the formal end. As platforms promote the entrepreneurial ethos, aspirational creators are taking inherent risks in creative production in the hope of moving up the tiers informed by data and algorithms. While the possibility of the formal interacting productively and profitably with the informal exists, there is also a dark side to the story. This includes a reductionist approach to value and the risk of skewed algorithms, which are linked to the role of platforms in steering both production and consumption in their own interest. Moreover, the impact is evident in the new 'fringe areas' (Parks, 2006) created by algorithms based on user-generated data, the standardisation of cultural production, and uneven and porous infrastructure available to creators.

Notes

1 The two platforms have maintained separate operations since the merger.
2 The bullet screen (*danmu*) refers to real-time comments projected directly onto the screen like a barrage of bullets, hence the name.

References

Anderson, C. (2006). *The long tail: Why the future of business is selling less of more*, Hyperion, New York, NY.

Beer, D. (2009). Power through the algorithm? Participatory web cultures and the technological unconsciousness. *New Media & Society, 11*(6), 985–1002.

Brady, A.-M. (2008). *Marketing dictatorship: Propaganda and thought work in contemporary China*, Rowman & Littlefield, Lanham, MD.

Chalaby, J. K. (2016). *The format age: Television's entertainment revolution*, Polity Press, London.

Chen, J. (2017). The next big thing in the screen industry: Investment in self-produced internet content increasing by 125% last year. Retrieved 30 July 2017 from www.ce.cn/xwzx/gnsz/gdxw/201707/20/t20170720_24321238.shtml.

China Media News (2015). One series, two satellite policy pushing ratings numbers for some channels. Retrieved 15 January 2015 from www.cmm-i.net/media-news/2015-01-12/one-series-two-satellite-policy-pushing-ratings-numbers-some-channels.

China.com.cn (2015). Youku launches zipindao to promote 100,000 video entrepreneurs. Retrieved 25 November 2015 from http://tech.china.com.cn/internet/20151124/210203.shtml.

CNTV (2010). CNTV profile. Retrieved 12 December 2013 from http://english.cntv.cn/20100609/102812.shtml.

Cunningham, S. and Craig, D. (2016). Online entertainment: A new wave of media globalization. *International Journal of Communication*, *10*, 5409–5425.

Cunningham, S. and Craig, D. (2019). *Social media entertainment: The new intersection of Hollywood and Silicon Valley*, New York University Press, New York, NY.

Davis, D. W. and Yeh, E. Y.-y. (2017). Zimuzu and media industry in China. *Media Industries Journal*, *4*(1). Retrieved 1 March 2018 from https://quod.lib.umich.edu/m/mij/15031809.0004.102/-zimuzu-and-media-industry-in-china?rgn=main;view=fulltext.

De Burgh, H., Zeng, R., and Chen, S. (2012). Chinese television 'internationalization' and the search for creativity. *Creative Industries Journal*, *4*(2), 137–154.

Dickson, B. J. (2007). Integrating wealth and power in China: The Communist Party's embrace of the private sector. *The China Quarterly*, *192* (December), 827–854.

Donald, S. H. and Keane, M. (2002). Media in China: New convergences, new approaches, in *Media in China: Consumption, content and crisis*, eds S. H. Donald, M. Keane and H. Yin, RoutledgeCurzon, London; New York, NY, pp. 3–17.

Feng, L. (2017). Online video sharing: An alternative channel for film distribution? Copyright enforcement, censorship, and Chinese independent cinema. *Chinese Journal of Communication*, *10*(3), 279–294.

Foucault, M. (1991). *Discipline and punish: The birth of a prison*. Penguin, London.

Gu, J. (2018). From divergence to convergence: Institutionalization of copyright and the decline of online video piracy in China. *International Communication Gazette*, *80*(1), 60–86.

Hallinan, B. and Striphas, T. (2016). Recommended for you: The Netflix Prize and the production of algorithmic culture. *New Media and Society*, *18*(1), 117–137.

Hu, K. (2012). Chinese subtitle groups and the neoliberal work ethics, in *Popular culture collaborations and co-productions in East and Southeast Asia*, eds O. Nissim and B.-A. Eyal, National University of Singapore Press, Singapore, pp. 207–232.

Hu, K. (2014). Competition and collaboration: Chinese video websites, subtitle groups, state regulation and market. *International Journal of Cultural Studies*, *17*(5), 437–451.

Karaganis, J. (ed.). (2011). *Media piracy in emerging economies*: Social Science Research Council, New York, NY.

Keane, M. (2002). As a hundred television formats bloom, a thousand television stations contend. *Journal of Contemporary China*, *11*(30), 5–16.

Lange, P. G. (2008). Misconceptions about YouTube, in *Video vortex reader: Responses to YouTube*, eds G. Lovink and S. Niederer, Institute of Network Cultures, Amsterdam, Netherlands, pp. 87–100.

Lash, S. and Urry, J. (1994). *Economies of sign and space*, Sage, London.

Lee, C.-C. (2000). *Power, money and media: Communication patterns and bureaucratic controls in cultural China*, Northwestern University Press, Evanston, IL.

Li, J. (2012). From D-Buffs to the D-Generation: Piracy, cinema, and an alternative public sphere in urban China. *International Journal of Communication, 6*, 542–563.

Liao, X. (2009). 162 inappropriate websites shut down. Retrieved 4 April 2010 from http://news.xinhuanet.com/news-center/2009-03/31/content_11103382.htm.

Lobato, R. (2008). The six faces of media piracy: Global film distribution from below, in *The Business of Entertainment*, Vol. 1: Movies, ed. R. C. Sickels, Praeger, Westport, CT, pp. 15–36.

Lobato, R. and Thomas, J. (2015). *The informal media economy*, Polity Press, Cambridge.

Lobato, R., Thomas, J. and Hunter, D. (2011). Histories of user-generated content: Between formal and informal media economies. *International Journal of Communication, 5*, 899–914.

Lu, J. and Weber, I. (2008). Chinese government and software copyright: Manipulating the boundaries between public and private. *International Journal of Communication, 2*(1), 81–99.

Lynch, D. C. (1999). *After the propaganda state: Media, politics, and 'Thought Work' in reformed China*, Stanford University Press, Stanford, CA.

Marwick, A. (2013). *Status update: Celebrity, publicity, and branding in the social media age*, Yale University Press, New Haven, CT.

Massey, J. A. (2006). The emperor is far away: China's enforcement of intellectual property rights protection, 1986–2006. *Chicago Journal of International Law, 7*(1), 231–237.

Meng, B. (2012). Undetermined globalisation: Media consumption via P2P networks. *International Journal of Communication, 6*, 467–483.

Mercurio, B. C. (2012). The protection and enforcement of intellectual property in China since accession to the WTO: Progress and retreat. *China Perspectives, 1*(89), 23–28.

Moran, A. and Keane, M. (2006). Cultural power in international TV format markets. *Continuum, 20*(1), 71–86.

Pang, L. (2006). *Cultural control and globalization in Asia: Copyright, piracy, and cinema*, Routledge, Abingdon.

Pang, L. (2012). *Creativity and its discontents: China's creative industries and intellectual property rights offenses*, Duke University Press, Durham, NC.

Parks, L. (2006). Where the cable ends: Television in fringe areas, in *Cable visions: Television beyond broadcasting*, eds S. Banet-Weiser, C. Chris and A. Freitas, New York University Press, New York, pp. 103–126.

Postigo, H. (2016). The socio-technical architecture of digital labor: Converting play into YouTube money. *New Media and Society, 18*(2), 332–349.

Potts, J., Cunningham, S., Hartley, J. and Ormerod, P. (2008). Social network markets: A new definition of the creative industries. *Journal of Cultural Economics, 32*(3), 167–185.

SARFT (2008). List of online audio-visual broadcasting license holders. Retrieved 20 December 2008 from www.sarft.gov.cn/articles/2008/12/19/20080618094603550698.html.

SARFT and MIIT (2007). The Administrative Provisions on Internet Audio-Visual Program Service. Retrieved 1 June 2014 from www.sarft.gov.cn/art/2007/12/29/art_1583_26307.html.

Sina.com (2015). Youku Tudou promotes channels as two becomes one. Retrieved 6 March 2015 from http://tech.sina.com.cn/i/2015-08-17/doc-ifxfxrav2535735.shtml.

State Council (2006). Regulations for the protection of the Right of Communication through the information network (Hulianwang deng xinxi wangluo chuanbo shiting jie mu guanli banfa). Retrieved 1 April 2015 from www.scio.gov.cn/zcfg/zcfg/Document/341492/341492_1.htm.

Striphas, T. (2015). Algorithmic culture. *European Journal of Cultural Studies*, *18*(4–5), 395–412.

Tudou (2011). Tudou debuts its second original drama 'Utopia Office'. Retrieved 5 May 2011 from www.prnewswire.com/news-releases/tudou-debuts-its-second-original-drama-utopia-office-120455924.html.

Van Dijck, J. and Poell, T. (2013). Understanding social media logic. *Media and Communication*, *1*(1), 2–14.

Voci, P. (2010). *China on video: Smaller-screen realities*, Routledge, London.

Vonderau, P. (2015). The politics of content aggregation. *Television and New Media*, *16*(8), 717–733.

Wang, Q. (2010). 'Xinxi wangluo chuanbo baohu tiaoli' zhong 'bifenggang' guize de xiaoli (The effectiveness of the safe hour protection clause in *Regulations for the Protection of the Right of Communication through the Information Network*), *Fa Xue* (Law Science), *6*, 128–140.

Wang, S. (2003). *Framing piracy: Globalization and film distribution in Greater China*, Rowman & Littlefield, Lanham, MD.

Yang, G. (2014). The return of ideology and the future of Chinese internet policy. *Critical Studies in Media Communication*, *31*(2), 109–113.

Yar, M. (2005). The global 'epidemic' of movie 'piracy': Crime-wave or social construction? *Media, Culture & Society*, *27*(5), 677–696.

Youku (2010). Youku launches copyright identification management platform. Retrieved 3 March 2011 from http://c.youku.com/abouteg/detail/_aid81686_1781.

Youku (2015). Details of Youku zipindao tiered system. Retrieved 1 September 2015 from http://club.youku.com/thread-37192-1-1.html.

Youku Tudou Inc. (2013). Tudou Video Festival empowers UGC talents with sponsors and marketing support. Retrieved 1 June 2014 from www.prnewswire.com/news-releases/tudou-video-festival-empowers-ugc-talents-with-sponsors-and-marketing-support-211350651.html.

Yu, H. (2015). After the 'Steamed Bun' e'gao and its postsocialist politics. *Chinese Literature Today*, *5*(1), 55–64.

Zhang, W. and Mao, C. (2013). Fan activism sustained and challenged: Participatory culture in Chinese online translation communities. *Chinese Journal of Communication*, *6*(1), 45–61.

Zhang, X. and Fung, A. (2010). Market, politics and media competition in China: Competing media discourses in TV industries. *Journal of the Oriental Society of Australia*, *42*, 133-154.

Zhang, X. and Fung, A. (2014). TV formatting of the Chinese Ugly Betty: An ethnographic observation of the production community. *Television and New Media*, *15*(6), 507–522.

Zhang, X. W. (2011). Online video sites set up new records in licensing cost: 1000 times growth within 5 years. Retrieved 9 September 2011 from http://tech.163.com/11/0831/00/7COCKDT5000915BF.html.

Zhang, Y. (2017). Ten years of internet variety shows and their influence on lifestyle and beyond. Retrieved 30 November 2017 from http://media.people.com.cn/n1/2017/1121/c40606-29657782.html.

Zhao, Y. (1998). *Media, market, and democracy in China: Between the party line and the bottom line*, University of Illinois Press, Urbana, IL.

Zhao, Y. (2008). *Communication in China: Political economy, power and conflict*, Rowman & Littlefield, Lanham, MD.

Zhou, L. and Xiong, Y. (2017). Internet variety shows: Boundaries still important for a bigger stage. Retrieved 22 December 2017 from http://epaper.gmw.cn/gmrb/html/2017-12/20/nw.D110000gmrb_20171220_4-11.htm.

Zhu, Y. and Berry, C. (2009). *TV China*, Indiana University Press, Bloomington, IN.

5 Aspirations, precarity and agency

Creative labour in the formalising internet literature market

From time travel to fantasy, warrior legends to teen romance, historical fiction to science fiction, internet literature has emerged and blossomed in China since the late 1990s. It all started with amateur writers and literary enthusiasts publishing original, long-form serialised writings mainly comprising fiction in online discussion forums and literary websites. With no financial ambitions, internet literature writers started writing online out of pure interest and the desire for self-expression and social communication (Hockx, 2015). In a country where literary production has long been regarded as a tool of propaganda and confined to elite professionals, internet literature has flourished owing to lower entry barriers and weaker censorship in the online space.

Over the years, China's online literature market has travelled far beyond its departure point. Digital platforms such as Qidian, Zongheng, Hongxiu, Jinjiang and Xiaoxiang have attracted a growing number of largely amateur writers to publish their works. Based on the freemium business model and with a massive influx of capital, the once non-commercial grassroots communities have now formalised into a rapidly growing industry. The market size exceeded US$1.3 billion (9 billion yuan), with a readership of over 333 million by the end of 2016 (*People's Daily*, 2017). Meanwhile, the market-dominating China Reading Group claimed over 5.3 million registered writers on its multiple platforms (People.cn, 2017), pumping out works with the aspiration of winning the hearts and pockets of readers.

While the accelerating commercialisation and concentration of the internet literature market in China indicates a formalising tendency, informal practices have always abounded and coevolved with the formal. Labour, a key constituent variable in disaggregating the spectrum of formality, provides a useful lens for understanding the informal and its interaction with the formal (Lobato and Thomas, 2015). This is particularly relevant as creative labour has coevolved with China's internet literature industry, which has become dominated by digital platforms.

As the creative economy discourse has gained traction with its potential contribution to economic growth and job creation, it has provoked heated debates on creative labour. On one hand, proponents such as Florida (2003) and Howkins (2001) paint a rosy picture. As Lobato and Thomas (2015) point out, informality in such discourses 'takes on a positive character, associated with freedom, autonomy and liberation from Fordist routinization' (p. 72). On the other hand, the work of Hardt and Negri (2000, 2004) in the Autonomist Marxist tradition provides a counter-perspective by pointing to a precarity inextricably linked to the process of capitalist accumulation under Post-Fordism. Their work has inspired a growing critique of the precarious conditions of creative labour (Caldwell, 2008; Deuze, 2007; Gill and Pratt, 2008; Hesmondhalgh and Baker, 2011; Mayer, 2011; McRobbie, 2002; Neilson and Rossiter, 2005; Ross, 2009). In the context of digital economy, while much literature has focused on the altruistic motivations and the democratic potentials of UGC (Burgess, 2006; Jenkins, 2005; Jenkins *et al.*, 2013; Yang and Jiang, 2015), pessimists have critiqued the mediocrity of amateur media and its potential effects in drowning out professionalism (Keen, 2007) and exploitation of user labour (Andrejevic, 2009; Fuchs, 2010, 2013, 2015; Terranova, 2000). All this work has been productive in revealing different realities of creative labour. To achieve a more textured understanding of media industry, it requires us to bring the creative labour debate and the informal economy debate into dialogue (Lobato and Thomas, 2015).

At the dawn of the new century, the agenda of the structural transformation from a resource-intensive economy to a knowledge-based one has led state and local governments in China to adopt and adapt the creative industries discourse, initially championed by the British New Labour government in the late 1990s (Cunningham 2009; Hartley and Keane 2006; Keane 2009). The idea of creative industries has had an uneven reception across China, more warmly welcomed in Shanghai and subsequently adopted with some caution in Beijing, followed up by local governments' adoption and adaptation of it as a development template elsewhere (Keane, 2009). While the creative industries idea was gaining momentum, Jing Wang (2004) expressed doubts about its acceptance in a country 'where creative imagination is subjugated to active state surveillance' (p. 13).

In analysing the social and economic impact of creativity in China, leading industrial economist and policy adviser Li Wuwei (2011) points out that creative industries are not only creating new employment opportunities for Chinese society but also changing the traditional employment structure of China, which has witnessed the growth of unregistered employment. In the digital media economy, a diversified range of informal labour practices has emerged, which are closely connected with formal economies. These include guild labour in online gaming (Zhang and Fung, 2013), volunteer subtitling communities (Hu, 2012), amateur online video production (Zhao, 2014) and informal circuits of labour attached to the iPhone (Qiu *et al.*, 2014). As digital platforms have become an important site for creative production, creative users' experiences and their coevolution with the market calls for further research.

This chapter adds to this emerging line of research with reference to internet literature production in China, an important site in the creative and digital economy where the market has become formalised yet labour practices remain largely informal. While a small number of top writers are courted by online platforms with prestige contract offerings and reap their share of revenue from the fan economy, the other side of this reality reveals precarious labour conditions. Meanwhile, creative practices have evolved in response to these precarious conditions, yet paradoxically perpetuate them. Drawing on in-depth interviews with internet literature writers in June and July 2014, supplemented with material collected from newspapers, research reports and online forums, this article approaches internet literature production as a case study of the interconnections and interactions between the formal and the informal in the wider context of creative labour in the platform economy. I begin with an analysis of the inception of internet literature as a grassroots alternative to the state-controlled publishing businesses in the context of the Chinese literary system. Then I analyse multiple dimensions of the formalisation of the space, reflected in the rise of online literature platforms based on the freemium business model and with the influx of capital, growing institutional recognition and increasing state oversight. Following this, I examine the often-neglected precarious experience of aspiring writers in the platform economy. Then I proceed to analyse ghost writing as an emerging form of the informal self-organised secondary market, to reveal the formality therein and to examine its economic and sociocultural impacts. The analyses reveal new forms of surplus value production and capital–labour relations as digital platforms refashion amateur creative labour in the context of increasing state oversight.

The inception of internet literature in China

The emergence of internet literature in China cannot be fully appreciated without reviewing the literary production system in the country. Under the formal system, all books published in print in China must have a book number, a number issued by the state to state-run publishing houses as a means of controlling book publishing. Private publishing houses can only obtain book numbers through joint ventures with state-owned publishers. As scarce resources, book numbers have long been the focus of illicit trading and exchanges among publishers (Latham, 2005). Another distinct feature of the Chinese literary system is the China Writer's Association (CWA, *zhongguo zuojia xiehui*), which has been unique worldwide since the disintegration of the Soviet Union as a nominal association of writers actually operated by a national government. The government provides financial support to the CWA, which gives writers 'iron rice bowls' to produce 'major melody' works in the centrally planned cultural production system (Martinsen, 2006). As an institutional mechanism, the CWA supports and solidifies elitism in literary production and meanwhile controls the production. Writers usually conduct self-censorship, which manifests the internalisation of party guidelines as a form of preventive censorship (Link, 2000). Since the 1980s the state has scaled back financial support, resulting in a market-driven literary field under state control. Nevertheless, publishers have retained power as gatekeepers in terms of what is publishable.

The centrally controlled system of cultural production since the establishment of the PRC and the instrumental use of literature mean that readers' demands remain under-addressed. While writers have to create works within the boundaries of state censorship to reach the market, readers have both the will and the way to obtain alternatives. The underground circulation of hand-copied entertainment fiction during the Cultural Revolution (Link, 2000) and parallel imports of books are telling examples here. The market gap not only triggered the informal circulation of books but also witnessed a growing number of market-oriented writers outside the official system. Since the mid-1990s, a large number of freelance writers have emerged in the Chinese literary market as a result of the market-oriented reforms. While not employed by any organisation, these writers earn their daily bread by publishing literary works and have relatively more creative freedom than professional writers fed by CWA. This institutional mechanism has encountered aloofness and even disdain from writers who are outside the official institution yet are well received on the market. The post-1980s writer Han Han is a paradigmatic example.

Similarly, internet literature production has its *raison d'être* in the literary production system it undermines and the market demand it satisfies. Outside the official literary system, it is free from the constraints of book number allocation and subject to weaker censorship as the sheer volume of works creates a loophole in the censorship mechanism. Meanwhile, it comes with a lower entry barrier. Once an undertaking confined to the elite, literary production has re-established its popular orientation as online space offers discourse power to the public, especially to non-professionals (Ouyang, 2011). As Ma (2013) points out, while the popularisation of literature in the 1980s was largely driven by the cultural elite in a top-down fashion by catering to the popular taste, the popular orientation of internet literature goes a step further as it opens up space for amateurs and enthusiasts.

One of the earliest internet literature publishing sites was Rongshu Xia ('Under the Banyan Tree'), hosted by a Chinese American, William Zhu. The website was established in 1997 as a space for literary enthusiasts to publish original work, from poetry and short prose to novels and autobiographies. Writing out of pure interest and the desire for self-expression and peer recognition, these authors had no intention of reaping financial gains. Submissions had to be reviewed for original and literary value before publishing. Therefore amateur writers perceived publishing on this site as something to be proud of. Notably, the site was deliberately maintained free of advertising for a long time. While it attempted to make profits through offline publishing, the difficulty of obtaining officially sanctioned book numbers became a major challenge. Therefore, while the site was well received among writers and readers, the website struggled to make any profit. Another popular destination was the online forum Tianya, where anyone could create an account and publish. This social media site had an even lower entry barrier to online publishing and created a more interactive environment for readers and writers.

As Li Xunhuan, a well-known internet literature writer, summarised the early stage of the internet literature, the ethos of online writing lay in freedom, equality, non-monetary motives and truthfulness (Ouyang, 2002). Born as a fan-generated, non-commercial alternative to its state-controlled printed cousin, internet literature has therefore become a grassroots alternative outlet for literary production and consumption. As amateur writers produce online writings in a rich and growing range of genres, they circumvent the largely state-sanctioned literature production system to express their creativity and address popular tastes. Therefore it serves the function of gap-filling for the formal publishing market.

Formalisation of the internet literature space

Despite its grassroots beginnings, internet literature in China has soon found a path to commercialisation. A successful business model was established by qidian.com, an online publishing platform launched in 2003 by Chinese Magic Fantasy Union, a group of amateur writers of fantasy novels. The site hosts internet literature published as serials, and derive revenue from user subscription to premium content. Readers can access initial chapters for free and usually pay 0.02 to 0.05 yuan per 1,000 words to access the following chapters of popular works moved behind the paywall. The time lags between publication of chapters in premium sections and release of the chapters to all readers are a major motivator for readers to pay for content (Tse and Gong, 2012). Moreover, the 'tipping' (*dashang*) feature gives authors opportunities to receive rewards from readers in the form of virtual currency. Such tips can be converted into real currency based on a certain ratio and usually split between websites and authors on a revenue-sharing basis. While some fans express their support through a micro amount of payment, others are not hesitant in flaunting their wealth for a sense of satisfaction. Some writers, such as Tangjia Sanshao and Mengru Shenji, have reportedly received a single reward of over one million RMB. According to the fan who rewarded Mengru Shenji, he just wanted to get a good feeling by beating another user, who rewarded the writer with 0.4 million RMB (Li, 2013).

While anyone can apply for an author's account and publish on internet literature platforms, not all can secure a contract with online platforms and profit from their works. Writers need to keep uploading new instalments to attract attention from online editors who review published works, monitor consumption data and offer contracts with various terms to writers with commercial viability. Once contracted and if consumption data remain strong, writers become 'VIP authors', with usually the initial chapters of their works available for free and the following ones moved behind the pay wall. Authors receive a share of revenue based on user subscription, usually a couple of cents per 1,000 words. Those perceived as more commercially viable may be approached with contracts offering guaranteed remuneration from online platforms based on their output regardless of subscription figures. Such guaranteed remuneration is usually calculated based on a fixed price per 1,000 words, which could vary significantly from case to case. Contracted writers at the top of the pyramid are referred to as 'platinum authors', who receive dedicated promotion from online platforms, which usually buy out all copyrights of their works and require them to produce new works at a certain rate. The tiered contracting system offers writers the possibility of different levels of remuneration, a prestige indicator and a 'career ladder' to climb.

The prospect of becoming signed writers with the digital platform and getting paid for publishing have lured many aspiring authors (Hockx, 2015). This is a social network market, where word of mouth and taste cultures rather than innate preferences and price signals dominate readers' choices (Potts *et al.*, 2008). Readers become more important than expert critics and assume a significant role in influencing creative production. The datafication of consumption practices in the form of clicks, subscriptions, favourites and commentaries constitutes a partially automated like economy (Gerlitz and Helmond, 2013). This allows editors and platform owners to understand readers' ephemeral tastes and identify promising writers and further commercialisation opportunities. In other words, popularity is conditioned by connectivity, user-generated data and algorithmic culture on digital platforms, which underlies the business model of the platform (Van Dijck and Poell, 2013). As such, readers as produsers/prosumers play an important part in capital accumulation (Andrejevic, 2009). The freemium model allows both authors and end-users to share the risks inherent in creative production, and this has been a key factor in its success (Xiang and Montgomery, 2012).

The success of the freemium business model together with the tiered contracting system and incentive mechanisms soon prompted other internet literature platforms such as Hongxiu, Jinjiang, Xiaoxiang and Zongheng to follow suit. This accelerated the commercialisation and concentration of the internet literature market. Only a year after the launch of the subscription service, Qidian was acquired by Shanda Interactive Entertainment, Ltd., a leading interactive entertainment media venture in China. Shanda offers a diversified portfolio of entertainment content including some of the most popular, massively multi-player online role-playing games (MMORPGs) and casual online games. Its nationwide payment platform further facilitated Qidian's business model based on reader subscription and revenue sharing with authors. It was not long before Shanda increased capital investment in the market and acquired more internet literature platforms before establishing its subsidiary Shanda Literature Corp. (later Cloudary Corp.) to capitalise on the booming market. This was a milestone in the development of internet literature market in China.

As the market formalises, copyright-driven operation has become a major capital accumulation strategy. Commercially viable internet literature works have become key resources for not only multi-platform distribution including over e-readers and mobile phones, but also downstream licensing and adaptation into animation, movies, TV series and games (Zhao, 2011). The rapidly expanding market has attracted China's internet behemoths, with mergers and acquisitions further consolidating the market. The social media giant Tencent established its subsidiary Tencent Literature in April 2014 with its 'pan-entertainment' strategy focusing on downstream licensing. In the same year, the country's biggest search engine Baidu acquired Beijing Huanxiang Zongheng Chinese Literature Website Co., Ltd. (zongheng.com), which was merged with two online reading platforms, Xiongmao Kanshu and Duoku Reading, to form Baidu Literature. The market witnessed further consolidation when Tencent Literature and Cloudary jointly established China Literature (also known as the Yuewen Group) in March 2015. The mobile commerce giant Alibaba also entered the market in 2015 with its internet literature division, keen to profit from the flourishing market. In 2016, the online game developer and operator Perfect World purchased Zongheng from Baidu.

As well as internet giants, state-run publishing houses have also come to tap into the market. Among these publishers are People's Literature Publishing House, Changjiang Literature and Arts Publishing House, Chunfeng Art and Literature Press, Zhejiang Literature & Art Publishing House and Blossom Press. In recent years, more than half of the 3,000 novels published in print every year have their origins online (Ma, 2013). This is in stark contrast with the scenario in the earlier times, when few traditional publishers were willing to publish internet literature in print because of varying quality, genres with inherent risks and questionable market potential (Tse and Gong, 2012).

As the internet literature space witnesses intense commercialisation, institutional recognition has also emerged. For example, China's prestigious literary awards, such as the Lu Xun Literary Prize and the Mao Dun Literary Prize awarded by CWA, have started to allow submissions of internet literature works in 2010 and 2011 separately. CWA has also assigned memberships to internet literature writers in recent years, with Tangiia Sanshao and Dangnian Mingyue sitting on the national committee. Further, internet literature commissions under local writers' associations have emerged including those in Guangdong, Hainan and Beijing. In 2014, Shanghai witnessed the establishment of an online writers' association, and Zhejiang province set up the first provincial-level online writers' association in the same year.

Formalisation is however never value-neutral (Lobato and Thomas, 2015). In the internet literature space in China, this has given a prominent status to genre fiction. In the highly risky business of creative production, authors produce these born-digital works within a framework of patterns for a specific target readership. All genres share a common characteristic, namely, creating a dream world for readers where they can identify with the protagonists and fulfil their desires for fame, fortune, love and sex, which are hard for them to attain in real life. This is why Chinese online genre fiction has earned the nickname of 'YY fiction', where YY stands for yiyin, or 'lust of the mind' (Hockx, 2015). In the capital-driven market where financial motivations are more prominent, super-rich internet literature writers have emerged by adopting this approach to expand readership. Noticeably, the Chinese Online Writers Rich List debuted in 2012, with Tangjia Sanshao, Wochi Xihongshi and Tiancan Tudou topping the chart with royalties in the previous five years reaching over 33 million RMB, 21 million RMB and 18 million RMB respectively (Yang, 2012). In 2016, Tangjia Sanshao became the first Chinese author to earn more than 100 million yuan (about US$14.5 million) a year, topping the list for the fourth consecutive year with royalties of 110 million yuan (around US$16 million) (*China Daily*, 2016).

The emergence of super-rich writers in the formalising market, however, should not eclipse the fact that creative labour in the market still sits towards the informal end. In fact, the other side of reality has little glamour. As writers including contracted ones are not formally employed by digital platforms, they are different from editors, lawyers and management working for the platforms and receiving regular salaries. They are also different from established writers who rely on CWA for their iron rice bowls in the print-based system. While love and passion drive amateurs to publish online, commercial motivations become equally if not more important in the formalising market. Essentially, many writers are producing content with aspirations to make money by doing what they love. The future-oriented mindset is evident in what Neff (2012) has conceptualised as 'venture labour', referring to the entrepreneurial behaviour exhibited by non-entrepreneurs as they invest in current work for future payoffs. While Neff focuses on employee behaviour, a similar mindset has been found in what Kuehn and Corrigan (2013) frame as 'hope labour' in voluntary social production, and in what Duffy (2016) refer to as 'aspirational labour' in amateur creative production. Similarly, based on her study of employees in internet industries, Neff (2012) uses the notion of 'venture labour' to describe entrepreneurial behaviour exhibited by non-entrepreneurs. The next section will analyse how aspirations meet reality as internet literature writers produce content in the formalising market in China.

Between aspirations and precarity: informal labour on commercialised platforms

As capitalist modes of production hold sway in the market, internet literature writers experience have transformed production process. While Marx (1976) had to limit his analysis of capitalist production based on the exploitation of industrial wage labour, the notion of surplus value, exploitation, alienation and subsumption is still relevant today in the context of the digital economy (Fuchs, 2010; Fuchs and Dyer-Witheford 2013). As the internet literature space becomes a commercially viable content industry, writers experience multiple forms of precarity as evident in inequitable temporalities, tensions over copyright negotiations and a diluted creative autonomy. These are closely connected with platform affordances and constraints.

Inequitable temporalities

Owing to the serialised nature of internet literature on digital platforms, timely updates are crucial to attracting and maintaining readership. Writers have to recalibrate to readers' time needs to expand readership and hopefully maximise earnings based on the meagre unit price. This is a condition of labour 'where people exist in a differential and inequitable temporal relation with another group with whom they are expected to synch up' (Sharma, 2014, p. 79). Uneven temporalities of lived time are entangled with 'labor arrangements, cultural practices and technological environments' (Sharma, 2014, p. 9). Time, as lived experience, is thus highly political and enmeshed in power relations. In the commercialised internet literature market, inequalities in temporalities result from the techno-economic design and sociocultural affordances of digital platforms, as well as the internalisation of platform logic by aspiring writers through self-discipline and self-exploitation.

Writers operate under a temporal architecture comprised of 'technologies, commodities, policies, plans, programs, and the labour of others' (Sharma, 2014, p. 139). These include the serialised nature of content, platform features, incentive mechanisms and the free labour of users. Most notably, many online platforms have introduced the 'all-attendance reward', which requires authors to maintain a daily upload of around 6,000 words to qualify for a nominal reward of around 500 yuan. This incentive mechanism is designed to motivate contracted writers to keep publishing on a daily basis with an expected word count. Failure to meet the daily update requirement attracts a penalty, which is calculated on a daily basis until the reward is exhausted. Moreover, interactive affordances of digital platforms allow readers to urge writers to upload new instalments. Failure to do so can attract readers' comments ranging from gentle reminders to vehement complaints. This allows readers to reinforce their privileged position in the temporal order. While their time is prioritised, readers' demand involves free labour generating value for digital platforms. This works in two ways. First, readers' calls for updates are a popularity indicator, used by editors and platform owners to measure the economic value of writers. In this sense, readers play a part in creating asymmetries of visibility and attention on platforms. As Fuchs (2013, 2014) points out, Smythe's (1977) notion of audience labour retains its continuing relevance in understanding prosumer labour in social media. Second, readers play a role in reducing turnover time in serialised internet literature production. In other words, by using interactive features on platforms, users discipline writers to serve platforms' purpose of accelerated capital accumulation. Over time, the logic of acceleration becomes a norm, institutionalised on digital platforms.

Indeed, regular and high-frequency updates are perceived by authors as a part of the formula for success. One interviewee's response is typical:

> It's not difficult to upload 10,000 words a day. What makes it challenging is to keep doing so for eight years. This is a major reason why Xuehong has so many fans.
>
> (Personal Interview, July 2014)

Many writers agreed that failure to keep up with the expected tempo is costly, not only financially but also in retaining readership (Personal Interview, 2014). The latter applies to both contracted and non-contracted writers. Consequently, writers frequently have to keep uploading new instalments to feed their readers, who usually expect daily updates or even multiple updates everyday (Tse and

Gong, 2012). As one author described her everyday life, 'I'm always on. Going shopping, travelling, and chatting with friends over afternoon tea have almost all become luxuries for me' (Personal Interview, June 2014). In fact, many writers have to work long hours continuously, and quite a few cases of sudden death from overwork have attracted much media and public attention in recent years (Wu and Zhang, 2013). Clearly, as aspiring writers internalise the acceleration logic of cultural production through self-discipline, they reinforce uneven temporalities at the expense of their own health and lifestyle.

While the need to sync up with readers' time demands is certainly physically demanding, failure to do so can be emotionally taxing at the same time. One author recounted the days when he failed to publish new instalments after experiencing a divorce. At the time, he explained to readers what had happened in his life to seek their understanding. While some readers sent condolence messages, many assaulted him with abuses and curses because of his failure to supply new instalments in time. As the author recalled:

> Insults and curses kept coming at me. These readers had no sympathy for me at all. From then on, the thought of quitting often crosses my mind. After all, I've been here for over 10 years. I'm old, and I'm tired now. Why should I stay to bear all this?
>
> (Personal Interview, 2014)

The emotionally charged account comes from an author, born in 1981, who receives good financial returns for his creative production. Despite commercial success he has started to question whether it is worth it.

Moreover, the strategically extended length of internet literature works extends the pattern of temporal recalibration. As discussed earlier, under the freemium business model, writers have to publish free content first. Once they become popular enough to charge for content, the authors' share of revenue is based on a unit price per 1,000 words in the premium section. In this context, more words mean more earnings. Most interviewees confided that they deliberately added non-essential descriptions, characters, dialogue and plots to extend the length of their work, or in their words, 'to inject meat with water' (Personal Interview, June 2014). As a result of strategic extension, it is typical for online fiction to reach several million Chinese characters. This is significantly longer than novels published in print, and the creative process becomes tedious for writers (Personal Interview, July 2014). As Hesmondhalgh and Baker (2013) point out, product, in addition to process, influences creative workers' experience of work. While such strategic extension carries the hope of delivering more economic returns, the creative process is characterised by a sense of drudgery owing to the non-essential and sometimes meaningless extension of the creative process. This reduces writers' satisfaction with their work and makes time recalibration even more challenging.

Further, any sign of popularity makes online writers work harder and update even more frequently. As one writer put it:

> I'd rather work harder for three years to make money that can sustain me for five years given people are following my work now.... Who knows what happens to my next book?
>
> (Personal Interview, July 2014)

The highly risky nature of creative production evidently drives online writers to seize the opportunity when they can. In other words, they have a sense of urgency to capitalise on any indication of market popularity as shown in clicks, likes, subscriptions and calls for more and faster updates. While many writers are still engaged in creative production with a future-oriented mindset (Neff, 2012; Kuehn and Corrigan, 2013; Duffy, 2016), any sign of initial success triggers a sense of urgency to catch the moment for others.

As market mechanisms, labour arrangement and interactive affordances of digital platforms work together to privilege readers' time demands, authors are compelled to negotiate uneven temporalities. By extending work time, keeping unsociable hours to maintain or accelerate update cycles, and accentuating the pattern in strategic extensions, they recalibrate their bodies to appeal to readers at the expense of their health and wellbeing, their work quality and their labour experience.

As such, internet literature production is as much associated with high-intensity physical labour as creative or intellectual labour. As Gill and Pratt (2008) point out, the emphasis on immateriality in the knowledge economy calls for a response that highlights the persistence of all-too-material forms of labour. A widely used term in addressing internet literature writers and online writers' self-reference is 'writing hands' (*xieshou*), which has connotations of low-level labour (Hockx, 2015, p. 5). This is in contrast to authors (*zuojia*), a term used to address established writers in the print-based system and indicates an elevated cultural status. It reflects the reality where exhaustion, frustration, anxiety and insecurity are constant companions, closely bound up with the pressure to sync up with readers' time demands and a sense of urgency to capture market opportunities.

As writers engage in temporal labour (Sharma, 2014), they create surplus value for digital platforms in the contemporary context of a transition from formal to real subsumption of labour (Marx, 1976, pp. 1019–1023; 1025–1034). As Fuchs (2014) points out, time is an important category for a digital labour theory of value, especially in relation to the blurring of production and consumption time, new forms of absolute and relative surplus value production, and the acceleration of consumption. Moreover, self-exploitation as a salient feature in cultural production (Hesmondhalgh and Baker, 2011; McRobbie, 2002; Ross, 2003) has become more pronounced on digital platforms in the formalising internet literature space. This is in sharp contrast to the time prior to commercialisation of the space, where online writing was more a worry-free hobbyist activity unburdened by strong commercial motivations.

Tensions over copyright

In the now copyright-driven industry, informality is often imbricated with tensions over copyright. First of all, the contracting process is littered with risks. Digital platforms often encroach on the interests of authors through strategic gaming of contracts. Authors, especially those with strong aspirations yet little knowledge of copyright, often find themselves lacking the capacity to differentiate different kinds of contracts and their associated rights and obligations. As one author put it, 'It is like telecom contracts, lacking clarity and notoriously difficult to understand' (Personal Interview, June 2014).

It is not uncommon that authors sign up for deals based on a fixed price per 1,000 words, in which they must relinquish all intellectual property rights including subsidiary rights. In such cases where authors are alienated from their work, downstream licensing means little for them in economic terms. Usually online platforms only give a nominal economic reward to appease writers and capture value from the work and subsequent adaptations. This provides potent evidence of how Marxian notions of primitive accumulation (Marx, 1976) remain alive and well as platform owners devise contracting mechanisms in their own interest.

Complicating the matter is the absence of transparent metrics available to writers when the terms of contract are applied. This is particularly evident in relation to mobile platforms and printed publications. Many interviewees mentioned that they had little idea of the distribution scenario on mobile media, and strongly doubted the figures given by internet literature platforms (Personal Interview, June 2014). The degree of transparency of the data received by writers is in sharp contrast to that of the data they produce for digital platforms. In the latter case, data surveillance operates, in connection with incentive mechanisms and performance management, in the interest of the platforms. Information asymmetries thus put writers at a significant disadvantage.

As Bettig (1996) points out, copyright, when combined with the control of distribution system, plays an important role in value extraction and capital accumulation. Therefore copyright politics is manifested not only in the ultimate ownership and control of the creative production output, but also in the terms and conditions of the employment of creative labour. As writers publish on online platforms, they do so on terms structured by those who own and control the means of production, interaction, communication and community building (Andrejevic, 2009). Therefore the choice to sell their labour power remains coercive as it 'internalise[s] the forms of violence and alienation that structured the terms of the choice itself' (Andrejevic, 2009, p. 49). As copyright becomes a major driving force for internet literature platforms, the terms and conditions upon which the creative process hinges becomes a site of contestation. Further, growing industry consolidation means that writers have increasingly weak negotiation power against publishers.

Diluted creative autonomy

In the commercialised space, precarity also manifests itself in writers' diluted creative autonomy, which has transformed the labour process and constitutes real subsumption of labour under capital (Marx, 1976: 1023–1025, 1034–1038). As mentioned earlier, readers exert significant influence over writers' creative production. Most writers discussed how they took readers' comments into consideration in their creative production (Personal Interview, 2014). Such attempts to cater to readers reflect a trade-off between creative autonomy and potential financial returns. The strategic extension of the works discussed earlier is also a salient example of how writers compromise their creative autonomy while at the same time being beholden to the techno-economic platform design and utilising it for financial gains.

Moreover, the copyright-driven logic of platforms operates in connection with platform governance, resulting in compromised creative autonomy for writers. As downstream licensing becomes a major capital accumulation strategy for online publishers, aspiring writers have to target specific genres with commercial viability. Given more stringent censorship in the print and broadcasting industry, certain genres such as fantasy fiction and Boy's Love (romantic or sexual relationships between male characters) are most unlikely to appear in print or on screen. As one writer recalled her experience,

> I started publishing Boy's Love fiction ten years ago. No longer now. Very few writers I know of still write this genre. Online publishers are more interested in adaptable work.
>
> (Personal Interview, June 2014)

This is confirmed by Liao Junhua, editor-in-chief at Qidian, 'We no longer sign authors who write Boy's Love fiction, as we do not see its commercial potential' (cited in Li, 2014). Evidently, the approach of downstream licensing in the context of uncertain state policies has curtailed the development of niche genres and constrained the creative autonomy of writers who are more motivated by financial gains. As platforms aim to maximise surplus value, their governance in the contracting process operates in connection with state policies.

Indeed, as well as the logic of capital, more stringent state regulation over internet literature has also impacted on writers' creative autonomy. During his speech at the Forum on Literature and Art in Beijing in October 2014, President Xi Jinping reiterated that literature and art should serve politics and reflect core socialist values such as patriotism (*China Daily*, 2014). Such tenets extend CCP's approach to literature and art, and echo Chairman Mao's lectures at the Yan'an forum on art and literature in 1942. Noticeably, representatives of internet literature writers joined a room of cultural workers at the forum. President Xi also urged writers to clean up 'undesirable styles' lurking on the internet. Soon after the forum, the State Administration of Press, Publication, Radio, Film and Television (SAPPRFT) (2014) issued 'Guiding Opinions concerning Promoting the Healthy Development of Internet Literature'. The document set out regulatory measures to put internet literature under closer state scrutiny. The authorities also urged digital platforms to implement the editorial responsibility system as a self-regulatory measure. The requirement to establish a real-name registration system in particular raised concern among writers, who perceive it as a call for promoting self-censorship (Personal Interview, 2014). As Wang (2004) poignantly asked, 'How do we begin to envision a parallel discussion in a country where creative imagination is subjugated to active state surveillance' (p. 13)?

Further, institutionalisation in the form of professional associations has raised similar concerns, although writers' attitudes are more ambivalent here. While some have questioned the nature of the association as soft governance, others have welcomed this official recognition (Personal Interview, July 2014). Some expressed hope that such professional bodies would provide a support framework, especially for small-time writers, to improve the precarious conditions (Personal Interview, July 2014). So far, such formalisation has however only opened arms to a limited number of renowned internet literature writers. For example, although Shanghai eWriters' Association claims to promote emerging talent, only 75 well-known internet literature writers were on its initial membership list (Sun, 2014). To what extent such institutionalisation impacts on creative production and writers' experience still remains to be seen.

Self-organised secondary market: invisible writing hands on the assembly line

As writers negotiate between aspirations and reality under platform affordances and constraints, a secondary labour market of ghost writing has emerged. This can be attributed largely to the strong market demand and the hierarchy among writers. While more successful writers with a large following of subscribers experience precarious conditions in maintaining their readership, many more writers are scratching their heads over the vexing question of how to become contracted writers. In the secondary market, contracted writers can buffer against the risk of failing to sync up with readers' time needs, and uncontracted yet aspiring writers receive a guaranteed income. Essentially, this is an attempt to reconcile reality and aspirations, between current payoffs and future possibilities. Therefore surrogate writing can be seen as an attempt by both contracted writers and their non-contracted peers to exercise agency and self-manage risks. Thus, Neff's (2012) notion of venture labour has its relevance beyond the workplace. As writers do this, the secondary market exhibits both informality and formality, which paradoxically reinforces the logic of capital accumulation.

A writer seeking a surrogate usually goes to relevant online forums and posts a plot scenario or chapter synopsis to invite submission of works, usually between 3,000 and 8,000 words long. Through an open call for submissions, the owner of the post selects those who can write efficiently with a similar writing style to work as the ghost writer. Following that the post owner sends the work-in-progress and creative guidelines to the ghost writer, who then begins the creative process. As writers subcontract the work to others on a work-for-hire basis, they release part of their creative responsibilities yet still claim authorship of the complete work and receive shared revenue and other incentives from online platforms. In doing so, writers who enlist the assistance of surrogate writers are themselves actively implicated in the establishment of a secondary labour market, which reinforce the platform logic of acceleration. This is to some extent similar to the constitutive role of television workers in the exploitative and commodifying processes of television production in the UK (Ursell, 2000).

For a large number of new entrants, ghost writing provides a gateway to the internet literature production with a more assured income. The rate is usually RMB5–35 per 1,000 characters, which is significantly higher than the usual quote for contracted writers. While surrogate writers do not receive any share of revenue, writing for an assured income at such a rate is better than working on something with little prospect of securing contracts from online publishers. The pricing strategy has therefore attracted an increasing number of uncontracted writers to the alternative path of ghost writing.

As one interviewee Liu recalled, his ghost writing career could be traced back to the time when he responded to a recruitment post in a well-known internet literature forum by submitting a 5,000-word chapter based on a synopsis. The client writer was satisfied with his submission, and invited him to join a group of ghost writers for further communication on QQ, a leading online instant messaging platform developed by China's internet giant Tencent. The client then offered him a 'job' and reached an oral agreement with him regarding the job description and payment. Under this agreement, Liu would write 10,000 words per day for RMB100 based on an outline with plot synopses. The payment was to be settled monthly, provided he could complete the 300,000-word workload. Liu's work would then be published on a leading internet literature site under the client's name. The supposedly smooth deal hit an unexpected turn when Liu discovered his work was revised. He felt it unacceptable and complained strongly about it in the QQ group. Shortly after the complaint, Liu found himself kicked out of the group. When he telephoned his client, he found out that he was to be replaced by someone else. According to the interviewee himself:

> Many internet literature writers often refer to themselves as writing hands who just keep churning out words. I'm at the bottom of the pyramid and one of many invisible hands doing so.
>
> (Personal Interview, June 2014)

Such experience reveals the precarious conditions experienced by surrogate writers. They result from both the informal contracting process and the nature of made-to-order work. As surrogate writers flesh out plot synopses into full-blown stories, they have to compromise their creative autonomy to meet the expectation of their clients. When their work is regarded as misaligned with expectations, this could lead to potential conflicts between the two parties.

Further, although surrogate writers cannot claim authorship of their creative work, their sense of ownership does not necessarily recede. This also gives rise to tensions. In some cases, surrogate writers face the risk of losing their 'jobs' at any time. While client authors and online publishers benefit from copyright-centric operation in the market, the use of ghost writing paradoxically betrays such logic. Therefore, for surrogate writers who have no contracts with online platforms, while ghost writing serves as an approach to self-managing risks, their experiences are still bound up with precarity.

Despite the risk of losing creative autonomy, copyright ownership and sometimes even their 'jobs', ghost writing has evolved over time. It has come to be characterised by systematic teamwork with clear division of labour, a form of codification of the creative process facilitating and controlling the underground practice. A large number of 'studios' have sprung up where surrogate writers work together for their clients. Many interviewees reported having seen recruitment posts on literature forums, instant messaging groups and the e-commerce site Taobao (Personal Interview, June 2014). Business developers in these studios are in charge of identifying and approaching writers who need ghost-writing services. Various roles of surrogate writers include 'ferrymen', who make sure main plots are interlinked with smooth transitions, 'inspectors', who spot inconsistencies and logical mistakes, and 'cosmetologists', who polish the draft (Chen, 2012).

As well as invisible writing hands filling the workstations along the assembly line, a crucial element in the production process is the pattern. Patterns are carefully designed to target a specific consumer segment to control the creative process and reduce inherent risks in the creative venture. Genres, sub-genres and plot guidelines used for the division of labour are important components of patterns. Like formats in TV production, they arguably downgrade autonomous creativity (Banks, 2007). Patterns also include instruction manuals developed by more experienced writers. Some manuals illustrate various plot development techniques for writers to meet readers' expectations. Others list many 'dos and don'ts' as a means of quality control. One widely circulated manual likens internet literature production to software development (Liangma, 2010). Targeting online writers who aspire to capture a large readership, the manual explains that both internet literature writing and software development are complicated system engineering, and only by following strict rules of operation can producers create products that satisfy readers. Thus patterns both facilitate and control the production process. Specifically, assembly workers use patterns to expedite the production process while complying with production guidelines for the purpose of quality control.

It is evident that the self-organised, informal market of ghost writing has its formal dimension in the organisation of labour. Indeed, informal activities are often much better organised and managed than policymakers understand (Guha-Khasnobis *et al.*, 2006). Atomisation of the creative process into tradable units, coupled with pattern development and time management, enables top-down planning with a market-oriented approach. This turns individual creative endeavour into integrated creative services, in which products are planned and produced through codification and delivered by ghost writers. Codification, while controlling informal media activity, also permits a certain scope of informality (Lobato and Thomas, 2015). In the case discussed here, codification facilitates the production process in the informal labour market.

While the secondary labour market allows the formalising market to acquire services from the informal zone, or under informal conditions, in order to increase efficiency (Lobato and Thomas, 2015), market realities limit possibilities for surrogate writers to progress along a 'career trajectory'. This results from the constraints associated with asymmetries of visibility and attention (Fuchs, 2013). According to most interviewees, as celebrity online writers are the key assets of internet literature sites, they have dedicated editors and receive more support than other writers in promoting their work (Personal Interview, June 2014). Moreover, while a range of mechanisms including monthly subscriptions and tips are in place with the purpose of discovering promising talent, celebrity writers collude with promotion agencies to buy their way up (Xu, 2013). The potential revenue from user subscription weighs more than promotion costs, encouraging authors to invest in promotion. Ranking charts in this context become a barometer more of promotion capacity than of readers' perception of the creative work. The logic of the metrics-driven popularity of digital platforms (Van Dijck and Poell, 2013) is thus hacked. As resource-intensive promotion becomes important in the increasingly homogeneous, formalised and consolidated market, ghost writing is more likely to perpetuate the hierarchy among writers.

Thus, as internet literature writers reorganise the production process and collude with online platforms to relocate the creative energies of surrogate writers to the formalising market, risks have emerged while opportunities of progressing along the formality spectrum are limited for surrogate writers. In Marx's (1976: 1023–1025, 1034–1038) words, this demonstrates the real subsumption of labour under capital, where the production process is reorganised to meet the dictates of capital. As a result, ghost writers are alienated from their creative work while surplus value is extracted from their labour. Ultimately, publishing platforms and author clients, rather than surrogate writers, benefit more from the secondary labour market.

On a broader level, the secondary industry results in a revaluation of the market, which is one of the effects of informal activities on formal markets (Lobato and Thomas, 2015). As workers produce tradable units based on patterns, which undergo a further processing, assembling and quality control process before being shipped to target consumers, the final products render the market increasingly homogeneous. Therefore ghost writing dilutes the economic value of the market over time, where workers' endeavours to follow tested recipe result in increasingly bland homogenisation and the loss of creative edge.

Conclusion

Creative labour has sparked intense debate in recent years, with scholars sitting on either the optimistic or the critical side. This chapter has attempted to explicate the argument by applying the lens of informality to the creative labour debate. The uniqueness and significance of China's internet literature space and the creative labour in it lies not only in its scale and business model in the digital economy, but also – and more importantly – in the deep insight it affords into the complex interactions between formality and informality. This chapter goes beyond the simple binary and offers a more nuanced and dynamic view of the relationship between the formal and informal in the broader context of the creative labour debate. Moreover, it reveals the relationship between capital and labour, commerce and creativity as digital platforms dominate the market.

While the internet literature space undergoes formalisation with the valid business model, an increasing flux of capital, growing institutional recognition and more state oversight, labour practices remain largely at the informal end. Writers experience precarious conditions including the risks resulting from inequitable temporalities, tensions over copyright and diluted creative autonomy. Datafication, connectivity, popularity and programmability (Van Dijck and Poell, 2013) operate in connection with technological configurations, the freemium business model and state oversight, leading to a power asymmetry between writers and readers, and between writers and platforms, and hierarchies among writers themselves.

While platforms come with affordances and constraints, users do manifest agency in negotiating between aspiration and reality. The self-organised secondary market in ghost writing is a salient example. Just as informality lingers in the commercialised market, formality also manifests itself in the informal site of the self-organised secondary labour market. This is evidenced in the sophisticated division and coordination of labour in ghost writing, where codification expedites the production process and reduces the inherent risks of the creative venture, thereby both facilitating and controlling the production process.

For surrogate writers, however, precarity remains in place despite the opportunity to enter the market with some assured income. It is not imposed from above but from the intersection of the formal and informal, where both contracted writers and ghost writers internalise the operational logic of digital platforms and play a constitutive role in it. This is where the 'democratic-sounding discourses surrounding precarity are particularly insidious' (Brophy and de Peuter 2007, p. 183). In tacitly allowing ghost writing, publishers who stress the pivotal importance of copyright to the industry paradoxically collude with author clients in extracting surplus value from surrogate writers. This constitutes a process of real subsumption of labour under capital, where the labour process is reorganised to increase market efficiency and accelerate capital accumulation. While ghost writing theoretically offers opportunities for surrogate writers to progress further, it is more likely to reinforce the hierarchy in the market where access to support and promotion is inequitable and the existing mechanisms of popularity favour deep-pocketed users. Consequently, publishing platforms and author clients benefit more from ghost writing in a market where efficiency is crucial. As Yúdice (2004) has noted, the subordinate classes of civil society, compared with entertainment conglomerates and the holders of intellectual property, benefit much less from the creative economy. However, such a self-organised secondary market may dilute the market value over the long term as a result of a bland homogenisation and loss of creative edge.

As internet literature writers navigate formal–informal boundaries, they are caught in ambivalent identities between writers and writing hands, between professionals and amateurs, between the glamorous creative class and humble labourers. Meanwhile, promises of democratisation and empowerment of creativity are adulterated by the precarious conditions. While it would be overly pessimistic to suggest a complete deprivation of pleasure in the amateur creative labour, the formalising market has witnessed new forms of surplus value production, where aspirations, precarity and agency are registered and negotiated in multiple ways.

References

Andrejevic, M. (2009). Critical media studies 2.0. *Interactions; Studies in Communication & Culture, 1*(1), 35–51.

Banks, M. (2007). *The politics of cultural work*, Palgrave, Basingstoke.

Bettig, R. (1996). *Copyrighting culture: The political economy of intellectual property*, Westview Press, Boulder, CO.

Brophy, E. and de Peuter, G. (2007) Immaterial labour, precarity and recomposition, in *Knowledge workers in the information society*, eds C. McKercher and V. Mosco, Lexington, Lanham, MD, pp. 177–192.

Burgess, J. (2006). Hearing ordinary voices: Cultural studies, vernacular creativity and digital storytelling. *Continuum, 20*(2), 201–214.

Caldwell, J. T. (2008). *Production culture: Industrial reflexivity and critical practice in film and television*, Duke University Press, Durham, NC.

Chen, J. (2012). Investigation into surrogate writing as established hidden rule in internet literature market. Retrieved 1 June 2014 from http://tech.sina.com.cn/i/2012-02-02/23586678303.shtml.

China Daily (2014). Role of art and literature. Retrieved 1 November 2014 from www.chinadaily.com.cn/opinion/2014-10/16/content_18745967.htm.

China Daily (2016). Top Chinese web-writer's income tops 100 million. Retrieved 1 September 2017 from http://europe.chinadaily.com.cn/culture/2016-03/25/content_24099404.htm.

Cunningham, S. (2009). Trojan Horse or Rorschach Blot? Creative industries discourse around the world. *International Journal of Cultural Policy, 15*(4), 375–386.

Deuze, M. (2007). *Media work*, Polity, Cambridge.

Duffy, B. E. (2016). The romance of work: Gender and aspirational labour in the digital culture industries. *International Journal of Cultural Studies, 19*(4), 441–457.

Florida, R. (2003). *The rise of the creative class*, Basic Books, New York, NY.

Fuchs, C. (2010). Labor in informational capitalism and on the Internet. *The Information Society, 26*(3), 179–196.

Fuchs, C. (2013). *Social media: A critical introduction*, Sage, London.

Fuchs, C. (2014). Digital prosumption labour on social media in the context of the capitalist regime of time. *Time and Society, 23*(1), 97–123.

Fuchs, C. (2015). *Digital labour and Karl Marx*, Routledge, New York, NY.

Fuchs, C. and Dyer-Witheford, N. (2013). Karl Marx @ Internet Studies. *New Media & Society, 15*(5), 782–796.

Gerlitz, C. and Helmond, A. (2013). The like economy: Social buttons and the data-intensive web. *New Media & Society*, *15*(8), 1348–1365.
Gill, R. and Pratt, A. (2008). In the social factory? Immaterial labour, precariousness and cultural work. *Theory, Culture & Soceity*, *25*(7–8), 1–30.
Guha-Khasnobis, B., Kanbur, R. and Ostrom, E. (2006). *Linking the formal and informal Economy: Concepts and policies*, Oxford University Press, Oxford.
Hardt, M. and Negri, A. (2000). *Empire*, Harvard University Press, Cambridge, MA.
Hardt, M. and Negri, A. (2004). *Multitude: War and democracy in the age of empire*, Penguin, New York, NY.
Hartley, J. and Keane, M. (2006). Creative industries and innovation in China. *International Journal of Cultural Studies*, 9(3), 259–262.
Hesmondhalgh, D. and Baker, S. (2011). *Creative labour: Media work in three cultural industries*, Routledge, Oxon.
Hockx, M. (2015). *Internet literature in China*, Columbia University Press, New York, NY.
Howkins, J. (2001). *The creative economy: How people make money from ideas*. Penguin, London.
Hu, K. (2012). Chinese subtitle groups and the neoliberal work ethics, in *Popular culture collaborations and co-productions in East and Southeast Asia*, eds O. Nissim and B.-A. Eyal, National University of Singapore Press, Singapore, pp. 207–232.
Jenkins, H. (2005). *Convergence culture: Where old and new media intersect*, New York University Press, New York, NY.
Jenkins, H., Ford, S. and Green, J. (2013). *Spreadable media: Creating value and meaning in a networked culture*, New York University Press, New York: NY.
Keane, M. (2009). Creative industries in China: Four perspectives on social transformation. *International Journal of Cultural Policy*, *15*(4), 431–434.
Keen, A. (2007). *The cult of the amateur: How today's internet is killing our culture*, Doubleday, New York, NY.
Kuehn, K. and Corrigan, T. (2013). Hope labor: The role of employment prospects in online social production. *The Political Economy of Communication*, *1*(1), 9–25.
Latham, K. (2005). Shuhao (book numbers), in *Encyclopedia of contemporary Chinese*, ed. E. L. Davis, Sage, London, pp. 758.
Li, L. (2013). The rise of reward culture in internet literature: A million-dollar reward from a reader. Retrieved 3 March 2014 from www.chinanews.com/cul/2013/08-30/5227350.shtml.
Li, W. (2011). *How creativity is changing China*, Bloomsbury Academic, London.
Li, X. (2014). An analysis of productive chain of internet literature. Retrieved 1 October 2014 from www.timeweekly.com/html/20140424/24644_1.html.
Liangma (2010). How to write a popular fiction: The perspective of software engineering. Retrieved 9 October 2014 from http://bbs.qidian.com/show/252756.
Link, P. (2000). *The uses of literature: Life in the socialist Chinese literary system*, Princeton University Press. Princeton, NJ.
Lobato, R. and Thomas, J. (2015). *The informal media economy*, Polity Press, Cambridge.
Ma, J. (2013). Wangluo wenxue: Wenxue de gerenhua yu minjianhua [Internet literature: Personalization and folk tendencies]. *Beijing Cultural Review*, *2013*(2), 132.
Martinsen, J. (2006). The Chinese Writers' Association: What good is it? Retrieved 10 October 2014 from www.danwei.org/state_media/china_writers_association_what.php.
Marx, K. (1976). *Capital*, Penguin, Harmondsworth.

Mayer, V. (2011). *Below the line: Producers and production studies in the new television economy*, Duke University Press, Durham, NC.

McRobbie, A. (2002). Clubs to companies: Notes on the decline of political culture in speeded up creative worlds. *Cultural Studies*, *16*(4), 516–531.

Neff, G. (2012). *Venture labour: Work and the burden of risk in innovative industries*. MIT Press, Cambridge, MA.

Neilson, B. and Rossiter, N. (2005). From precarity to precariousness and back again: Labour, life and unstable networks. *Fibreculture*, *5*. Retrieved 1 June 2017 from http://five.fibreculturejournal.org/fcj-022-from-precarity-to-precariousness-and-back-again-labour-life-and-unstable-networks/.

Ouyang, Y. (2002). Lun wangluo wenxue de jingshen quxiang [On ethos of the internet literature]. *Literature and Art Studies*, *5*, 74–77.

Ouyang, Y. (2011). Chinese literature's transformation and digital existence in the new century. *Social Sciences in China*, *32*(1), 146–165.

People.cn (2017). Internet literature platforms grow rapidly with the aim of going for IPO and upgrading the entertainment industry chain. Retrieved 1 September 2017 from http://media.people.com.cn/n1/2017/0822/c40606-29485061.html.

People's Daily (2017). China's online literature market booming. Retrieved 1 June 2017 from http://en.people.cn/n3/2017/0704/c90000-9237068.html.

Potts, J., Cunningham, S., Hartley, J. and Ormerod, P. (2008). Social network markets: A new definition of the creative industries. *Journal of Cultural Economic*, *32*(3), 167–185.

Qiu, J. L., Gregg, M. and Crawford, K. (2014). Circuits of labour: A labour theory of the iPhone era. *TripleC: Communication, Capitalism & Critique*, *12*(2), 564–581.

Ross, A. (2003). *No-collar: The humane workplace and its hidden costs*, New York University Press, New York, NY.

Ross, A. (2009). *Nice work if you can get it: Life and labour in precarious times*. New York: New York University Press.

SAPPRFT (2014). Notice on issuing 'Guiding Opinions concerning Promoting the Healthy Development of Online Literature'. Retrieved 1 February 2015 from www.gapp.gov.cn/news/1663/236795.shtml.

Sharma, S. (2014). *In the meantime: Temporality and cultural politics*, Duke University Press, Durham, NC.

Smythe, D. W. (1977). Communications: Blindspot of Western Marxism. *Canadian Journal of Political and Social Theory*, *1*(3), 1–27.

Sun, L. (2014). Internet literature in China says good bye to the era of disunity. Retrieved 1 June 2015 from http://media.people.com.cn/n/2014/0706/c14677-25244634.html.

Terranova, T. (2000). Free Labor: Producing culture for the digital economy. *Social Text*, *6*(18), 33–58.

Tse, M. S. C. and Gong, M. Z. (2012). Online communities and commercialization of Chinese internet literature. *Journal of Internet Commerce*, *11*(2), 100–116.

Ursell, G. (2000). Television production: Issues of exploitation, commodification and subjectivity in UK television labour markets. *Media, Culture & Society*, *22*(6), 805–825.

Van Dijck, J. and Poell, T. (2013). Understanding social media logic. *Media and Communication*, *1*(1), 2–14.

Wang, J. (2004). The global reach of a new discourse: How far can 'creative industries' travel? *International Journal of Cultural Studies*, *7*(1), 9–19.

Wu, Y. and Zhang, Z. (2013). Sudden death of a contracted writer at Qidian in a rented apartment, producing over 1.6 million-character work in a year. Retrieved 1 October 2014 from http://tech.sina.com.cn/i/2013-07-02/02198498171.shtml.

Xiang, R. and Montgomery, L. (2012). Chinese online literature: Creative consumers and evolving business models. *Arts Marketing*, *2*(2), 118–130.

Xu, M. (2013). My view of buying authors' way up in internet literature. Retrieved 10 October 2014 from www.chinawriter.com.cn/wxpl/2013/2013-06-28/165699.html.

Yang, F. (2012). Rich list of online writers in China shows the richest online writer receiving 33 million RMB in 5 years. Retrieved 3 March 2014 from http://news.xinhuanet.com/zgjx/2012-11/26/c_131999170.htm.

Yang, G. and Jiang, M. (2015). The networked practice of online political satire in China: Between ritual and resistance. *The International Communication Gazette*, *77*(3), 215–231.

Yúdice, G. (2004). *The expediency of culture: Uses of culture in the global era*, Duke University Press, Durham, NC; London.

Zhang, L. and Fung, A. Y. (2013). Working as playing? Consumer labor, guild and the secondary industry of online gaming in China. *New Media & Society*, *16*(1), 38–54.

Zhao, E. J. (2011). Social network market: Storytelling on a Web 2.0 original literature site. *Convergence: Journal of Research into New Media Technologies*, *17*(1), 85–99.

Zhao, E. J. (2014). The micro-movie wave in a globalising China: Adaptation, formalisation and commercialisation. *International Journal of Cultural Studies*, *17*(5), 453–367.

6 Between entrenched and 'smart' informalities

Ride-hailing platforms and governance challenges

Ride-hailing platforms are often deemed as a poster child for the growing on-demand economy. Best represented by Uber globally, these platforms tout the capacity to improve market efficiency in urban transportation by exploiting slack capacity based on mobile, locative and data-driven technologies. For Srnicek (2016, p. 49), these are 'lean platforms' that operate on a business model of minimal asset ownership. Moreover, the rhetoric of algorithm-driven innovation, flexibility in labour relations and 'entrepreneurial opportunities' for its 'driver-partners' figure prominently in self-promotional discourses. Since its launch in 2009, Uber has witnessed exponential growth. As it expands to different geographic markets, its service lines have also diversified, including the low-cost UberX, the ride-sharing service, UberPOOL, and the most luxurious UberBlack. Yet as many innovations do, it remains controversial and encounters significant regulatory hurdles. While in some jurisdictions it is defined and regulated as transportation network companies, it is illegal in other parts of the world. Its most vocal opponents come from the taxi industry. As taxi companies lobby the government to crack down on their emerging competitor, taxi drivers paralyse various cities by protesting against the ride-hailing platform.

In China, over 30 ride-hailing apps have emerged since late 2011, including Didi Dache, Kuaidi Dache, Yaoyao Zhaoche and Dache Xiaomi. The sector soon attracted investment from bullish venture capitalists both in China and overseas, including GSR, Matrix, Softbank China, DST, Hillhouse and internet giants such as Tencent, Alibaba, Sina and Apple, have also put down heavy stakes. Among a growing list of investors, the state-owned China Investment Corporation (CIC) is particularly noticeable given its role as the country's sovereign wealth fund. Unlike their overseas counterparts, many of these apps in China relied heavily on the recruitment of taxi drivers in their initial development. Very soon, Didi Dache and Kuaidi Dache became market leaders, with the former dominating in Beijing and the latter claiming leading positions in Hangzhou and many second-tier cities. Backed respectively by two of China's internet giants, Tencent and Alibaba, Didi Dache and Kuaidi Dache spent extravagantly on subsidies for drivers and riders to expand the market. The intense competition in the ride-hailing market connected closely to the intention of Tencent and Alibaba to promote their mobile payment apps, namely, WeChat Pay and AliPay. Indeed, a competitive edge in the key component of mobile payment infrastructure is crucial in the battle of e-commerce and digital ecology more broadly.

As these two service providers continued competing against each other, Uber embarked on the Chinese market in August 2013 by launching the higher-end service UberBlack. It recruited drivers from employees working for fleet at five-star hotels. These drivers offered rides in Audis, BMWs and Benzs, and worked on a daily basis for Uber in their free time. In order to expand beyond the niche market of UberBlack in China, the firm launched People's Uber (Renmin Youbu) in August 2014. This more affordable service connected private car owners with riders, and by doing so, Uber has made a further foray into a grey area.

Intense competition eventually drove Didi Dache and Kuaidi Dache into each other's arms, as the two called a truce on the fierce subsidies war in a merger on Valentine's Day, 2015. The merger has seen Didi Kuaidi rapidly expanding its service lines, which include private car hailing through express cars (*kuaiche*) and premium cars (*zhuanche*), social ride sharing (Didi Hitch) and personal chauffeur services (Didi Daijia). In conjunction with service line expansions, the venture rebranded itself as Didi Chuxing in September 2015. While *dache* means 'catch a cab' in Chinese, *chuxing* means 'commute', indicating multiple means of transport. The dust finally settled when Didi Chuxing's acquired Uber China in August 2016. Thus Didi Chuxing (hereafter Didi) established a dominant position in China's emerging on-demand hailing market, which claimed 217 million users in China by mid-2017 (CNNIC, 2017). The merger has turned the venture into the only enterprise receiving investment from each of China's three major internet companies – Baidu, Tencent and Alibaba, collectively known as BAT (*China Daily*, 2016a). By the end of 2017, Didi became the most valuable start-up in the world, being worth about $56 billion (Fortune, 2018).

Despite increasing capital investment and market consolidation, ride-hailing platforms remained a grey area in China for about five years before it became legalised eventually in 2016. While many discussions focus on the disruptive effects of the on-demand or gig economy, the connection with existing informalities and the legalisation process have received little attention. This chapter focuses on Didi (including its trajectory from Didi Dache to Didi Kuaidi and Didi Chuxing), and starts by tracing entrenched forms of the informalities that ride-hailing platforms exploit to expand their market. These include informal labour practices in the oligopolistic taxi industry, labour dispatch and the unlicensed taxi market. I then examine the lengthy and complicated legalisation process, which was imbricated with departmental interests and central–local dynamics in government regulation. Following this, I turn to the impacts of government regulation and explain how social inequalities have resurfaced in the platform economy. I also examine the platform's algorithm-driven governance and the contested negotiation of power in platform labour. The chapter draws on publicly available documents such as government regulations, news reports, corporate websites and interviews with drivers between 2014 and 2016. Employing the strategy of guerrilla interviewing, which sociologist Thomas Gold (1989) defined as 'unchaperoned, spontaneous but structured participant observation and interviews as opportunities present themselves' (p. 180), I conducted interviews while I was a passenger of the drivers. This allowed me to interview drivers when opportunities presented themselves, and proved useful at the time of regulatory uncertainty. While some drivers were cautious, others were willing to share their views in the space they were familiar with (i.e. inside cars).

Exploitation of entrenched informalities

Informality and precarity in the oligopolistic taxi industry

In China, the booming ride-hailing market owes much to taxi drivers, who were early adopters of many apps including the now dominant Didi. As well as the promotional message of technology-facilitated market efficiency, promotional incentives propelled the adoption of apps by taxi drivers. Unlike driver-users that later joined Didi's service lines such as *kuaiche* (express car) or *zhuanche* (premium car), taxi drivers can keep the total fare, as the platform sought to increase market share in its initial development with Didi Dache. Moreover, the platform showered a huge amount of subsidies on taxi drivers as well as passengers so as to drive adoption. Thus, a promotion strategy focusing on exemption from commission, substantial subsidies and the technology-facilitated market efficiency claimed by the platform, persuaded many taxi drivers to adopt the app. This has much to do with the stubborn ills of the taxi industry, which is characterised by informalities and precarity.

Since the introduction of licensing controls in the taxi industry in the mid-1990s, taxi drivers in China have witnessed the creation of an oligopolistic market (Wang, 2002). Occupying the scarce resource of operational permits, taxi firms rely on drivers for finance, as the latter pay monthly franchise fees and management fees, or *fenziqian* in Chinese.[1] As economist Buchanan (1980) points out, governmental licences, quotas, permits, authorisations, approvals and franchise assignments have long been vehicles for creating scarcities, which in turn generate rent-seeking activities. In China, rent seeking is not only a result of economic transition, but is also intertwined with industrial policymaking (Ngo and Wu, 2009). The highly sought-after licences provide a rent-seeking space for both taxi firms and local authorities (Wang, 2002). These are evident in the inflated franchise fees charged by taxi firms, and local governments' capitalisation of taxi firms' purchasing power in industrial policymaking to support local automobile manufacturers.

For taxi drivers, the oligopolistic market has bred informal practices resulting in precarious work conditions. This is particularly evident in private taxi firms, which receive licences based on the status of being subsidiaries of or affiliated with government agencies or collective firms. Although local governments do not allow arbitrary increases of *fenziqian*, many taxi drivers mentioned that their firms often collect a higher amount than the figures published under their various names (Personal Interviews, July 2014). In provincial cities, *fenziqian* ranges from 5,000 to 15,000 yuan. Usually two drivers share a taxi and these expenses. As one driver put it, 'I have to work for the taxi firm and the oil company before I work for myself' (Personal Interview, June 2014). Specific items described as management fees are many and convoluted, and frequently drivers do not receive receipts. The collected fees are used to cover operational costs of various kinds including management salaries. Under intense pressure to garner enough fares to meet the lease, these drivers perceive their cabs as a kind of 'iron cage' to which they are confined (Notar, 2012). While taxi drivers slog long hours on the roads for a meagre income under this mechanism, managers receive much higher salaries while sitting in their offices. Many drivers have pointed out that so-called management involves little more than routine meetings to stress service standards and handle customer complaints (Personal Interviews, July 2014). Moreover, while drivers pay *fenziqian* to taxi firms, the latter often transfer the responsibilities of car maintenance and insurance to the former.

While *fenziqian* comes under various names resulting from the oligopoly created by licensing regulations, fare regulation adds to drivers' woes. As the state government positions taxi services as quasi-public transportation services offering an important supplement to large-capacity public transportation (Feng *et al.*, 2008), it curtails the growth of taxi fares in order to protect consumer welfare. Dismissing the market-oriented demand–supply balance, the state's regulation of taxi fares is in effect a means to maintain the legitimacy of the CCP regime. Thus both taxi firms and drivers lament taxi fare regulation. In this context, taxi firms further transfer the financial pressure to drivers through exorbitant *fenziqian*, and informalities become aggravated in relation to the amount and nature of such fees.

Although taxi drivers used to be among the high-income earners in the 1980s and 1990s, they have fallen to the lower end of the income ladder since 2000 as a result of regulated prices, growing oil costs, persistent *fenziqian* and rising inflation. What makes things worse for many taxi drivers is the lack of social benefits in informal employment, especially for those who work for private taxi firms. Many of these firms obtain operation licences owing to their ties with the authorities, yet they are characterised by informality. As Notar (2012) points out, many people lack better choices and feel compelled to become taxi drivers to stave off further marginalisation in society. Among these are many migrant workers. Ding's (2014) study on migrant taxi drivers in Shenzhen revealed their precarious conditions, working long hours, paying a high amount of *fenziqian*, and unlearning their original dialects in order to seek livelihoods in the city. The long hours and arduous work led Ding to describe these migrant drivers as footless birds, which keep flying until death.

This has triggered strings of strikes[2] by taxi drivers over the years. Most notably, in November 2008, rolling taxi strikes occurred in multiple cities including Chongqing, Sanya, Yongdeng, Chaozhou and Shantou, registering as the longest sustained chain reaction of labour unrest to date. Major triggers of the action included 'gouging by the taxi companies from whom they rented their cars and collusion between the companies and corrupt local officials' (Elegant,

2008). In 2011, taxi drivers in cities including Hangzhou, Shanghai and Changsha parked their cars in downtown areas to protest over low pay, reduced oil subsidies and inadequate social benefits (*China Labour Bulletin*, 2011). Despite drivers' protests, informalities and precarity remain firmly embedded in the industry. This provided room for Didi as well as other similar platforms to drive adoption among taxi drivers based on the perceived higher income prospects owing to zero commission and subsidy programs at the initial market development stage.

Boundary-skirting in the expansion of platform labour market and emerging tensions

While initially focusing on taxi-hailing services, Didi and its then-competitor Kuaidi have expanded the platform labour market beyond taxi drivers. An informal practice crucial to such expansion is labour dispatch. The practice of labour dispatch has been adopted in China since the 1990s, and has played a key role in the expansion of informal or non-standard labour in China (Huang, 2017b). Under this arrangement, organisations hire workers through dispatch agencies, and contracts are signed between workers and dispatch agencies. Thus, labour relationship does not exist between workers and the organisations they work for. Widely exploited by both state-owned enterprises (SOEs) and foreign-invested enterprises, labour dispatch allows organisations to shirk responsibilities as employers pass on the risks to workers who fall outside the labour safety net, or 'workers without benefits' (Brown, 2016). Although labour dispatch was written into the Labour Law in 2007, and the Chinese government tightened the regulation over the practice in 2013, the relevant terms lack clarity and informal practices remain prevalent. For Huang (2017a), the legalisation of dispatch labour is a 'peculiar mixing of informal employment with formal legislation, and capitalist expediency with the discourse of labor legislation inherited from a socialist era' (p. 8).

For digital ride-hailing platforms, labour dispatch agencies and car rental firms were key intermediaries in their market expansion. Kuaidi and Didi launched Kuaidi One and Didi *zhuanche* services in July and August 2014, both connecting private car owners with higher-end riders. To deliver these services, digital platforms collaborated with car rental companies. The latter leased vehicles to their contracted drivers to provide ride-hailing services for digital platforms. This allowed digital platforms to circumvent licensing and pricing regulation in the taxi industry in order to expand their market. However, a more controversial part was the platforms' practice of contracting drivers of privately owned cars through labour dispatch companies and car lease firms. This allowed platforms to play edge ball, skirting the boundaries of government policies for the purpose of market expansion, specifically, to connect private car owners to platforms. First, as private cars cannot provide rental services, the digital platform would connect a private car owner with a rental car company so that the driver can be affiliated to and get backed (*guakao*) by the firm. The car rental firm would charge a certain fee and register the private car as one that can provide rental services under the firm. Second, the driver, the rental car firm, the labour dispatch company and the digital platform would enter a four-party agreement. Under this agreement, the private car owner would become an employee of the labour dispatch company rather than of the digital platform, with the vehicle registered as eligible to provide rental service under the rental firm. This provided a solution for digital platforms to circumvent the cap on the number of vehicles a rental firm could own under the tight regulations in China. It explains why digital platforms adopted this informal practice over direct collaboration with car rental companies. Equally importantly, labour dispatch served the platform's purpose of treating drivers as independent contractors rather than employees, thus shirking employer responsibilities, gaining flexibility and maximising profits in the on-demand economy. Moreover, this informal practice through the key intermediaries such as car rental companies and dispatch agencies allowed ride-hailing digital platforms to capitalise on both private car owners and their vehicles in value production. This was crucial to support the market expansion of lean platforms based on the model of minimal asset ownership (Srnicek, 2016).

A further crossing into the shadows with legal uncertainty was evident in the launch of a new service line that allowed private car owners to sign up to ride-hailing platforms directly. This was Didi's express car (*kuaiche*) service, a response to People's Uber (Renmin Youbu). The service allowed private car owners to sign up as full-time or part-time drivers by simply clicking 'yes' to terms of service. Thus, ride-hailing platforms played a crucial role in the structural expansion of contingent labour. According to Van Doorn (2017), digital ride-hailing platforms should be conceived as 'new players in a dynamic temporary staffing industry whose traditional business-oriented approach is being augmented by a more austere and zero-liability, peer-to-peer model that leverages software to optimize labor's flexibility, scalability, tractability, and its fragmentation' (p. 901).

Notably, the emerging market attracted many migrant workers. According to data published by Didi in 2016, less than 10,000 out of over 410,000 registered drivers in Shanghai held local *hukou* (People.com.cn, 2017). In Beijing, only 10 per cent of the Didi drivers were local permanent residents. As well as rural migrants, inter-urban migrants, including laid-off workers from SOEs, also joined the market. Some rented cars while the more entrepreneurial ones purchased their own cars. Cars were usually cheap to purchase, priced at between 80,000 and 100,000 yuan. At the time of policy indeterminacy, drivers worked long hours in the hope of paying off their rentals or loans faster. As one migrant driver in Beijing said about his experience:

> It's a norm for people like me to work for 13 or 14 hours a day. In the first ten hours I am working for the bank. I only get to start working for myself in the last three or four hours. The days when the license plate restriction applied to mine were the days I took a break.
>
> (Personal Interview, December 2016)

When I asked him how he felt about Beijing, he paused and then said,

> Well, I don't know much about Beijing. I'm either in my car transporting passengers or I'm at home.... It doesn't matter. I'm here for the money. It's more likely to earn more money here.
>
> (Personal Interview, December 2016)

Evidently, migrant workers in platform-mediated labour faced strenuous and precarious labour conditions and lacked a sense of belonging in the cities. In spite of that, they had strong motivations and found some comfort in the economic prospects offered by the emerging platform-mediated economy.

While Didi started out by optimising the taxi market through technology, it became a disruptive force to the taxi industry especially since their expansion into private car-hailing services. This turned many taxi drivers, including early adopters, into vocal opponents. They started to question the legality of the ride-hailing platform, denouncing it as 'invaders to the taxi market', or 'a serious threat to their business' (Personal Interview, July 2015). Many compared the platform-mediated service to unlicensed taxis, and complained vehemently about the alliance between the digital platforms and rental car companies, as well as the dispatch agencies, in 'whitewashing' unlicensed taxis (Personal Interview, July 2015). Many shared a feeling of being betrayed by Didi. As one driver put it,

> We (taxi drivers) helped them build the market, and now they bring private car owners to the market. They are ditching us. We were simply paving way for others.
>
> (Personal Interview, July 2015)

Another taxi driver shared this sentiment:

> Now I regret the decision to use Didi last year [2014]. The subsidies for us taxi drivers were short-lived, and gradually they became harder to obtain. We helped them promote the software, but now it's eating into our own business.
>
> (Personal Interview, July 2015)

This sentiment is mixed with their reflections on the taxi industry. As one taxi driver put it:

> Isn't this legalising unlicensed cabs? Why do we need licenses then? Why do we have to pay *fenziqian*?
>
> (Personal Interview, July 2015)

Heiche: Predecessor to platform-mediated informal urban mobility

Indeed, as the predecessors of on-demand ride-hailing platforms, unlicensed taxis (*heiche*) have played a visible role in the informal urban market. As urban areas continue to sprawl in China, public transport infrastructure is struggling to keep up, particularly in the new suburbs and urban–rural fringes. This has fuelled the growth of unlicensed taxis, filling under-addressed demands. Government crackdowns, often through special audits, enforcement blitzes and surprise raids feature a strong element of administrative coercion and campaign-style enforcement (Cai and Wang, 2010). Local officials are often reluctant to support consistently strict enforcement as they see job creation and economic development as higher priorities, therefore allowing informality a certain room to develop (Liu *et al.*, 2015). In the context of strong market demand and weak enforcement, the informal urban market has remained resilient.

The supply side is as strong. While many taxi drivers have long-standing grievances against *heiche*, some are pressured to moonlight by driving *heiche*. Without the burden of *fenziqian*, unlicensed taxis are perceived as a gig generating higher returns to complement drivers' meagre income from day jobs. Some even quit their jobs and start anew in the informal urban market. This can be seen as a mild resistance to the stubborn ills of the formal sector. In other words, the informal market has emerged largely as a result of the informality and precarity embedded in the formal market, discussed earlier. As well as taxi drivers, displaced former SOE workers have also found the informal transportation market an alternative way to support their livelihoods. Once holding the 'iron rice bowl' and receiving cradle-to-grave security provided by the work unit (*danwei*), former SOE employees faced a major shock when they became laid-off workers as a result of China's economic restructuring in the 1990s. Many of these displaced workers have subsequently entered the informal sector, where they are subject to precarious conditions (Betcherman and Blunch, 2008).

As well as taxi drivers and laid-off workers, many migrant workers also strive to make a living in cities by driving *heiche* (Zhang, 2014). The unrelenting pace of urbanisation has witnessed not only many new suburbs and urban–rural fringes where transportation infrastructure lags behind, but also a massive wave of rural migrants flooding into cities to seek livelihoods. However, the government has maintained its control over the right to the city: *hukou* (official residential status) is such a crucial system of social control created by the state in the planned economy to control rural–urban migration, denying fundamental citizenship rights to rural residents. In the pre-reform era, urban *hukou* was birth-ascribed, and tied with principal public goods such as housing, employment, healthcare, education and social welfare. This has resulted in rural–urban apartheid within the country (Alexander and Chan, 2004; Wu and Treiman, 2004; Cheng and Selden, 1994). In reform-era China, the *hukou* system has been characterised by conditionally opening urban residency to rural populations, where migrants remain in vulnerable positions caused by social exclusion (Chan and Zhang, 1999; Li, 2006). As Zhang (2010) insightfully points out, such control emphasises eligibility rather than entitlement, and underpins city governments' broader project of entrepreneurial city building in their own interests. While city governments welcome rural migrants as labour resources, they attempt to avoid social responsibilities and exclude rural migrants from the right to the city. In this context, there is little chance for rural migrants to obtain urban *hukou*, which formalises the conditions for full integration into the city (Zhang, 2010). Without *hukou*, rural migrants face considerable challenges in landing jobs in the formal economy even when they enjoy more freedom to move to urban areas.

As Merton (1968) notes, 'Social structures exert a definitive pressure upon certain persons in the society to engage in nonconforming rather than conforming conduct' (p. 140). Existing literature has documented various groups of this subaltern population as it migrates to cities, including iSlaves labouring on assembly lines in Foxconn (Qiu, 2016), maids working as 'intimate strangers' in urban homes (Sun, 2008) and construction workers steeped in a culture of violence generated by the labour subcontracting system (Pun and Lu, 2010). Zhang (2009) regards the urban-based self-help settlement of temporary population as a key feature of China's informal urbanisation. In response to the social inequality resulting from the rigidities and limitations of state regulations, these people are contesting and reproducing socio-spatial divisions in the domains of the labour market as well as housing, social welfare and social order in the city (Zhang, 2009). While usually stigmatised as 'trouble-makers' or 'headaches' for the government, *heiche* as an informal, urban street market provides a livelihood for less privileged people (Zhang, 2014). As unlicensed taxis operate at the intersection of mobile technologies and urbanisation as symbols of modernity, they are a part and a symbol of an alternative modernity as a microcosm of China's informal urban economy (Greenspan, 2014).

Similarly, ride-hailing platforms have developed by addressing the imbalance between supply and demand in the urban transportation market. As they do so, they have attracted taxi drivers and private car owners, including migrant workers joining the trade in the broader context of socio-economic realities in China's urbanisation. Yet the differences between *heiche* and platform-mediated markets are evident. Adapting the Silicon Valley-born Uber model to China by cutting into the taxi market first, Didi attracted both domestic and transnational capital funding, and quickly achieved scale. Moreover, Didi designed a futuristic vision of urban transportation by drawing on innovation-centred promotional discourse. This centres on the role of datafication, algorithms and cloud computing in increasing market efficiency of urban transportation and improving economic prospects for drivers (Didi Chuxing, n.d.). In doing so, the platform aimed to establish the legitimacy of the operational model and its superiority over the incumbent industry while still operating in a grey area. Meanwhile, informal labour practices have extended to the platform economy, refreshed with technological innovation and datafied for value production.

As discussed above, the rise of on-demand ride-hailing platforms represented by Didi in China is closely connected to multiple forms of informality grounded in the social context. These platforms rely on taxi drivers as early adopters, as a result of the perceived advantage over the persistent informality and precarity in the oligopolistic taxi industry. Their expansion into the private car-hailing service exploits labour dispatch to shirk employer responsibilities and expand platform labour while playing edge ball with government policies. Their growth benefits from refreshing and consolidating the existing informal urban market in which *heiche* has played a key role in addressing unmet demand and providing livelihoods for less privileged populations. While *heiche* operates in the black economy, ride-hailing platforms were shrouded in multiple shades of grey.

Regulating on-demand ride-hailing platforms

Regulatory uncertainty amid central–local dynamics

While skirting boundaries of existing regulation, on-demand ride-hailing platforms have raised significant controversies in terms of legality. In times of regulatory uncertainty, the practice of setting up operations first and striking deals with the authorities later has many other media precedents (Lobato and Thomas, 2015, pp. 120–122). As the largest ride-hailing service provider in China after the merger with Uber China, Didi asserted that it wanted to be regulated by the authorities. As its CEO Cheng Wei said, 'Technological innovations almost always outpace law, but they must be regulated as they evolve' (Tencent, 2016). This is similar to Uber's welcoming attitude to government regulation, as it attempts to seek legitimacy through explicit standards of regulation and some measure of protection from future competitors (Witt *et al.*, 2015).

Reality is less optimistic for ride-hailing platforms, at least initially, as evidenced in the local regulations. The platformisation of part of key urban transport infrastructure (Plantin *et al.*, 2016) adds complexity to the governance equation. In China, as discussed earlier, government interests, particularly at a local level, are closely connected with those of the taxi industry. Since late 2014, the regulatory bodies in many cities, including Beijing, Shenyang, Nanjing, Shanghai, Qingdao, Chongqing, Tianjin, Hangzhou, Guangzhou and Chendu, prohibited private cars from offering private car hailing services very soon after the emergence of such services on digital platforms (*China Daily*, 2014). These authorities essentially declared private car-hailing services as outlaws. Local governments staged police raids targeting these services, although not on a large scale. Such enforcement activities were based on the Provisions on the Administration of Taxi Business Operations and Services, prohibiting unlicensed private car drivers from providing rental and taxi services. Yet whether on-demand ride-hailing should be regulated under such a legal framework remained a contested issue. Despite the controversies, for local authorities this approach served the purpose of maintaining entry barriers to the taxi industry. It protected their vested interest, as taxi firms are operated by a limited number of licensed companies, many of which are owned by local or state enterprises. As discussed earlier, the interests of local governments and taxi firms are closely entwined.

While multiple local governments outlawed platform-mediated private-car hailing services, the ministerial-level regulator sent a mixed message. On 8 January 2015, the Ministry of Transport (MOT) expressed for the first time its attitude to the emerging service. While it urged ride-hailing app firms to ban private cars from operating on their platforms, it acknowledged the positive role that ride-hailing platforms can play in working with licensed operators to serve differentiated market demands (*Xinhua News*, 2015b). For drivers who were providing services with cars leased from rental companies, this was reassuring news. As one such driver recalled:

> I was relieved to hear the news. I rent the car from a lease firm. This makes me different from those private car owners who are attached to lease firms through dispatch agencies.
>
> (Personal Interview, 2015)

The MOT's recognition of the positive role of ride-hailing apps and the suggestion of a collaborative approach has left some leeway for digital platforms. It indicated a more nuanced approach than the outright ban of the apps by some local governments. However, clearly articulated regulatory measures remained absent.

The MOT's attitude to ride-hailing platforms triggered strong endorsement for ride-hailing platforms from the state media. Yet calls for reform in the taxi industry ran counter to the MOT's will. *People's Daily* published commentaries commending the potential benefits of innovative ride-hailing apps in optimising market efficiency, reducing climate pollution and prompting reforms in the taxi industry (Zhou, 2015). It called for the need to 'advance market reforms, smash the monopoly of vested interests, challenge conservatism, and kickstart the transport reform' (Zhou, 2015). *Xinhua News* (2015a) pointed out that hope for reform could lie in local explorations, which often tend to step beyond existing boundaries. Notably, it raised the example of Xiaogangcun, the village in Anhui Province where local farmers set off the land reforms by secretly dividing communal land in 1978, and consequently ended widespread starvation. The official media discourse thus indicated a push back from within the central government against the MOT's position, which banned private cars from operating on ride-hailing platforms. For Liu Yuanju, a Shanghai-based economist, this reflects a much wider context where behind-the-scene tensions between conservative and innovative factions within the Chinese state play out (quoted in *Financial Times*, 2016). For reformists, innovations emerging from informalities provide a significant opportunity to remedy the ills of the incumbent industry and drive transformation. Meanwhile, local experimentation seemed to be encouraged.

While the legality of platform-mediated private car hailing raised much debate, state capital noticeably entered the consolidating market. Funding bodies included Ping An Ventures, the venture capital arm of China's Ping An Insurance Group, China Merchants Bank, China Investment Corp., CITIC (the China International Trust Investment Corporation) Industry Investment Fund, CICC Alpha (a subsidiary of China International Capital Corporation Limited (CICC)), Beijing Automotive Group and Sailing Capital, backed by the Shanghai Municipal Government (Tencent News, 2016). This injected a shot of confidence into digital platforms amid regulatory uncertainty.

Against this backdrop, local experimentation did occur. Didi was brought out of the shadows at a local level when it received China's first internet car-hailing licence from the Shanghai Municipal Transportation Commission (SMTC) in October 2015. The licence was meant to be valid for one year. To obtain it, companies need to meet certain criteria, including screening and certifying drivers and vehicles, providing mandatory insurance to carriers and passengers, and having servers located inside China. A major breakthrough was the permission to allow private car owners to offer ride-hailing services via digital platforms, provided they met certain standards set by platforms in relation to age, driving history and vehicle safety (*The Paper*, 2015b). Crucially, local government required the licence holders to develop a differentiation strategy by offering better-quality vehicles and services than traditional taxis and charging premiums (*Xinhua News*, 2015c). Therefore, while providing some leeway for ride-hailing platforms, the regulatory approach here had strings attached so that the vested interest of the taxi industry could be protected.

At a time when national legislation was yet to be established, the Shanghai model carried the hope of being considered by central regulators as a reference point. Indeed, Didi's CEO Cheng Wei explicitly expressed the hope of seeing more cities consider the regulatory approach taken in Shanghai (*South China Morning Post*, 2015). For Cheng, the Shanghai model demonstrates 'a very market-oriented philosophy' and leaves room for further experimentation with big data analysis and algorithms to achieve a more reasonable equilibrium (quoted in *Xinhua News*, 2015d). In China, according to Breznitz and Murphree (2011), the tension in central–local relations, or what they characterise as 'structured uncertainty', has enabled local adaptation of ambiguous central mandates to build an innovative economy through 'trial and error based experimentation' (p. 19). Similarly, Ang (2016) argues that weak institutions can be harnessed to build markets, and reveals how Chinese reformers crafted enabling conditions for effective improvisation when faced with roadblocks to adaptation.

However, the hope ignited by the Shanghai model was soon dampened in the complex local–central dynamics. On 10 October 2015, two days after Shanghai awarded the first municipal internet car-hailing licence in China to Didi, MOT (2015) issued the draft of the Guiding Opinions on Deepening Reform to Promote Sound Development of the Taxi Industry (draft 'Guiding Opinions') and of Interim Measures for the Administration of the Online Car-hailing Operation and Services (draft 'Interim Measures'), to solicit public comments. The draft 'Guiding Opinions' categorised taxi services into two types: cruising taxis and taxis subject to online booking. As Lobato and Thomas (2015) point out, codification as a mechanism for managing informal activities is an important part of the debate around ride-hailing apps (pp. 122–123). This involves 'creating new categories, rights and limitations around informal activities, thus allowing them to be controlled while also permitting a certain scope of informality' (ibid., p. 36). Coding an on-demand ride-hailing service as a sub-category of taxi services indicates an intention to bring it into the existing framework governing the taxi industry. In association with codification, the draft 'Interim Measures' put forward a mandatory licensing requirement for platforms, vehicles and drivers as a form of authorisation to provide online ride-hailing services. While the draft 'Guiding Opinions' encouraged ride-sharing for non-commercial purposes, the draft 'Interim Measures' banned private cars without taxi licences from providing online ride-hailing services for commercial purposes. This negated the more lenient approach of the Shanghai model to private car owners. Moreover, the 'Interim Measures' allowed local authorities regulatory power over pricing and quantity, and required digital platforms to sign labour contracts with drivers to establish formal employment relationships.

The drafts soon provoked challenges from industry experts and observers. Many opinion leaders criticised the approach of codifying online ride-hailing services as taxis subject to online booking (*The Paper*, 2015a), cautioned against regulatory approaches based on departmental interest, and called for room to be left for emerging innovations (Caijing.com.cn, 2015). Meanwhile, Didi published its response to the draft 'Interim Measures', requesting more room for development, especially in relation to the eligibility of private car owners to participate in the market (*China Daily*, 2015). It also called for room for local experimentation and cited the Shanghai model as an example. The platform further emphasised its role in 'managing' and 'upgrading' black cabs by connecting them to the digital platform. Interestingly, the platform in the shadows hoped to gain legal status by differentiating its service from the existing black market, and more importantly, by emphasising its role as a quasi-regulator of the 'undesirable' informal market. Ironically, the platform would not have dominated the emerging market without exploiting existing informalities.

Legalisation and deep-rooted social inequality

The drafts became finalised and issued by the central authorities almost a year later, in July 2016 (the State Council of China, 2016). Notably, the revised 'Interim Measures' are more accommodating than the earlier draft in two dimensions. First, private cars that meet certain requirements may provide car-hailing services via online platforms. However, central authorities did not specify the requirements, leaving it to local governments to formulate further terms in relation to the eligibility of drivers and vehicles. For Ho (2001), deliberate institutional ambiguity is the lubricant on which the system runs, avoiding social conflict, and meanwhile creating leeway for the central leadership to react to societal development. Second, formal employment relationships are no longer a requirement as proposed in the draft.

The 'Interim Measures' quickly generated responses from local governments. First-tier cities, including Beijing, Shanghai and Shenzhen, simultaneously released specific measures relating to the eligibility of drivers and vehicles on 8 October 2016 (*Xinhua News*, 2016). By introducing more stringent requirements on vehicles, local governments aimed to differentiate the platform-mediated ride-hailing service from the incumbent taxi service so as to protect the interests of the latter. Moreover, local authorities in Shanghai and Beijing stipulated that drivers registering with ride-hailing platforms must have local residency (*hukou*) and use locally registered vehicles to provide their service. In Shenzhen, drivers can provide a platform-mediated service as long as they possess a local residential permit (*juzhuzheng*),[3] or what was previously known as a temporary residential permit (*zanzhuzheng*).

The local residency requirement needs to be understood in connection with the approach of both exploiting and controlling the floating population. While China's 13th Five-Year Plan propels continued urbanisation based on the National Plan on New Urbanisation (2014–2020), the government has encouraged only those rural people who are able to work and live without the aid of government subsidies to register in cities and to change their *hukou* status to 'urban' (*China Daily*, 2016b). Moreover, it has lifted registration requirements only in third- and fourth-tier cities, which offer limited job opportunities and public resources (*China Daily*, 2016b). Meanwhile, central authorities see urgency in strictly controlling the size of permanent resident populations in mega-cities. This is perceived as a potential cure for 'mega-city diseases', from traffic congestion and air pollution to prohibitive apartment prices and a shortage of public services, including education and medical care. At the local level, Beijing and Shanghai have outlined plans to phase out non-capital functions or non-core functions for mega-cities. The cities have reiterated their determination to cap the population at 23 million and 25 million respectively by 2020 (Shanghai Municipal Government, 2016; Beijing Municipal Government, 2016). Existing measures, such as demolishing and redeveloping informal settlements in large cities, indicate the strong push from the authorities to purge the cities of unwanted people and to 'optimise' their labour force (Chung, 2009; Hao, 2015).

Such projects betray the logic of derogating migrant labour, which serves as a mobile reserve of cheap labour for urban areas. This is evident in the discourse of *suzhi* (roughly translated into English as 'quality'), which circulates in reform-era China as a value articulation of bodies as human capital/human subjectivity (Yan, 2003). Yan's (2003) study on migrant women in the domestic service market reveals the centrality of the cultural production of the post-Mao notion of *suzhi* to the economic production of surplus value, and the use of *suzhi* as an intangible operator in the labour contract. Similarly, Anagnost (2004) explicates how valuing migrant labour operates according to a circular logic of value coding. Specifically, migrant labour is devalued as 'low quality' (*suzhi di*), which justifies the extraction of surplus value enabling capital accumulation and serves to legitimate new regimes of social differentiation and governmentality. Sun (2009) uncovers the ways in which the quality of individuals increasingly take on an external, spatial and geographic dimension with reference to *suzhi* discourses on domestic workers. In regulating ride-hailing platforms, local authorities have inherited such logic and deprived migrant drivers of the right to participate in the so-called on-demand economy. Deep-rooted social inequality thus resurfaces in the platform economy.

The approach of allowing room for local authorities to develop by-laws according to local situations is widely used in policy development in China.

Researchers have pointed out the role of institutional adaptability in local development patterns, performance and the potential to nurture innovation (Breznitz and Murphree, 2011; Shen and Tsai, 2016). While it makes sense to consider local situations in policy development, especially in a vast country like China, it could also become an impediment to reform and innovation. Local authorities can capture the opportunity and tweak the measures to nullify innovation potential and protect local interests. In the context of land policy making, for example, Ho (2001) highlights the risk of such institutional ambiguity being exploited by economically more developed regions. The concerted moves of local authorities in first-tier cities in regulating the ride-hailing market attest to such a possibility. This further indicates the will at local levels to exploit structured ambiguity that is evident in central regulations to protect the incumbent interest. Consequently, for drivers, structured inequality in society becomes entrenched in the emerging platform economy.

The predicament of migrant drivers

Following the introduction of local measures, the supply side started to see a sharp decline. One out-of-town driver in Shanghai mentioned the declining activity of the WeChat group of fellow *kuaiche* drivers:

> There's good money to be made here last year. I earned 20,000 yuan in November, and earlier this year my monthly income was over 10,000 yuan. I was in a WeChat group for drivers like me. It was quickly filled up with 500 people within a week. There were constant flows of voice messages, when people updated the traffic situation, or even chatted with each other. It was busy. Nowadays it's much quieter. The latest message was from yesterday afternoon. Looks like many have quit. I'll also quit, probably after the busy winter season.
>
> (Personal Interview, December 2016)

A sense of disappointment and helplessness permeated migrant driver communities. As another driver put it:

> If it became legal, I would think about how to increase my income from it. Now that non-locals are excluded from the game, there is not a ray of hope
>
> (Personal Interview, December 2016)

However, migrant drivers were not completely at a loss. When asked about their plans for next steps, many did not consider going back to their hometowns. The majority of migrant workers from rural areas, particularly second-generation migrants, do not have much experience or skill in farming. Moreover, there is not enough arable land or alternative opportunities for most farmers to make a basic living in the countryside (Chan, 2010). Similarly, inter-urban migrants do not see any future back in the sluggish economies of their hometowns. In this context, migrant workers keep drifting into cities as they seek the next gig. As one driver remarked:

> I don't have any specific plans. I can't really plan. You see? I was planning to make some good money here in the app-enabled car-hailing business, but now what? I can only drift from gig to gig.
>
> (Personal Interview, 2016)

For others who had a vague idea of what to do next in the city, the examples usually mentioned were driving *heiche* or going back to their former trade, such as a removal service, where they faced various kinds of precarity (Personal Interviews, December 2016).

These remarks vividly capture the plight of migrant workers. In the context of deliberate institutional ambiguity in central government coupled with local policies in first-tier cities, the emerging platform-mediated ride-hailing market reflects a long-standing structural problem in the Chinese economy. Migrant workers in the Chinese system are treated much like the Marxian 'industrial reserve army': they are flexible, temporary, and disposable (Harvey, 2005). By building on existing informalities, digital platforms can exploit and discard labourers at a minimal cost while complying with state regulations. As a marginalised group, migrant workers are made to absorb the risks as they drift rootlessly from gig to gig. Class inequalities are thus reproduced in the platformisation of labour.

Algorithmic governance and digital inequality

While structured inequality is inscribed in local policies, it would be simplistic to place the sole blame for the inequality experienced by drivers on government regulation. In negotiating regulatory measures with the government, Didi's CEO Cheng Wei has emphasised the strength of big data and algorithms, which may help the platform to achieve market efficiency, and by extension, its governance capacity (*Xinhua News*, 2015d). As Witt and her colleagues (2015) point out, the argument mounted by digital ride-hailing platforms is not about regulated versus unregulated systems; rather it is essentially about whether market-based systems that rely on data, ratings and algorithms can deliver better social outcomes than the formal co-regulatory structures in the existing taxi industry. Algorithms, however, are never neutral (Gillespie, 2014). In the words of Van Doorn (2017), 'in the world of platform labour, inequality is a feature rather than a bug' (p. 10).

Indeed, algorithmic governance by platforms, which tends to be obfuscated by restrictive government regulations, can accentuate inequality in platform labour. For instance, the algorithmic logic behind the order dispatch system put taxi drivers at a disadvantage when the platform introduced new service lines connecting private drivers with passengers. Soon after connecting private car owners to the platform, Didi started to promote a '100% response rate' to taxi-hailing users in May 2015. Specifically, when a user did not receive any response to a taxi-hailing request within 60 seconds, the request was to be forwarded to other service lines where private car owners operated. This initiative coincided with an investment of one billion yuan's worth of a subsidy program to promote *kuaiche* service across 12 major cities in the country (Jin, 2015). For taxi drivers, the alarm rang loud. As one taxi driver commented:

> The commitment to 100% response rate looks like an effort to deliver better service for taxi-hailing users and boost such orders. What really happens is we are put side by side with *kuaiche* as well as *zhuanche* and face more competition. Passengers are directed to those services. Plus, Didi is heavily subsiding *kuaiche*, which makes it more appealing.
>
> (Personal Interview, July 2015)

Another taxi driver held a similar view, 'This is simply using us to promote *kuaiche*' (Personal Interview, July 2015). Clearly, algorithmic tweaking worked in concert with the evolution of the business model of the platform. Unlike other private hire drivers, taxi drivers did not need to pay commission to the platform. Therefore, by directing requests to other service lines, the platform could achieve a higher profit margin. In this context, taxi drivers, as early adopters, were sidestepped. While drivers in all service lines contribute data to train the algorithm that drives the operation of the platform, the algorithm betrayed an obvious bias against taxi drivers. Thus, taxi drivers were mobilised more for the purpose of cultivating consumer habit and collecting real-time data, but they were rendered more substitutable as the platform expanded the market. The algorithm-conditioned hierarchy enhanced the platform's flexibility and nimbleness, serving the purpose of capital accumulation.

Another notable example is the separate pricing systems for drivers and passengers introduced by Didi on its *kuaiche* and *zhuanche* service lines in August 2016, following its acquisition of Uber. Under this mechanism, passengers and drivers see different figures on their separate interfaces. On the driver's interface, instead of showing the actual transaction amount for a ride, the new system shows the actual income going to the driver. The platform promoted the change as a move to bring 'more stable income for drivers with no price fluctuations at the passengers' end' (*The Paper*, 2016). This is a misleading message. In fact, the revenue split remains solidly in place. More precisely, as the drivers' interface no longer shows the actual transaction amount, revenue-sharing details become *hidden*. This is deeply problematic. By artificially constructing such information asymmetry between drivers and passengers, the platform gained more pricing power in transactions. Previously, the platform charged a commission from the driver when the driver and the passenger agreed on a price and reached a deal. Separate pricing systems mean the platform can buy low, sell high and profit more. Actual commission can be much higher than the 20 per cent previously stated. In fact, algorithms have been found to serve the logic of discriminative pricing. This constitutes what Joseph Turow (2006) describes as 'marketing discrimination', where businesses treat different niches differently so as to maximise efficiency and profit. In other words, when artificial information asymmetry becomes bound up with artificial scarcity and discriminative surge pricing, opacity is doubled and platforms derive hidden benefits at the expense of users.

This has provoked questions about the true character of the digital platform. As one driver said with much disappointment:

> Crows under the sun are all black. Commissions and surging pricing are no more transparent that *fenziqian* in the taxi industry.
>
> (Personal Interview, November 2016)

Clearly, information asymmetry in algorithmic labour ultimately benefits the platform more as it aims to extract maximum value from users. This runs counter to the rhetoric of 'drivers as partners' and a sharing economy, which suggests a common goal and mutual benefits (Gregg, 2011).

While algorithm-driven platform governance exacerbates inequality, drivers manifested their negotiation power when they could. To motivate drivers in a market witnessing a declining supply following government regulation, Didi introduced a 'recommended tips' feature, encouraging taxi-hailing users to offer tips valued between five and 20 yuan, with the full amount of tips going to drivers. This feature did motivate drivers to some extent, but not exactly as the platform hoped for. In fact, drivers tended to keep ignoring requests until higher tips kicked in. In other words, drivers exploited the tipping feature embedded in the logic of order dispatch for their own benefit. Thus, while real-time algorithms govern labour as datafied asset (Rossiter, 2015), they can encounter hacking by labourers. This brings challenges to platforms, which tout the capacity to achieve market efficiency based on real-time data and algorithms. In Didi's case, the platform received widespread complaints from passengers as a result of drivers' disruptive exploitation of the tipping feature. In this context, the platform eventually terminated the feature, but kept allowing passengers to offer tips on a voluntary basis.

Conclusion

Self-portraits of on-demand digital platforms often centre on their novelty, their strength in facilitating more autonomous and flexible labour and their algorithmic power in enhancing market efficiency. This chapter has traced the connection between on-demand ride-hailing platforms and existing informalities in China, upon which they build in market expansion. Such informalities are deeply grounded in Chinese social realities. Specifically, taxi drivers who are subject to informal and precarious employment have become an easy target as early adopters of emerging digital platforms in initial market expansion characterised by zero commissions, heavy subsidies and ground promotion. The practice of labour dispatch aligns with the logic of platform labour, where platforms aim to shirk employer responsibilities, offload risks, and optimise flexibility and scalability as they continue to expand the market by connecting private car owners with passengers. The existing underground market of *heiche* plays an important role in addressing unmet demand in urban mobility, and provides an informal market to be further exploited, 'smartened up' and consolidated. In other words, entrenched informalities have been repackaged into digital platforms, which paradoxically reinforce the precarity embedded in their predecessors.

As the on-demand ride-hailing market evolves, it raises significant governance challenges. While platforms employ the rhetoric of technology-driven innovation to improve urban transportation in the hope of establishing superiority over the incumbent taxi industry, and by extension, legitimacy, the legality of ride-hailing platforms has triggered much controversy. Government regulatory processes have witnessed the uncertainty and ambiguity imbricated in departmental interest and central–local dynamics. The key debate revolves around two issues in the formalisation process: the codification of emerging digital platforms, and the licensing scheme as a form of authorisation. At the central level, reformists' will to introduce competition and transform the incumbent industry through emerging innovations conflicts with the industry regulator's wish to utilise such potential in the incumbent while establishing thresholds in the emerging market. The ambiguity of central policies has resulted in local authorities swinging between restrictive and lenient approaches at the initial stages. When the central authorities' message becomes clearer, some local governments use the manoeuvring room left by central government to impose restrictive measures to localise central policy. This proves to be aligned with local regulators' initial reactions to the emerging market, although to a different degree. Thus the legalisation process is one where multiple parties negotiate. While the outcome confers legality on ride-hailing platforms, the platforms have to reconfigure their strategies, especially labour utilisation, within regulatory boundaries. Meanwhile, structured inequality in society is reproduced in the emerging platform economy.

While it is tempting to focus critique on government regulations, the role of algorithm-driven platform governance and its social consequences should not be obfuscated. As this chapter has shown, inequality and discrimination as reflected in order allocation and pricing mechanisms are bound up with information asymmetry and artificial scarcity. While the operation of algorithmic power relies on multiple forms of data contributed by drivers and passengers, users are not treated equally. As algorithms serve the production regime of platform capitalism, users manifest their negotiation power by turning algorithms on their head. In the context of centralised private firms gaining more power through algorithmic governance by platforms, their often-touted role in improving market efficiency, and more importantly, better social outcomes, should be carefully scrutinised. After all, as informalities become 'smartened up' on digital platforms, the more important questions are: who benefits from this, at what cost, and can it be otherwise?

Notes

1 Except for a very limited number of drivers who own individual taxi operational licences, most drivers have to pay *fenziqian.*

2 Official media usually employ the less confrontational forms of expression such as 'mass incidents' (*quntixing shijian*) to refer to strikes, or *ting yun* to refer to strikes by taxi drivers specifically. While the Constitution enacted in 1975 and 1978 stipulate that citizens in China have the freedom to strike, the 1982 Constitution removed the regulation about the freedom to strike.

3 Shenzhen adopted a new residential permit (*juzhuzheng*) in 2006, to replace the previous temporary residential permit (*zanzhuzheng*), as the required ID card for any migrant staying longer than one month.

References

Alexander, P. and Chan, A. (2004). Does China have an apartheid pass system? *Journal of Ethnic and Migration Studies*, *30*(4), 609–629.

Anagnost, A. (2004). The corporeal politics of quality (suzhi). *Public Culture*, *16*(2), 189–208.

Ang, Y. Y. (2016). *How China escaped the poverty trap.*. Cornell University Press, Ithaca, NY.

Beijing Municipal Government (2016). Report on the work of the government 2016 (part II). Retrieved 6 August 2017 from www.ebeijing.gov.cn/Government/reports/t1467515.htm.

Betcherman, G. and Blunch, N.-H. (2008). The limited job prospects of displaced workers: Evidence from two cities in China. *Economic Change and Restructuring*, *41*(3), 187–207.

Breznitz, D. and Murphree, M. (2011). *Run of the Red Queen: Government, innovation, globalization, and economic growth in China.* Yale University Press, New Haven, CT.

Brown, R. (2016). Chinese 'workers without benefits'. *Richmond Journal of Global Law & Business*, *15*(1), 20–53.

Buchanan, J., M. (1980). Rent seeking and profit seeking, in *Toward a theory of the rent-seeking society*, eds J. Buchanan, M. R. D. Tollison and G. Tullock, Texas A&M University Press, College Station, TX, pp. 3–15.

Cai, D. and Wang, C. (eds). (2010). *China's journey towards the rule of law: Law reform, 1979–2008*. Brill, Leiden.

Caijing.com.cn. (2015). Experts regard drafts of regulatory measures regarding ride-hailing services highly problematic and urges further deliveration. Retrieved 10 October 2016 from http://yuanchuang.caijing.com.cn/2015/1022/3990729.shtml.

Chan, K. W. (2010). The global financial crisis and migrant workers in China: 'There is no future as a labourer; Returning to the village has no meaning'. *International Journal of Urban and Regional Research*, *34*(3), 659–677.

Chan, K. W. and Zhang, L. (1999). The hukou system and rural–urban migration in China: Processes and changes. *The China Quarterly* (160), 818–855.

Cheng, T. and Selden, M. (1994). The origins and social consequences of China's Hukou System. *The China Quarterly* (139), 644–668.

China Daily (2014). Car-hailing apps encounter bumpy roads. Retrieved 1 March 2015 from www.chinadaily.com.cn/china/2014-12/27/content_19179513.htm.

China Daily (2015). Didi issues a statement against MOT's requirement for private cars to change oerational nature to use ride-hailing apps. Retrieved 10 October 2016 from http://caijing.chinadaily.com.cn/2015-10/20/content_22228507.htm.

China Daily (2016a). Didi Chuxing confirms merger with Uber China. Retrieved 15 August 2016 from www.chinadaily.com.cn/business/motoring/2016-08/01/content_26298821.htm.

China Daily (2016b). Major centers look for ways to cure 'big city disease'. Retrieved 30 December, 2016 from www.chinadaily.com.cn/china/2016-12/23/content_27752378.htm.

China Labour Bulletin (2011). Taxi. Retrieved 1 June 2014, from Document 4.

Chung, H. (2009). The planning of 'Villages-in-the-city' in Shenzhen, China: The significance of the new state-led approach. *International Planning Studies*, *14*(3), 253–273.

CNNIC (2017). The 40th China statistical report on internet development. Retrieved 6 January 2018 from www.cnnic.net.cn/hlwfzyj/hlwxzbg/hlwtjbg/201708/P020170807351923262153.pdf.

Didi Chuxing. (n.d.). About Didi. Retrieved 10 December 2017 from www.didiglobal.com/about-didi/about-us.

Ding, W. (2014). *Mobile homelands: Community communication and identity practices of the 'You county cab driver village'*. Beijing: Social Sciences Academic Press.

Elegant, S. (2008). China's taxi strikes: A test for the government. Retrieved 1 June 2014 from http://content.time.com/time/world/article/0,8599,1862718,00.html.

Feng, J., Zhang, J. and Gao, S. (2008). Analysis of and judgment on several major issues related to China's taxi industry. Retrieved 1 June 2014 from http://en.drc.gov.cn/2008-12/09/content_22521067.htm.

Financial Times (2016). Uber's battle for China. Retrieved 1 August 2016 from https://ig.ft.com/sites/uber-in-china/

Fortune (2018). After Softbank investment, Uber is no longer world's most valuable unicorn. Retrieved 21 January 2018 from http://fortune.com/2018/01/19/uber-softbank-didi-worth-most-valuable-startup/

Gillespie, T. (2014). The relevance of algorithms, in *Media technologies: Essays on communication, materiality, and society*, eds T. Gillespie, P. J. Boczkowski and K. A. Foot, MIT Press, Cambridge, MA, pp. 167–193.

Gold, T. B. (1989). Guerrilla interviewing among the getihu, in P. Link, R. Madsen and P. Pickowicz (eds), *Unofficial China: Popular culture and thought in the People's Republic*, Westview Press, Boulder, CO, pp. 175–192.

Greenspan, A. (2014). *Shanghai future: Modernity remade*. London: Hurst.

Gregg, M. (2011). The doublespeak of the gig economy. *The Atlantic*. Retrieved 6 June, 2016 from www.theatlantic.com/business/archive/2015/09/gig-economy-doublespeak-new-labor/404779/.

Hao, P. (2015). The effects of residential patterns and Chengzhongcun housing on segregation in Shenzhen. *Eurasian Geography and Economics*, *56*(3), 308–330.

Harvey, D. (2005). *A brief history of neoliberalism*. Oxford University Press, New York.

Ho, P. (2001). Who owns China's land? Policies, property rights and deliberate institutional ambiguity. *The China Quarterly*, *166*, 394–421.

Huang, P. C. C. (2017a). China's informal economy, reconsidered: An introduction in light of social-economic and legal history. *Rural China*, *14*(1), 1–17.

Huang, P. C. C. (2017b). Dispatch work in China: A study from case records, part I. *Modern China*, *43*(3), 247–287.

Jin, L. (2015). Didi's answer to Uber: Subsidy program for Kuaiche and 100% response to taxi hailing. Retrieved 30 May 2015 from http://zjnews.zjol.com.cn/system/2015/05/23/020664902.shtml.

Li, B. (2006) Floating population or urban citizens? Status, social provision and circumstances of rural–urban migrants in China, *Social Policy and Administration*, *4*(2), 174–195.
Liu, N., Lo, C. W.-H., Zhan, X. and Wang, W. (2015). Campaign-style enforcement and regulatory compliance. *Public Administration Review*, *75*(1), 85–95.
Lobato, R. and Thomas, J. (2015). *The informal media economy*. Polity Press, Cambridge.
Merton, R., K. (1968). *Social theory and social structure*. Free Press, New York, NY.
MOT (2015). MOT publishes drafts of guiding opinions on deepening reform to promote sound development of the taxi industry and interim measures for the administration of the online car-hailing operation and services for public comments. Retrieved 20 October 2015 from www.mot.gov.cn/jiaotongyaowen/201510/t20151014_1898235.html.
Ngo, T.-W. and Wu, Y. (2009). *Rent seeking in China*. New York: Routledge.
Notar, B. E. (2012). 'Coming out' to 'Hit the road': Temporal, spatial and affective mobilities of taxi drivers and day trippers in Kunming, China. *City and Society*, *24*(3), 281–301.
People.com.cn (2017). Car hailing is getting difficult again. Retrieved 26 January 2017 from http://travel.people.com.cn/n1/2017/0124/c41570-29045675.html.
Plantin, J.-C., Lagoze, C., Edwards, P. N. and Sandvig, C. (2016). Infrastructure studies meet platform studies in the age of Google and Facebook. *New Media & Society*, *20*(1), 293–310.
Pun, N. and Lu, H. (2010). A culture of violence: The labor subcontracting system and collective action by construction workers in post-socialist China. *China Journal*, *64*, 143–158.
Qiu, J. L. (2016). *Goodbye iSlave: A manifesto for digital abolition*. University of Illinois Press, Urbana; Chicago; Springfield, IL.
Rossiter, N. (2015). Coded vanilla: Logistical media and the determination of action. *South Atlantic Quarterly*, *114*(1), 135–152.
Shanghai Municipal Government (2016). Beijing Shanghai, and Guangzhou draws the line to cap residential population. Retrieved 26 March 2016 from www.shanghai.gov.cn/nw2/nw2314/nw2315/nw17239/nw17241/u21aw1099711.html.
Shen, X. and Tsai, K. S. (2016). Institutional adaptability in China: Local developmental models under changing economic conditions. *World Development*, *87*, 107–127.
South China Morning Post (2015). Didi Kuaidi grabs China's first internet car-booking licence from Shanghai while rival Uber sets up local company in city's FTZ. Retrieved 10 October 2016 from www.scmp.com/tech/start-ups/article/1865260/didi-kuaidi-grabs-chinas-first-internet-car-booking-license-shanghai.
Srnicek, N. (2016). *Platform capitalism*, Polity, Cambridge, UK; Malden, MA.
State Council of China (2016). Guiding opinions on deepening reform to promote sound development of the taxi industry Retrieved 10 October 2016 from www.gov.cn/zhengce/content/2016-07/28/content_5095567.htm.
Sun, W. (2009). Suzhi on the move: Body, place and power. *Positions*, *17*(3), 617–642.
Sun, W. (2008). *Maid in China: Media, morality, and the cultural politics of boundaries*. Routledge, London; New York, NY.
Tencent (2016). Didi CEO Cheng Wei comments on new regulations: Regulation usually lags behind innovations, but must cover innovations as the latter evolve. Retrieved 19 November 2016 from http://tech.qq.com/a/20161118/017887.htm.
Tencent News (2016). State capital heading into Didi Chuxing: A sure win? Retrieved 17 August 2016 from http://tech.qq.com/a/20160817/005385.htm.

The Paper (2015a). MOT responds to criticism towards new regulations for lacking internet ethos. Retrieved 23 October 2015 from www.thepaper.cn/newsDetail_forward_1388156.

The Paper (2015b). Shanghai releases the first zhuanche license in China: A private car in the morning can be a zhuanche on the digital platform in the afternoon. Retrieved 10 October 2015 from www.thepaper.cn/newsDetail_forward_1382991.

The Paper (2016). Didi adjusts pricing model. Retrieved 20 August 2016 from www.thepaper.cn/newsDetail_forward_1515766.

Turow, J. (2006). *Niche envy: Marketing discrimination in the digital age*. MIT Press, Cambridge, MA.

Van Doorn, N. (2017). Platform labor: On the gendered and racialized exploitation of low-income service work in the 'on-demand' economy. *Information, Communication & Society*, *20*(6), 898–914.

Wang, K. (2002). The inside story of the taxi industry in Beijing. *China Economic Times*, pp. 1–5.

Witt, A., Suzor, N. and Wikström, P. (2015). Regulating ride-sharing in the peer economy. *Communication Research and Practice*, *1*(2), 174–190.

Wu, X. and Treiman, D. J. (2004). The household registration system and social stratification in China: 1955–1996. *Demography*, *41*(2), 363–384.

Xinhua News (2015a). Key moment for overall and thorough reforms in the taxi industries. Retrieved 1 October 2016 from http://news.xinhuanet.com/mrdx/2015-01/11/c_133910723.htm.

Xinhua News (2015b). Ministry of Transport encourages innovation but bans private cars from providing zhuanche service via digital platforms. Retrieved 10 January 2015 from www.xinhuanet.com/politics/2015-01/08/c_1113930632.htm.

Xinhua News (2015c). Shanghai issues the first ride-hailing platform license with a validity period of one year. Retrieved 10 October 2016 from http://news.xinhuanet.com/fortune/2015-10/09/c_128298636.htm.

Xinhua News (2015d). Taxi-hailing app Didi Kuaidi receives official license. Retrieved 10 October 2016 from http://news.xinhuanet.com/english/video/2015-10/10/c_134699458.htm.

Xinhua News (2016). Beijing, Shanghai, Guangzhou, Shenzhen releases specific measures regarding platform-mediated ride-hailing services. Retrieved 9 October 2016 from www.xinhuanet.com/city/2016-10/09/c_129314638.htm.

Yan, H. (2003). *Neoliberal governmentality and neohumanism: Organizing suzhi/value flow through labor recruitment networks. Cultural Anthropology*, *18*(4), 493–523.

Zhang, D. (2014). Shanghai's unlicensed taxis (Hei Che) as informal urban street market, in *Informal urban street markets: International perspectives*, eds C. Evers and K. Seale, Routledge, New York, NY, pp. 158–166.

Zhang, L. (2009). China's informal urbanisation: Conceptualisation, dimensions and implications. *Post-Communist Economies*, *21*(2), 203–225.

Zhang, L. (2010). The right to the entrepreneurial city in reform-era China. *China Review*, *10*(1), 129–155.

Zhou, R. (2015). Let zhuanche to kickstart taxi industry reform. Retrieved 1 March 2017 from http://auto.people.com.cn/n/2015/0112/c1005-26364557.html.

7 Conclusion

China's growing digital economy has attracted increasing spotlight in recent years. The trajectory is characterised as much by formal circuits as by informal ones and the interaction between the two. While the rise of digital platforms has witnessed formalising tendencies as evidenced in increasing commercialisation, market consolidation and regulatory oversight, it has also made the informal elements more visible. From open source cultures and piracy, to amateur media and on-demand labour, multiple forms of informality travel along the circuits of cultural production, distribution and consumption and labour utilisation. The diversity of informality refutes the common assumption that casts it in a polemic light. Moreover, the formal and informal often interpenetrate each other, which calls for a dynamic perspective.

In this book, I have analysed various interactions between formal and informal media economies in the broader context of the rise of digital platforms, contingent and complicated state–market interactions, and the evolving roles of users. Understanding the connection and dynamics between the formal and the informal requires us to disaggregate the spectrum of formality along multiple dimensions such as entry barriers, state regulation, centralisation and labour (Lobato and Thomas, 2015). Further, a historical perspective reveals how organisations can move across the spectrum of formality in different dimensions. Formalisation in one dimension does not mean the elimination of informalities. Strategic navigation between formal and informal both empowers and challenges platforms, at both discursive and operational levels. This raises significant governance challenges.

Platforms rising across the formal/informal divide

The rise of digital platforms has opened up new circuits of cultural production, distribution, consumption and labour utilisation, with accelerating market consolidation and profound impacts on society. This book has highlighted the intimate connections between these platforms and informal circuits of cultural production, distribution, consumption and labour utilisation evident in *shanzhai* production, open source cultures, parallel trade, hacking, unofficial content distribution, amateur creativity, unlicensed cabs and precarious labour. Xiaomi has built up market dominance with a forked Android OS, relying on open source cultures and fan labour. The story of 91 Wireless started with the creation of a secondary market to the informal device market in app distribution. The inception of online literature and online video sites owes as much to the unfulfilled gap left by state-controlled cultural production and distribution system as to amateur creativity. Ride-hailing platforms have carved their share of market by capitalising on the existing underground urban transportation market and informal labour practices.

Indeed, multiple publics participate in these informal circuits, including profit-motivated entrepreneurs, enthusiastic fans, creative users and necessity-driven, on-demand labourers. Some are pressured into the informal economy with little option otherwise, while others venture there to seek entrepreneurial gains. Some step into the informal zones for fun while others are subject to precarious conditions. Some are located in the illegal zone while others are in the grey area, which can be more innovative than is generally assumed. Indeed, between black and white are many shades of grey.

The navigation of digital platforms between formal and informal space is accompanied by trans-border flows of capital, technology, content and labour. In analysing informality, researchers have foregrounded geographic tensions (O'Regan, 1991, 2012; Johns, 2009; Lobato and Thomas, 2015). Geographic boundaries trigger informality, where enterprises and consumers leverage regulatory or pricing differences, or variances in content availability. While transnational capital evidently provides the financial buttress to digital platforms in China, some platforms have developed by connecting with formal and informal actors transnationally. As Xiaomi intends to build a platform on the architecture of Android, it involves users as developers and testers in product development and counts on amateur developers to expand its ecology in and beyond the domestic market. The app distribution platform 91 Wireless has gained its market share by developing a trans-border value network incorporating parallel dealers, hackers, enthusiastic users, developers and incumbents such as telecom operators and internet giants. In the case of video streaming, overseas content has played a crucial role in attracting users to digital platforms in China, witnessing an evolving approach towards the formal end via licensing. On-demand ride-hailing platforms have repackaged informal and precarious labour conditions in new forms. As well as on-demand service platforms supported by transnational capital, labour dispatch firms, drivers and consumers all constitute the circuit of platform-driven value production. In this sense, digital platforms extend the circuit of value production constituted by multinational corporations, local subcontractors, workers toiling under informal labour practices and consumers craving gadgets and producing content and data (Qiu, 2016). Movement along the spectrum of formality and across borders is closely tied to the circuit of value production in the interest of digital platforms.

Discursive work and its discontents

When digital platforms navigate formal/informal boundaries, they apply delicate treatment to such connections. This reflects a broader tendency where firms are working discursively to frame their services and technologies (Stern, 2003). They do so for the purpose of maximising profits, navigating the regulatory landscape and promoting a self-serving cultural imaginary (Wyatt, 2004). A typical example is the strategic use of the term 'platform' to appeal to multiple audiences while eliding the tensions (Gillespie, 2010).

Discursive work involves trumpeting some connections with informalities while downplaying or even negating others. Xiaomi for example explicitly distinguishes itself from *shanzhai*, although it inherits and appropriates the networked production culture among *shanzhai* enterprises while riding on the wave of open source software and mobile tinkering cultures. Meanwhile, it highlights open source cultures in order to carve out a brand identity of high quality, technological innovation and a co-creative culture, which aligns with the state project of rebranding the 'Made in China' label and moving up the global value chain. This is a privilege of IPR-legible brands. In the case of 91 Wireless, the platform employs metaphorical strategies to highlight its underground status to users to solicit sympathy and support; to stress the function it serves for the authentic brand and to emphasise its role in content aggregation rather than production in order to reduce the threat of litigation. For online literature platform owners, amateur writers are a significant part in the freemium business model. However, as platform owners shine the spotlight on successfully commercialising writers, hierarchies, shadows and precarity are elided. Such discursive work aims to entrench among writers the platform logic including the freemium business model and associated mechanisms to measure the economic value of creative works.

Apart from highlighting, downplaying or even negating the informal, discursive work involves reconfiguring relationships with the informal, in other words, repositioning. For example, while Didi exploits existing informal labour practices and the unlicensed taxi market, it stresses the platform's capacity to deliver technology-mediated market efficiency and by extension better prospects for drivers on one hand, and to formalise and regulate unlicensed taxis on the other. Thus, what was widely perceived as competition has been transformed into a site of potential incorporation and formalisation. The purpose of this positioning approach based on platform governance lies in differentiating itself from unlicensed market participants, appealing to the authorities and obtaining legitimacy.

Discursive work also involves taking different approaches to the same elements at different times. On video-streaming sites, UGC has met with enthusiasm, frustration and eventually revalidation with a more dynamic perspective. From an industry buzzword connoting creative participation on digital platforms, UGC soon became a debased currency comparable to 'industrial waste water' before picking up steam again, this time couched in a broader discourse on professionalisation and entrepreneurship. Meanwhile, many streaming platforms have carved out a position not only in content hosting and nurturing but also in content production. The once hotbed of copyright infringement has witnessed aggressive investment in licensing deals despite the rapid escalation of costs. Licensed content, together with content produced in-house or in collaboration with partners, features heavily in the self-promotion of streaming platforms. The evolving attitude to informal circuits of content production and circulation is intimately bound up with platforms' endeavour to carve out a profitable position as they negotiate with multiple parties including viewers, creators, advertisers and regulators.

The capacity to manoeuvre between the formal and the informal lends power to digital platforms to build networks, amass users, seek revenues and align with evolving policy contexts. A dynamic and historical perspective of the informal helps highlight the nature and logic of digital platforms in value production. As digital platforms intermediate between different groups, inheritance, appropriation, exploitation or purging of informalities are highlighted, negated, whitewashed or repositioned to suit the strategic purposes of platforms.

Untenable promotional narratives and practices do not go uncontested. Xiaomi, for example, encountered challenges from transnational developer and user networks and informal, norm-based copyright governance. Contestation arising at the conjunction of control, value and ownership have raised questions about the promotional narrative that employs the metaphor of the internet as playground, and the rhetoric of a platform for co-creation. As multiple actors negotiate brand meanings, values and legitimacy, the process highlights the tensions that result from power asymmetry, the fragmentation of ethical positions and the incommensurability of standards for data curation, as the brand attempts to capture value from the co-creation process. For online video platforms hoping to move UGC towards its formal end, turning rights into privileges by tying copyright enforcement to a classification of users in terms of popularity has met resistance. Similarly, in the ride-hailing market, drivers have challenged the legitimacy of ride-hailing platforms as soon as they discovered platforms' inequitable treatment of driver-users in different service lines, and manifested negotiating power against the algorithm-driven platform governance of market and labour.

Contestations exist, not without ambivalence, contradictions and paradoxes. In the case of 91 Wireless, it encountered ambivalent and divided perceptions of its attempt to seek legitimacy through metaphorical strategies, the biased copyright enforcement approach and its influence on app production culture. This highlights the asymmetric power between the platform and developers. While the platform commands the gateway to the mobile internet by building a value network incorporating both formal and informal actors, developers face the challenge of enhancing the discoverability of their apps. In the online literature market, while digital platforms shine a spotlight over successfully commercialising writers, hierarchies, shadows and precariousness characterise many writers' experience. In spite of this, writers have developed their own informal labour networks to participate in the market, which paradoxically sustains inequality. Moreover, many users have internalised the platform logic of data-informed popularity and much-trumpeted entrepreneurship as they discipline themselves to climb up the hierarchies and contribute data to train algorithms.

Therefore, while platforms often fulfil the gap-filling function in the market and employ the rhetoric of user empowerment, a hastened conclusion that equates the heroic character with the nature of the platform is dangerous. In order to understand the nature and politics of platforms as they navigate across formal/informal boundaries, it requires us to scrutinise platforms at both discursive and operational levels, and with a historical perspective.

Platform labour and redrawn formal/informal boundaries: aspirations, precarity and inequality

Labour, as a key component of the media system, affords important opportunities to investigate formal/informal interactions. As creative amateurs, enthusiastic fans, 'ordinary' users and on-demand labourers become a vital part of capitalist accumulation for digital platforms, they are co-evolving with platforms, shaping the growing media ecology and reconfiguring the market. The meeting point of the formal and the informal is often a site of incubation or outsourcing (Lobato and Thomas, 2015). Ideas and skills among users are taken up by Xiaomi in product development, testing and promotion, and contribute to the organisation's rapid prototyping, iterative design and market expansion. The evolution of the once amateur project 91 Wireless involves networking parallel dealers, jailbreaking and rooting service providers, app developers and consumers, who interact across formal/informal boundaries and across geographic borders. Its initial success has resulted in its acquisition by the internet giant Baidu, where the outcome of networked labour is absorbed into the formal market. On online video platforms, UGC has moved from the centre to the fringes before claiming an important position in the content matrix, driving new modes of content curation. Literary enthusiasts and amateur writers have contributed significantly to the inception of online literature platforms, which have challenged the incumbent publishing industry. In this sense, UGC does not always stay as informal. As well as content creation and knowledge production, the platform-mediated, on-demand service is also characterised by labour outsourcing. As a typical case of lean platforms, ride-hailing platforms reduce their liabilities while relying on outsourced labour as well as assets in capitalist production.

While users engage in cultural production and service delivery on digital platforms, their experiences are highly uneven. Some aspirational amateurs are professionalising, receiving a share of the sizeable revenue from advertising or user subscriptions, and attracting capital investment in creative entrepreneurship. Others derive social and/or cultural capital from the labour process. Many more, however, are subject to precarity and inequality. In other words, it is a great leap to equate platform labour with empowerment and value co-creation, which often features in platform rhetoric. As discussed earlier, users engaging in creative and cultural production experience tensions around copyright and autonomy while sharing risks with platforms. For drivers who are subject to informal and precarious labour practices in the incumbent market players, digital platforms have become a site of repackaged informality and precarity based on smart technology. While opening up opportunities for users to participate in the platform economy, platform owners tend to shirk employer responsibilities, offload risks and optimise flexibility in market expansion and capital accumulation. The prospect of turning passions into professions and profits thus coexists with the risk of forced conformity, precarity and inequality.

Further, the platform-mediated labour of creative production or service delivery as well as platform usage by less active users is at the same time datafied labour. As well as relocating informal energy, digital platforms play a prominent role in evaluating, steering and policing platform labour based on datafication and algorithms. The capacity to harvest, use and reuse data, and conduct algorithmic assessment of information, or the logic of datafication and programmability in Van Dijck and Poell's words (2013), have become paradigmatic characteristics of platforms. Together with datafication, algorithm-driven governance steers and manipulates user experiences in producing and consuming content and services (Beer, 2009; Bucher, 2012; Van Dijck and Poell, 2013; Gillespie, 2014; Rosenblat and Stark, 2016).

While data harvesting and measurement indicate a formalising tendency, algorithms usher in informality owing to their notorious secrecy and opacity. In Pasquale's words (2015), the dominance of the logic of datafication and algorithms has given rise to the 'black box society'. Both the formalising and informalising tendencies as evidenced in data harvesting, analytics and algorithms are closely bound up with the capitalist production regime of digital platforms. According to Van Dijck and Poell (2013), datafication and programmability are intricately intertwined with popularity and connectivity as the underlying logic that empower social media platforms' business models. Various performance indicators and ranking charts manifest the capital accumulation logic, which influence the commercial prospects of creative users and on-demand labourers and underlie platforms' business models. Both the techno-economic and cultural logic of platforms thus construct entrepreneurial subjectivity among aspirational labourers. As creative users and on-demand labourers internalise such logic and endeavour to boost popularity metrics, only a minority can climb to the top of the ladder, leaving many more behind experiencing precarity and inequality. Further, while tying performance metrics with support and nurturing mechanisms as incentives to users, digital platforms (re)create and reinforce hierarchies and inequalities. This approach becomes more contentious when platforms confer rights as privileges on those who meet performance criteria. The application to copyright governance in mobile app distribution and online video markets are typical examples of this approach.

The power of datafication and algorithmic governance is augmented when they operate in connection with the terms of service of digital platforms. Terms of service have quasi-legal effects, as users cannot choose an alternative if they wish to use the service offered by platforms (Braman and Roberts, 2003). The increasingly concentrated market exacerbates this tendency. It enforces conformity among users even when the underlying logic is illegitimate or opaque, as their accounts can otherwise be suspended or terminated by platforms. Having said that, some users do manifest varying degrees of power in resisting or hacking the design of measurement and algorithmic mechanisms in their own interest. Some creative users have left online video platforms that treat user rights as priorities tied to performance metrics. Online literature writers have created a secondary market to reconfigure the organisation of labour, which paradoxically perpetuates hierarchies and precarity. Taxi drivers on ride-hailing platforms have exploited the tipping feature to maximise profit. While circumvention or hacking does exist, users are essentially caught in asymmetric power relations when they remain platform users.

Platforms are inescapably value-laden, privileging some values and interests over others (Beer, 2009; Bucher, 2012; Van Dijck and Poell, 2013; Gillespie, 2014; Rosenblat and Stark, 2016). The values embedded in platform logic are intimately intertwined with the platform governance of cultural production and labour utilisation in self-serving ways. As platforms deploy measurement mechanisms and algorithm-driven labour governance, they push users to subscribe to platform values, some of which are more visible than others. Therefore, as users engage in creative production, on-demand service and datafied labour, they play a role in accentuating platform values, sometimes willingly, other times unconsciously. In the platform economy, the promises of empowerment, value co-creation and democratisation coexist with the risks of reinforcing precarity, discrimination and inequality. Meanwhile, the capitalist accumulation process is also a process where digital platforms produce and reproduce cultural and social values.

Multidimensional and multiscalar governance in platformisation

As the formal–informal dynamics play out in the platform economy, the Chinese state plays its role in various ways in the broader context of state-led digital capitalism. Indeed, while there is a parallel process of platformisation in China, the role of the state necessitates a critical engagement with the connection between the platform society and global capitalism, which Srnicek (2016) theorises through the notion of 'platform capitalism'. As China continues to defend and progressively advocate cyber sovereignty, it is crucial to understand the approaches of the sovereign state and government organisations to governing the internet, including digital China's informal circuits. As Flew and Waisbord (2015) compellingly argue, the nation-state assumes a continuing centrality to media processes and the national space remains significant in an age of media globalisation.

While the state places much hope in the internet as the new engine of growth and innovation, this economic logic is complicated by three factors. First, the state is both a market regulator and a market participant. State capital, while commanding incumbent industries, is seeking entry into the burgeoning platform-led digital economy, which has so far been dominated by transnational private capital. Thus, state participation in the market and interaction between incumbent industries and the emerging platform economy have become intervening factors in state regulation. Second, economic logic coexists with the long-standing political and cultural logic in the state's approach to internet governance. In other words, the rising importance of economic logic does not overwrite political and cultural control. A noteworthy development is a proposal by SAPPRFT in 2016 for the state to acquire 'special management shares', which can be as low as 1 per cent, in China's internet giants in exchange for a controlling or veto power over the management and operation of these firms. The push for equity investment, put forward under the Provisions on the Administration of Online Publishing Services (SAPPRFT, 2016), clearly indicates the state's intention to exert more influence on the internet sector, which has been heavily funded by transnational private capital. Third, as the state asserts its geo-economic and geopolitical visions in internet governance, it persistently blocks major global internet players, with few exceptions, from the domestic market. The approach serves the dual purpose of protecting Chinese-born platforms and fencing off inconvenient content in the domestic market.

In this context, the state shapes formal/informal dynamics in the digital media economy in various ways. Its stringent regulation of the formal market has triggered various informal activities. *Shanzhai* mobile phones, the informal circulation of content including piracy and unlicensed taxies are only a few examples here. User demand for contents or services that are otherwise unavailable, unappealing or restrictive has to a large extent fuelled the growth of informal activities including entrepreneurial activities of digital platform owners.

Informal activities in the digital media economy can mean different things for the state and relevant regulatory authorities. They can be the source of development and innovation to be utilised, disruptive elements to be curtailed, unruly energies to be disciplined, or uncertain phenomena to be monitored. The diversity of informality and the perceptions of authorities can therefore lead to different approaches. As such, regulatory authorities steer the dynamics between formal and informal energies strategically. There are times when the regulators attempt to constrain undesirable informal activities, although with varying degrees of success. There are other times when the authorities leave some leeway for informal activities to develop. This can result from a perception of informality as potentially productive or innovative, or from geopolitical/geo-economic considerations to nurture Chinese-born platforms in inter-capitalist competition. The regulators mediate formal/informal dynamics by various means. These include adjusting entry barriers to the formal economy, configuring the strength of enforcement mechanisms, determining the codification of and legal frameworks for emerging forms of informality, monitoring the evolution of informal activities, or pressing for state investment. These measures have introduced both formalising and deformalising tendencies to the digital media economy.

Complicating the scenario further are ambiguity, uncertainty and informality in policy development and enforcement. These result from multifarious governance logics, tensions between the central state and local governments, and overlapping and sometimes competing bureaucratic interests. In other words, the state is not a monolithic unit. Further, given that technology is a fast-moving beast, regulation often lags behind.

In this context, corporate actors respond to or intervene in policy development strategically. Some hope to derive power from aligning their interests with those of state actors. Xiaomi's attempt to build on the state project of rebranding 'Made in China' to strengthen its brand power is a typical case here. Adopting commercial nationalism as the underlying logic connects the state and the digital platform to the same cause. Corporate actors can also challenge existing regulation and influence policy making, especially at times of regulatory uncertainty and tensions. In other words, informal enterprises do not always evade government regulation. In fact, they sometimes wish to be incorporated into the regulatory scope and gain legal status. Some platform owners have demonstrated such negotiating power in policy development. Ride-sharing platforms have gained some leeway for development before obtaining legality, although not without compromise, after long-winded debate and conflicting regulatory tendencies at local and central levels. Thus, state–market relations are characterised by complexity, contingencies and constant power negotiations.

The multifaceted state–market interactions become more complicated considering the governing capacity of digital platforms. As Gillespie (2017) insightfully point out, along with the question of the governance of platforms, an equally important question is governance by platforms. For digital platforms, self-regulation can serve the purpose of aligning with government regulations, enhancing their own legitimacy or establishing a competitive advantage. This is evident in online video platforms' self-regulation at a time when the state strengthened copyright enforcement and the platforms started aggressive investment in content licensing. Self-regulation served the purpose of solidifying the commercial interest of resourceful platforms, maintaining raised market entry barriers, and establishing legitimacy despite the history of informal activities. Thus the converged interest between these platforms and the state in copyright enforcement has led to regulatory collaboration. In fact, collaboration between industry and the state in regulation is not unusual. Market-dominant internet giants have acted as surrogates of the state in the regulation enforcement in China. A very clear example is the management of public opinion (Hu, 2017). When performing such important social functions for the state, the internet giants exploit their market-dominant power over the internet to serve their own interests (Chen and Ku, 2016).

Governance capacity features prominently in digital platforms' self-promotional discourse in their power negotiations with the state. A salient example here is the discursive work of ride-hailing platforms. These platforms not only emphasise the capacity to increase market efficiency by optimising resource allocation, including labour utilisation, via smart technologies, but also highlight the de-facto regulation of the existing unlicensed taxi market by absorbing and reorganising the informal labour force. Ironically, it is by capitalising on existing informalities that ride-hailing platforms have expanded their market share. By promoting governance capacity, platforms wish to build legitimacy, purchase goodwill from local authorities and pre-empt possibly more stringent government regulation.

Yet governance by platforms has raised questions in relation to legitimacy and effectiveness. As discussed earlier, the privatisation of regulatory capacity is increasingly manifested in code, protocol and algorithms (Lessig, 1999; Braman and Roberts, 2003; Galloway, 2004; Beer, 2009; Van Dijck and Poell, 2013; Gillespie, 2014). The power of datafication and algorithmic cultures is augmented when it operates in connection with terms of service of digital platforms. Increasing market concentration exacerbates the tendency. More problematically, when values and ideologies are encoded into algorithms, they become as notoriously hidden as trade secrets. Therefore, while increasing measurement is a move towards the formal, algorithmic culture manifests informality because of its opacity. Operating in connection with digital platforms' business model, information asymmetry allows platforms to mediate interactions between different parties to serve their own economic interests. While platforms trumpet the role of real-time and predictive algorithms in catering to personal needs and optimising market efficiency, algorithm mechanisms can hurt cultural diversity, produce inequality and enforce conformity (Hallinan and Striphas, 2016; Rosenblat and Stark, 2016). The governance of labour by digital platforms also raises questions in relation to the risks of not only replicating existing precarious conditions but also creating new hierarchies. Having said that, platform power does not go uncontested as users discover the underlying operational logic and start to hack the algorithms in their own ways. Considering datafication and algorithms are crucial underlying logics of digital platforms and empower their business models (Van Dijck and Poell, 2013), governance by platforms and their social and cultural consequences should be scrutinised more closely.

This requires us to understand how platform logics interact with different logics dominating other institutional contexts (Van Dijck and Poell, 2013). Problematically, as this book has shown, governance by platforms can operate in connection with the state's coercive power over digital platforms or existing measures of social sorting, which impacts on cultural diversity or creative freedom, or reinforces bias, discrimination and inequality. For example, as the state takes an increasingly stringent approach to internet content regulation, aspiring creative users are pressured to stay within the boundaries mapped out by the state and enforced by platforms. Taxi drivers or migrant workers, as typical examples of vulnerable populations in society, are conveniently exploited and equally conveniently disposed of by on-demand ride-hailing platforms as need be. This results when platforms prioritise their own interest, and in doing so, value some users over others as their strategies evolve and the regulatory climate changes. While authorities play an important role in regulating the market, digital platforms have the capacity to work in conjunction with existing measures of social sorting, which extend social inequalities to the platform economy.

Beyond state agencies and digital platforms, informal institutions such as norms, customs and traditions must not be neglected. In fact, bottom-up, norm-based regulation plays an important role in governance structure. As shown by the case of Xiaomi, informal, norm-based regulation has been powerful in holding the brand accountable for non-compliance with copyright norms within open source communities and for inconsistency between brand promises and practices. Marsden (2011) has revealed the potential of user-generated regulation in a multi-stakeholder approach to internet governance. Similarly, Crawford and Lumby (2013) point out the weakness of understanding governance as the work of government and industry, and emphasise the role of users as stakeholders in the governance equation. This however does not mean negating the need for formal regulation. Interactions between user communities, platform providers and government policies are characterised by complex negotiations (Burgess and Green, 2009). When platforms have commercial imperatives and users are fragmented and ineffective, user-generated regulation could be perilous and ineffective (Marsden, 2011). Indeed, the issue is not a choice between whether or not to regulate, but how best to combine formal and informal modes of regulation (Hess and Ostrom, 2005; Lobato and Thomas, 2015).

Towards a holistic view of digital transformation

Digital transformation in China is rapidly evolving, with profound economic, cultural and social consequences. A holistic view of digital transformation requires us to take into account informal circuits and unearth their intricate interactions with the formal. The metamorphoses of various digital platforms in China have highlighted informal circuits at various levels, in different dimensions from cultural production to service delivery, both within the country and across borders. Informal media activities come in different sizes and shapes, involving multiple participants and challenging polemic views. Some informalities endure. Some subside. Others transform.

Rather than being a dichotomy, the informal are inevitably interwoven, enmeshed and entangled with the formal. The interactions are complex, with different outcomes. State actors, market players and multiple publics all play their roles in the processes of formalisation and informalisation in their own ways. These dynamics have brought major shifts in cultural production, distribution, consumption and labour utilisation. Hopeful signs of growth, innovation and empowerment coexist with concerning cultural and social consequences.

The impacts of formal/informal dynamics including those on cultural diversity, fair labour, data justice and social equality raise significant governance challenges. These challenges call for a solid understanding of informal circuits, their interactions with formal ones and their cultural, social and economic impacts. This becomes more urgent considering digital platforms' monopoly tendencies driven by network effects (Bratton, 2016; Srnicek, 2016), and the governance capacity of platforms through code and protocols. As digital platforms continue to penetrate society including key infrastructures that used to be provided by government monopolies (Plantin, Lagoze, Edwards, and Sandvig, 2016), the evolving state–market dynamics add complexity to governance challenges. Crucially, governance operates not only from the top down, but also from the bottom up and sideways, involving multiple actors negotiating in the space where collaborations, contentions and compromises coexist.

Much like acupuncture, multiple publics move around positive, negative or neutral energies, through and between formal and informal circuits, with their own purposes, situated in complex power dynamics and influenced by the broader context. These processes invite us to look further into the crucial questions arising here. How do these processes occur? What consequences do they deliver? What do better alternatives look like? And how can we drive change? As digital transformation continues to unfold in and beyond China, future research should further unpack how the formal and the informal collide and coalesce in a constant metamorphosis in different social, cultural and political contexts, and in transnational flows of capital, media, labour, technologies and ideas. Such a holistic view is essential for us to capture the complexity and nuance of digital transformation on a broader scale and China's evolving role in the global economy.

References

Beer, D. (2009). Power through the algorithm? Participatory web cultures and the technological unconsciousness. *New Media & Society*, *11*(6), 985–1002.

Braman, S. and Roberts, S. (2003). Advantage ISP: Terms of service as media law. *New Media & Society*, *5*(3), 422–448.

Bratton, B. H. (2016). *The stack: On software and sovereignty*, MIT Press, Cambridge, MA.

Bucher, T. (2012). Want to be on the top? Algorithmic power and the threat of invisibility on Facebook. *New Media & Society*, *14*(7), 1164–1180.

Burgess, J. and Green, J. (2009). YouTube: Online video and participatory culture, Polity, Cambridge and Malden, MA.

Chen, T.-J. and Ku, Y.-H. (2016). Rent seeking and entrepreneurship: Internet startups in China. *Cato Journal*, *36*(3), 659–688.

Crawford, K. and Lumby, C. (2013). Networks of governance: Users, platforms, and the challenges of networked media regulation. *International Journal of Technology Policy and Law*, *1*(3), 270–282.

Flew, T. and Waisbord, S. (2015). The ongoing significance of national media systems in the context of media globalization. *Media, Culture & Society*, *37*(4), 620–636.

Galloway, A. R. (2004). *Protocol: How control exists after decentralization*, MIT Press, Cambridge, MA.

Gillespie, T. (2010). The politics of 'platforms'. *New Media & Society*, *12*(3), 347–364.

Gillespie, T. (2014). The relevance of algorithms, in *Media technologies: Essays on communication, materiality, and society*, eds T. Gillespie, P. J. Boczkowski and K. A. Foot, MIT Press, Cambridge, MA, pp. 167–193.

Gillespie, T. (2017). Regulation of and by platforms, in *The Sage Handbook of Social Media*, eds J. Burgess, T. Poell and A. Marwick, Sage, Los Angeles, pp. 254–278.

Hallinan, B. and Striphas, T. (2016). Recommended for you: The Netflix Prize and the production of algorithmic culture. *New Media & Society*, *18*(1), 117–137.
Hess, C. and Ostrom, E. (eds). (2005). *Understanding knowledge as a commons: From theory to practice*. Cambridge, MIT Press.
Hu, Y. (2017). From Yulun (public opinion) to Yuqing (public intelligence): Their history and practice in China's information management, in *The Routledge Companion to Global Internet Histories*, eds G. Goggin and M. McLelland, Routledge, New York, pp. 516–528.
Johns, A. (2009). *Piracy: The intellectual property wars from Gutenberg to Gates*, University of Chicago Press, Chicago, IL.
Lessig, L. (1999). *Code and other laws of cyberspace*, Basic Books, New York, NY.
Lobato, R. and Thomas, J. (2015). *The informal media economy*, Polity Press, Cambridge.
Marsden, C. T. (2011). *Internet co-regulation: European law and regulatory legitimacy in cyberspace*, Cambridge University Press, Cambridge.
O'Regan, T. (1991). From piracy to sovereignty: International VCR trends. *Continuum*, *4*(2), 112–135.
O'Regan, T. (2012). Remembering video: Reflections on the first explosion of informal media markets through the VCR. *Television and New Media*, *13*(5), 383–398.
Pasquale, F. (2015). *The black box society: The secret algorithms that control money and information*, Harvard University Press, Cambridge, MA.
Plantin, J.-C., Lagoze, C., Edwards, P. N. and Sandvig, C. (2016). Infrastructure studies meet platform studies in the age of Google and Facebook. *New Media & Society*, *20*(1), 293–310.
Qiu, J. L. (2016). *Goodbye iSlave: A manifesto for digital abolition*, University of Illinois Press, Urbana; Chicago; Springfield, IL.
Rosenblat, A. and Stark, L. (2016). Algorithmic labor and information asymmetries: A case study of Uber's drivers. *International Journal of Communication*, *10*, 3758–3784.
SAPPRFT (2016). Answers to frequently asked questions regarding Provisions on the Administration of Online Publishing Services. Retrieved 1 December 2016 from www.sapprft.gov.cn/sapprft/govpublic/6685/282655.shtml.
Srnicek, N. (2016). *Platform capitalism*, Polity, Cambridge, UK; Malden, MA.
Sterne, J. (2003). Bourdieu, technique, and technology. *Cultural Studies*, *17*(3/4), 367–389.
Van Dijck, J. and Poell, T. (2013). Understanding social media logic. *Media and Communication*, *1*(1), 2–14.
Wyatt, S. (2004). Danger! Metaphors at work in economics, geophysiology, and the internet. *Science, Technology, & Human Values*, *29*(2), 242–261.

Index